W9-BCK-410

Ancient Peoples and Places

THE GREEKS

UNTIL ALEXANDER

General Editor

DR. GLYN DANIEL

Ancient Peoples and Places

THE GREEKS

UNTIL ALEXANDER

R. M. Cook

89 PLATES
36 LINE DRAWINGS
3 MAPS
AND 1 TABLE

FREDERICK A. PRAEGER
Publisher
New York

THIS IS VOLUME TWENTY-FOUR IN THE SERIES

Ancient Peoples and Places

GENERAL EDITOR: DR. GLYN DANIEL

BOOKS THAT MATTER *Published in the United States of America*

in 1962 by Frederick A. Praeger, Inc.

Publisher, 64 University Place

New York 3, N.Y.

Library of Congress Catalog Card Number: 62-8380

Printed in Great Britain by Hazell Watson & Viney Ltd.

Aylesbury and Slough

CONTENTS

LIST OF ILLUSTRATIONS 7

FOREWORD 12

CHRONOLOGICAL TABLE 14

I THE BACKGROUND

Greece 17
The Greeks 20
Greek Civilisation 21
Sources of Knowledge 21

II THE EARLY IRON AGE

The Greek States 23
Political Systems 25
Economics 28
Society 29
Religion 30
War 36
Architecture and Art 38
Homer and Hesiod 46
Historical Events 49

III THE ARCHAIC PERIOD

The Surrounding World 56
Colonisation 57
Economics 59
Politics 65
Relations between the Greek States 72
War 74
Society 80
Athletic Festivals 83

Religion and Thought 85
Literature 87
Music 89
Pottery and Painting 89
Sculpture 99
Architecture 102
Historical Events 116

IV THE CLASSICAL PERIOD
Historical sketch 117
Politics 121
Population 123
Public Finance and Administration 125
Society 127
Economics 129
Technology 132
War 134
Religion 138
Thought and Knowledge 139
Literature 144
Painting 146
Pottery 148
Sculpture 150
Other Arts 159
Architecture and Planning 160
Conclusion 172

NOTES ON THE FIGURES 175
BIBLIOGRAPHY AND ABBREVIATIONS 183
THE PLATES (48 pp.) 193
NOTES ON THE PLATES 241
INDEX 258

ILLUSTRATIONS

PLATES 1 Mount Olympus
2 Patmos
3 Seriphos, air view
4 View from Delphi to sea
5 Meteora
6 Perachora, from east
7 Perachora, harbour
8 Lycosura
9 Watercourse on Mt Olympus
10 Bay near Sunium
11 The plain of Sparta
12 Delphi, air view
13 Delphi, stadium
14 Delphi, theatre and temple of Apollo
15 Sunium, air view
16 Epidaurus, air view of site
17 Epidaurus, air view of theatre
18 Olympia, model of sanctuary
19 Olympia, air view of sanctuary
20 The Acropolis of Athens, model
21 The Acropolis of Athens, air view
22 Antissa, apsidal building
23 Larisa, fortification wall
24 Seriphos, modern houses
25 Aegosthena, fortification wall
26 Olympia, temple of Hera
27 Athens, reconstruction of Stoa of Zeus
28 Aegina, elevation of temple of Aphaia

PLATES 29 Athens, 'Theseum'.
30 The Doric order
31 The Ionic order
32 Athens, temple of Nike
33 Sarcophagus of the Mourning Women
34 Athens, choregic monument of Lysicrates
35 Athens, model of west end of Agora
36 Priene, model
37 Geometric bronze horse
38 Geometric bronze bird and disc
39 Geometric terracotta figurine
40 Early Archaic bronze soldier
41 The Auxerre goddess
42 Bronze statuette at Delphi
43 The Apollo of Tenea
44 The Critian boy
45 Relief with ball-players
46 Athena from the temple of Aphaia, Aegina
47 Statue of a woman from the Acropolis of Athens
48 Part of the frieze of the Siphnian Treasury
49 The Artemisium statue
50 Front of the Ludovisi throne
51 Bronze mirror in Copenhagen
52 Head of the Delphi Charioteer
53 The Alba head
54 Head of a charioteer from the Mausoleum
55 The Bartlett head
56 Part of the frieze of the Parthenon
57 Part of the frieze of the Mausoleum

PLATES 58 Attic gravestone
59 Part of the Nike Balustrade
60 The Demeter of Cnidos
61 The Hermes of Praxiteles
62 Attic Protogeometric cup
63 Corinthian Protogeometric jug
64 Attic Protogeometric amphora
65 Corinthian Geometric cup
66 Attic Geometric jug
67 Attic Geometric amphora
68 Detail of Attic Geometric bowl
69 Detail of Corinthian oil flask
70 Detail of Corinthian olpe
71 Corinthian olpe
72 East Greek jug
73 Detail of Attic Black-figure bowl
74 Corinthian olpe
75 Attic Black-figure amphora
76 Attic Black-figure hydria
77 Inside of Attic Red-figure cup
78 Inside of Attic Red-figure cup
79–80 Details of Attic White-ground lekythos
81–82 Details of Attic Red-figure ceremonial pot
83 Attic Red-figure stamnos
84 Detail of Attic Red-figure calyx-krater
85 Silver-gilt plaque from Duvanli
86 Chalcedony gem by Dexamenos
87 Bronze mirror case
88 Inscription on marble slab
89 The Lion of Chaeronea

FIGURES 1 *Physical map of Greece, p. 18*
2 *Political map of Greece, p. 19*
3 *Section of grave at Athens, about 740* BC, *p. 34*
4 *Soldier, about 750* BC, *p. 37*
5 *Warship, about 750* BC, *p. 38*
6 *Model of temple, late eighth century* BC, *p. 39*
7 *Gold diadem, about 725* BC, *pp. 40–41*
8 *Spectacle brooch, eighth century* BC, *p. 40*
9 *Brooch with square catch-plate, about 700* BC, *p. 41*
10 *Bronze tripod, mid eighth century* BC, *p. 42*
11 *Map of Greek colonisation, pp. 52–53*
12 *Alphabets, p. 56*
13 *Inscription at Abu Simbel, p. 60*
14 *Helmet, p. 75*
15 *Back of bronze corselet, p. 76*
16 *Warship, about 570* BC, *p. 79*
17 *Athenian gentleman, about 690* BC, *p. 81*
18 *Relief with drinking scene, p. 82*
19 *Bronze cauldron and stand, about 700* BC, *p. 91*
20 *Bronze head of griffin, about 650* BC, *p. 92*
21 *Corinthian cup (kotyle), p. 93*
22 *Corinthian oil flasks, p. 94*
23 *Archaic cups, p. 95*
24 *Plans of temples, p. 103*
25 *Reconstruction of the 'Theseum', p. 105*
26 *System of masonry, p. 106*
27 *System of roof-tiling, p. 107*
28 *Aeolic capital, p. 113*
29 *Plan of fortifications of Athens and Piraeus, p. 136*
30 *Statue of the Doryphorus, p. 152*
31 *Plan of grave, fifth century* BC, *p. 155*
32 *Family plot in cemetery, fourth century* BC, *p. 156*

FIGURES 33 *Statue of the Apoxyomenus, p. 157*
34 *Restoration of palace at Larisa, p. 164*
35 *Restoration and plan of house at Priene, p. 165*
36 *Plan of sanctuary of Aphaia in Aegina, p. 167*
37 *Plan of part of irregular town (Lato), p. 168*
38 *Plan of regular town (Priene), p. 169*
39 *Plan of Agora at Elis, p. 171*

Foreword

THE READER of this survey may well think that art and architecture have been allotted too much space and the Greeks outside Greece itself too little. The reasons are that it is a principle of the series *Ancient Peoples and Places* to lay emphasis on material remains and that other volumes have been commissioned on the Eastern and the Western Greeks. This is not a complaint. In fact these conditions made my job easier.

As is natural and prudent, I have exploited my family and friends. Dr M. I Finley, Mr G. S. Kirk, Mr A. G. Woodhead, Professor J. M. Cook and Mrs K. Cook have read all or most of the text and given their advice. From Dr W. H. Plommer, Mr R. V. Nicholls, Mr M. H. Bräude, Mr J. N. Coldstream, Professor H. A. Harris and Mrs S. A. Adam I have had criticism and information on special topics, and there are other colleagues whom I have pestered with questions.

The illustrations proved more troublesome than I expected, and it was especially difficult to find photographs of ecological scenery. The persons and institutions who have let me use their photographs and drawings are mentioned in the 'Notes on the Illustrations'. Among others who have helped me in one way or another are Dr J. Papadimitriou, Mr R. Johnson and Mr S. C. Collard, whose services have been many, Miss S. Benton, Mr J. Boardman, Dr N. Breitenstein, the Managing Committee of the British School of Archaeology at Athens, Mr J. K. Brock, Mr B. F. Cook, Mr P. E. Corbett, Mrs P. Demoulini, Dr H. Diepolder, Dr J. Dörig, Mr J. W. Hayes, Professor A. Greifenhagen, the Hellenic Society, Mr R. A. Higgins, Professor A. W. Lawrence, Dr R. Lullies, Professor F. Matz, Professor H. Möbius, Mr G. Pollard, Professor K. Schefold, Mr Cecil Stewart, Miss V. Verhoogen, Dr C. C. Vermeule, and Dr F. Willemsen. Mr H. A. Shelley redrew Figures 1, 2 and 11, Mr S. Schotten Figures 19 and 29, Mr P. R Ward Figures 7, 8, 9, 10, 14, 15, 20 and 28, and Messrs P. P. Pratt and M. E. Weaver Figures 6, 15, 27, 34, 35, 36 and 38.

This list of those to whom I am indebted is long and there are others whom I have not mentioned. To all I offer my sincere thanks.

R. M. C.

Period	Date	GREEK HISTORY		ORIENTAL HISTORY
	1100			
		Dorian invasion		
EARLY IRON AGE	1000			
		Ionian migration		
	900			
	800			
		Colonisation begins (*c.* 750)		
		Spartan conquest of Messenia (*c.* 725–05)		Assyrian expansion to Mediterranean
ARCHAIC	700			
		First Law codes (*c.* 660)	First Lydian attacks on Ionia	
		Tyranny at Corinth (*c.* 655)		
				Assyria destroyed by Medes, etc. (612)
	600			
		Peloponnesian league founded (*c.* 550)	Lydian conquest of Ionia, etc. (*c.* 550)	
		Tyranny at Athens (*c.* 546)	Persian conquest of Lydia, Ionia, etc. (546–5)	
		Democracy at Athens (507)		
	500			
			Ionian revolt (499–3)	
		Persian attack on Athens (490)		
		Persian invasion of Greece (480–79)		
CLASSICAL		Athenian alliance founded (478)		
			Athens makes peace with Persia (449)	
		Peloponnesian war (431–04)		
				Expedition of Cyrus and the 10,000 (401–400)
	400		Spartan expedition in Asia Minor (400–394)	
			Sparta makes peace with Persia (387)	
		Thebes defeats Sparta (371)		
	350			
		Philip II of Macedon conquers Greece (338)		
		Alexander III succeeds Philip (336)		
			Alexander attacks Persia (334)	

A CHRONOLOGICAL TABL

LITERATURE			PHILOSOPHY	ART & ARCHITECTURE		
					1100	
PIC				Protogeometric pottery begins	1000	PG
					900	
				Geometric pottery begins		GEOM.
					800	
omer				Orientalising and Black-figure pottery begins		
	LYRIC				700	
esiod						
	Archilochus			Sculpture begins		
	Tyrtaeus			Architecture begins		
	Alcaeus				600	
	Sappho, Solon		Thales			ARCHAIC
			Anaximander	Bronze casting mastered		
			Anaximenes			
	Anacreon					
			Pythagoras	Red-figure pottery begins		
			Xenophanes			
AGEDY			Heraclitus		500	
	Pindar					
schylus			Parmenides			
				Polygnotus		
	COMEDY	PROSE	Anaxagoras			
phocles		Herodotus	Leucippus			
			Hippocrates	Phidias (Parthenon)		CLASSICAL
ripides		Gorgias		Polyclitus		
	Aristophanes		Socrates			
		Thucydides	Democritus			
					400	
		Lysias				
		Plato	Plato			
		Xenophon				
				Praxiteles	350	
		Demosthenes		Lysippus		
			Aristotle			
				Apelles		

EVENTS AND PERSONS

CHAPTER I

The Background

GREECE
Figs. 1, 2
Plates 1–12, 15

GREECE is a country as poor as it is picturesque. Most of the mainland and the islands consists of mountains of limestone, which run in general from north to south. Macedonia and Thessaly have large and rich plains. Elsewhere fertile patches are small; the best are in Boeotia, along the north coast of the Peloponnese, near Argos, round Sparta and in Messenia. In the winter there is rain, heaviest on the west coast, or snow in the high mountains; the long summers are hot and dry. In ancient times the climate seems to have been much as it is now.

About a fifth of the land can be cultivated, and much of that is steep and stony. In the flatter bottoms there are small fields, meagre terraces climb some way up suitable hillsides, the higher ground at best allows summer pasturage for sheep and goats. In a few, till recently remote places some forest survives; in antiquity, anyhow at first, there was more on the nearer mountains. The chief crops were corn, grapes and olives. Sea fishing was good. A few, mostly very small deposits of iron, copper and silver were worked at one time or another, and there was plenty of building material – clay, limestone, and in some places marble.

Communications were difficult, until indeed the making of the modern motor roads. Such natural routes as there were ran mostly north and south. A determined man could, of course, cross the mountains, but in continental Greece south of Macedonia there were only four good tracks from east to west and those impassable by wheeled traffic. Travel by sea was better, though much of the coast is rocky and there are very few good natural harbours with access inland. Many of the rivers dry up in summer and none is navigable.

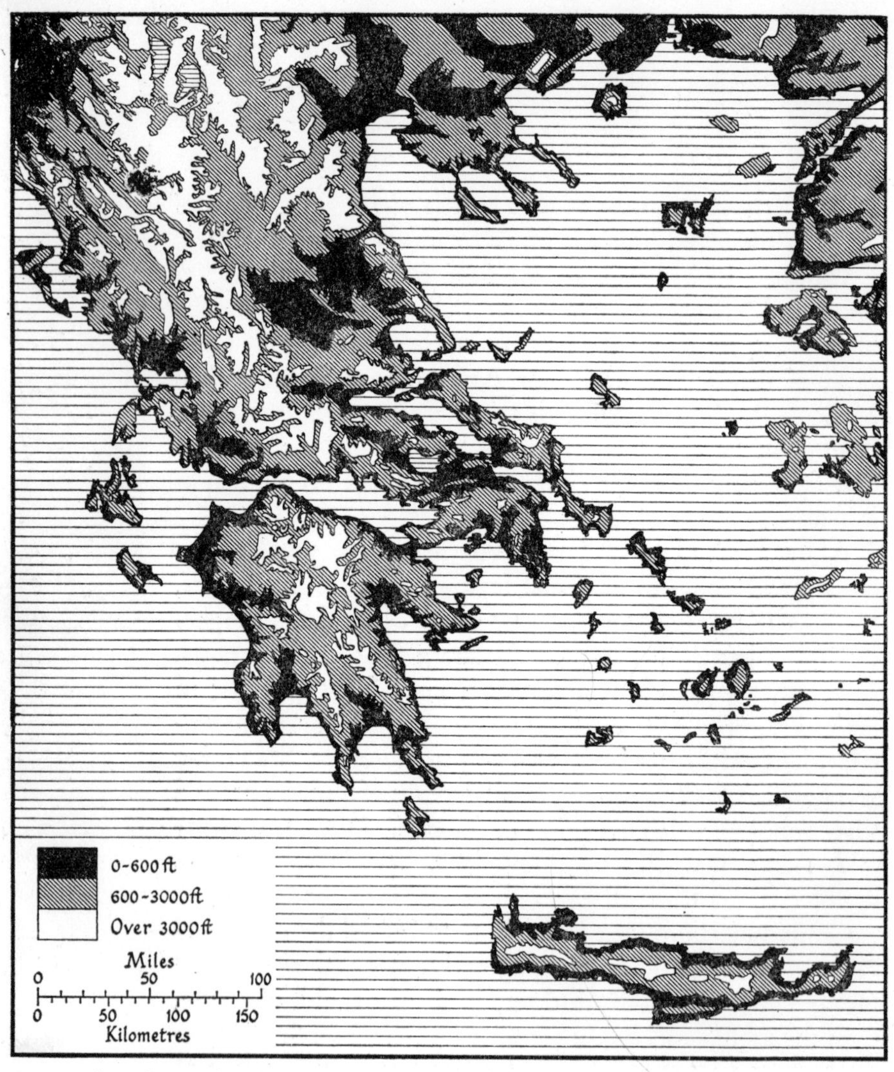

Fig. 1. Physical map of Greece

Its geography had decisive effects on the history of Greece. Lack of local resources was an obstacle to the growth of larger communities, lack of accessibility to the linking of small

Fig. 2. Political map of Greece

communities into larger states. Secondly, the convergence of routes both by land and sea tended to give some importance to the districts near the Isthmus of Corinth.

THE GREEKS

The Greeks were mixed racially, as might be guessed even without their skeletons. Some of the earlier inhabitants of Greece seem to have spoken a language very different from Greek; at least the later Greeks had names of places and Mediterranean plants that were not Greek in origin. But by the Late Bronze Age (the Mycenaean period) Greek was the speech of most of southern Greece and the islands, and other Greek-speakers occupied the regions further north. The last big shift of population in Greece, before the immigration of Slavs in the seventh century AD, was the invasion of the Dorians and other backward Greeks about the end of the Bronze Age. This Dorian invasion is attested by later tradition and by the distribution of Greek dialects in the seventh and sixth centuries BC. Curiously, it has left no positive archaeological record. Presumably it is connected with the destruction of the Mycenaean palaces and civilisation, though this destruction (which is not mentioned in the later tradition) could be wholly or partly explained by internal revolution.

The Dorians and related peoples conquered most of the Peloponnese except Arcadia in the mountainous centre, where older inhabitants kept their independence. In some places the Dorians became a ruling class, in others they fused with their predecessors. About the same time, so tradition says, the Boeotians moved into Boeotia and the Thessalians into Thessaly. Attica escaped invasion.

Propagandists sometimes explain later Greek achievements by racial causes, or contrast the inborn qualities of Dorian discipline and Ionian versatility. Here at best there is a confusion between race and culture, at worst such perversions as the cult of Nordic man. Greek is an Indo-European language, but there was never an Indo-European race. Nor has anyone yet proved that race has special qualities of mind or character.

In appearance the ancient Greeks probably varied over much of the same range as their modern successors. It is useless to rely on Archaic or Classical statues or drawings which are idealised; lifelike portraiture did not begin till the Hellenistic period in or after the time of Alexander.

GREEK CIVILISATION

The word 'Greek' has several meanings, but by 'Greek civilisation' is most usually and usefully meant that civilisation which began in the Iron Age and reached its greatest brilliance, though not extent, in the fifth and fourth centuries BC. By this definition the Mycenaean civilisation was not Greek, and indeed archaeologists distinguish between the Bronze Age and the Iron Age in Greece by calling one 'Helladic' and the other 'Hellenic'. This may seem paradoxical since the Mycenaeans spoke Greek and many of the later Greeks were descended from them. But Mycenaean civilisation, so far as we can judge yet, was of a type that was widespread in the eastern Mediterranean countries during the Late Bronze Age, and its higher and characteristic achievements did not survive the Dorian invasion. The new civilisation that eventually arose in Greek lands is ancestral to all Western civilisations, but itself – so it appears – had no true ancestor.

It is convenient to divide the history of Greek civilisation, so defined, into five periods. The divisions are, of course, much too precise. The Early Iron Age, which comprises the Protogeometric and Geometric periods of the archaeologists, runs from the eleventh to the second half of the eight century BC. It is succeeded by the Archaic period, which lasts to 480 BC. Next comes the Classical period, with which this book ends. The Hellenistic period begins at some date between 338 and 323 BC and continues till 27 BC. The final period, the Roman, begins to pass into Byzantine and the Medieval in the fourth century AD.

SOURCES OF KNOWLEDGE

In the Archaic period the Greeks had learnt to write, and many of their writings have survived. Poetry goes back at least to the eight century BC, but our earliest historians and other prose-writers are of the fifth century. Roughly speaking, we have on the literary side fairly good records from about 500 BC, though the cultural eminence of Athens has attracted too much attention to the history of that one city; for the sixth and seventh and even the late eighth centuries BC we have an unsatisfactory and diminishing assortment of statements and traditions; and the preceding centuries are almost blank. The archaeological evidence too is fullest for the Classical period (and later) and scantiest for the Early Iron Age, and even when more is available it must be remembered that excavation may reveal much about the works of men's hands, but little about the workings of their minds. So in the early period inference from later institutions must be important. If it was not so troublesome, it would be more logical to expound Greek history by tracing it backwards from the Classical period.

CHAPTER II

The Early Iron Age

ELEVENTH–LATE EIGHTH CENTURY BC

THE GREEK STATES

THE DORIAN and other invasions began about the end of the Bronze Age. They were followed by the migration of malcontent Greeks across the Aegean Sea to the west coast of Asia Minor. These movements must have taken some time, but tradition is not clear and excavation has been insufficient.

When Greece had settled down we find Dorian states in the south and east Peloponnese – one in Messenia, one in Laconia, several in the Argolid, and others at Corinth and Sicyon. Dorians were established also in Crete, Megara, and Aegina. Along the north Peloponnesian coast the Achaeans, if one may judge by their name, were survivors from the Mycenaean population. Further west the Eleans were newcomers related to the Dorians. In the centre the Arcadians believed themselves aboriginal. To pass to continental Greece, Attica resisted invasion, as did the big island of Euboea, where the most important states were close together at Chalcis and Eretria. In Boeotia, as it was now called, Thebes and other states were inhabited by Boeotians. North and west were the unimportant communities of the Phocians and the western and eastern Locrians and a small enclave of Dorians. Further north the Thessalians of Thessaly were divided into four groups. Beyond them the Macedonians spoke a Greek or near-Greek dialect, but were not reckoned as Greek until in the fourth century they could be ignored no longer. On the west side of mainland Greece the Aetolians, Acarnanians and Epirots remained unimportant. Macedonia and Epirus were the buffers of Greece in Europe: the Illyrians to the north and the Thracians to the east, peoples of lower civilisation and more loosely organised, were not Greek, even in speech.

The islands of the Aegean, the Greek Archipelago, were occupied by Dorians to the south, Aeolians to the north, and Ionians between. Melos and Thera were the chief Dorian states, Naxos and Paros the chief Ionian, and little Delos ranked as a common sanctuary of all the Ionians. These Ionians, incidentally, were not connected with the Ionian Sea and Islands on the west of Greece; in ancient Greek the two names were pronounced and spelt differently.

The pattern was repeated along the west coast of Asia. Lesbos and the mainland opposite became Aeolian; Ionians settled from the gulf of Smyrna to the foothills of Mount Latmus, most notably at Miletus and Ephesus and on the islands of Chios and Samos; the Dorians took Rhodes and Cos, where Mycenaean Greeks were already established, and some places on the Carian coast. Since the Ionian settlements were the most successful, this movement across the Aegean is often loosely called the Ionian migration. During the period of migration there was no strong power to oppose the Greeks; the Phrygian kingdom did not reach the west coast and of the local peoples only the Carians resisted effectively. At Miletus, Herodotus says, the Greeks married native women, but though there was some mixture there was little assimilation. The Greeks came here as conquerors.

The character of settlement varied from place to place. In Laconia, Crete and Thessaly the newcomers reduced the earlier inhabitants to serfdom. In many states there was amalgamation, with or without privileges. In the new foundations refugees from different parts must often have united. This mixing helps to explain the considerable uniformity in the arts and crafts of the Early Greek Iron Age.

When the Greeks – or, as they called themselves, Hellenes – became curious about their nationality, they observed (most obviously in Asiatic Greece) three main groups – Dorians, Ionians and Aeolians, with the Achaeans somehow to be attached. The criteria were dialect and institutions, though interested politicians afterwards insinuated the notion of race. This grouping is not mentioned in Homer, whose themes admittedly are set in an earlier period; but Hesiod not much after 700 BC, using a genealogical formula of a type popular with the Greeks, makes Hellen the father of Aeolus, Dorus and Xuthus, and Xuthus in turn the father of Ion and Achaeus. If, as now seems likely, the Ionic dialect is in origin intimately related to Arcadian, the connection of Ionians and Achaeans may be justified historically.

POLITICAL SYSTEMS

The standard constitution at the beginning of the Iron Age was the same both in the states formed by the new invaders and those where the earlier inhabitants maintained independence. The hereditary king was commander in war, chief religious functionary, and head in civil affairs. A council, advisory or deliberative, was formed from the aristocracy. The common people met in an assembly to approve or not approve the king's proposals. There might also be serfs, some personal slaves, captured in war or by piracy, and perhaps a few foreign residents; but none of these had any share in the state. The expenses of government, such as they were, came from the king's property, supplemented by an occasional levy.

The Mycenaean kings, to judge by their castles and the clay tablets recently deciphered, had been autocrats with an efficient centralised administration. The kings of the Early Iron Age had no such power or resources, and Homer shows even heroic rulers living in unfortified palaces and obliged to take advice from their nobles. Certainly by the end of the period monarchy had been abolished in most Greek states. The title of king might be kept for the successor to his religious duties, but power had passed to the permanent aristocratic council and its officers, appointed annually and so unlikely to become too powerful. Presumably the common people suffered by the revolution, since now there was no counterweight against the nobility. In the backward communities of Epirus and Macedonia strong hereditary kingships survived through Classical times. In Thessaly the former kingdoms jointly elected a military commander-in-chief for war. In Laconia there were two hereditary kings as far back as local memory went; during the Early Iron Age they should have been even more powerful than they were later. In Argos an effective monarchy lasted well down the seventh century. But in general the institution was vanishing between the tenth and the eighth centuries BC. According to tradition the refugees who settled Ionia brought kingship with them; but almost all the new colonies of the eighth and seventh centuries began as republics. The dominant system had become aristocracy or, perhaps more accurately, squirearchy. The cause of this change cannot have been simply urban growth, as some have suggested; it occurred among such unurbanised peoples as the Eleans and Locrians. More significant was the lack of centralised organisation and also, perhaps, of continuing danger of outside attack or internal revolt.

The social structure of Greek communities, old and new, was fairly uniform. The nobles were grouped in clans; each clan ('genos') was united by family ties. They had their adherents among the commoners. Both commoners and nobles were distributed into tribes, normally three in Dorian and four in Ionian states. The tribe ('phyle') was not a geographical entity, and it is hard to see that it ever had been, even before the disturbances of the Early Iron Age; at least the same tribal names recur in most of the new Dorian states, and yet in each state these tribes were of roughly equal size. But whatever the origin of the tribe, its earliest known function was as a military unit. Later, as constitutions developed, it became a civil unit too. The Greeks had a weakness for historical and genealogical claims, and they provided their tribes with ancestors; thus the three Dorian tribes – the Hylleis, Pamphyli and Dymanes – were descended from Hyllus, Pamphylus and Dymas. But such tidy fictions of kinship were not believed deeply, or it would have been less easy for later reformers to rearrange and rename these ancient divisions of the community. On the other hand, genuine blood ties were (and remained) important; homicide, for instance, was a family concern, though in many disputes the king or aristocracy dealt out justice, or as Hesiod complained, injustice.

Since Classical times the city state ('polis', from which comes our 'politics') has been considered – and rightly so – as the indispensable basis of the Greek way of life. The independent city was not, of course, peculiar to the Greeks. It existed already in Syria and Phoenicia, sometimes even with a republican constitution. But the eastern cities inherited an old and elaborate civilisation, and they lived under the shadow of Assyrian and Egyptian aggression; the Greek cities had much weaker and simpler traditions and could experiment without interference. In the Early Iron Age they were small or embryonic, the home of the king and of specialised craftsmen, a market in peace and a place of refuge in war; indeed the name 'polis' was restricted at first to the citadel or, as it was called later, the 'acropolis'. But, as graves in Attica show, many of the nobles lived – or were buried – on their country estates. Not much is known about fortification. Some of the citadels had been Mycenaean castles and, as at Mycenae and Athens, their defences were kept up. But it is not likely that the lower town, if there was one, had walls yet. It is sometimes said that the new settlements on the Asiatic coast led in the development of cities; the invading Greeks needed to shelter together against the natives, and Smyrna (the only well-explored site) was walled already in the ninth century. More field-work is wanted before such problems can be solved; unfortunately excavators are not much interested in the unimpressive remains of the Greek Early Iron Age.

ECONOMICS

The contrast between the remains of the Mycenaean civilisation and those of the Early Iron Age is very striking. The Mycenaeans have left us spectacular ruins, showy painting, elaborate metalwork and written records, and they traded widely overseas. Their successors seem to have had little foreign trade, were illiterate, and are best known for their painted pottery. But it does not follow, as is so often asserted, that the Early Iron Age was a time of abject poverty. The Mycenaean architects, artists and scribes worked for the monarchy, and probably trade was for luxuries and bronze but hardly for food; when the monarchy fell, so did its attendant crafts and services. But in the new order power and so, presumably, wealth were more widely shared, and the combined riches of the Iron Age aristocracy might have equalled those of the Mycenaean kings. After all, the main source of wealth was in agriculture, and the land was still there. During the years of invasion and settlement agriculture no doubt suffered, but the Iron Age had one technological advantage – it had iron.

The basis of the economy was peasant agriculture – even the subject populations, it seems, had (as serfs) their own plots to till – and the herding of flocks. The nobles had larger estates, worked often by free labour. Of specialised craftsmen there were blacksmiths, bronze-smiths, goldsmiths (though perhaps not till the end of the period), carpenters, shipwrights, potters, and poets. To judge by walls that remain, masons were rare. Spinning, weaving and dyeing were done at home by the women. Payments, when required, were in kind.

Trade with other districts was, so Hesiod suggests, casual and, to judge from Homer, not very reputable. A few objects of Eastern manufacture have turned up in Greek graves and probably some iron was imported, so that there must have been a little foreign commerce. Perhaps the carriers were the Phoenician and Sidonian merchants whose occasional visits are mentioned by Homer; if Greek ships sailed to the East, it cannot have been often enough to keep close contact with Cyprus, where the descendants of Mycenaean settlers were still flourishing.

A simple, self-sufficient economy of this kind has the inherent weakness that if its population grows, there may not be enough food to support it. Shortage of land was perhaps one cause of the emigration overseas that followed the Dorian invasion. It was pretty certainly the main cause of the colonising movement that began in the eighth century.

SOCIETY

The nobles of the Early Iron Age did not do so badly. According to Homer, whose society though set in the past presumably made sense to his audience, they looked after their estates and were not above working themselves, hunted, raided, indulged in piracy, visited distant nobles, and kept chariots. The Mycenaeans seem to have used chariots in war, unsuitable though the Greek terrain is for fast wheeled traffic; perhaps Homer was not misunderstanding tradition when he made his heroes drive up to battle and then dismount to fight. But as riding, in contrast to driving, became regular, the chariot survived as an object of prestige or sport. The cost of maintaining a chariot and its team of horses must have been high, especially as horses were not used for farm work; for oxen were the normal draught animals, and the standard by which wealth was measured. The harder life of the peasants, some richer and some poorer, is described in the *Works and Days* of Hesiod; it did not change much till the nineteenth century AD.

To the Greeks marriage was a serious business, but men who could afford the indulgence might supplement a wife by a concubine. In Homer we hear of gifts made to the father of the bride as well as of the dowries which later were normal.

Women's work was primarily domestic – spinning, weaving, and cooking – and in larger houses one part was reserved for them. Homer and later practice in backward communities suggest that in the upper class they had more liberty than in Classical cities. Peasant women, of course, were too busy for strict seclusion.

Religious festivals and the funerals of notables, which included competitions in sport and poetry, were the public entertainments. Hesiod speaks of going for funeral games from Ascra to Chalcis, more than thirty miles away; and the *Homeric Hymn to Apollo* describes the festival on Delos, where the Ionians came 'with their children and chaste wives' and, presumably, camped out.

RELIGION

The religious beliefs of the Greeks were composed of many strands, which even they could not disentangle. Still less can we, for all our knowledge of comparative religion. There were the gods and rituals the Greeks brought with them to Greece, those they found already established there, and those they adopted or invented later. All this was combined in different ways in different places and was, besides, liable to develop like the Greeks themselves.

The principal gods belonged to the Olympian family. Its head was Zeus, 'father of men and gods', whose original domain was the sky and whose attribute was the thunderbolt. His consort Hera presided over marriage and the respectable occupations of women. Athena appears as the divinity of wisdom and handiwork, and also of battle. Apollo, a god of light, took over healing, purification and poetry. His maiden sister Artemis was goddess of the moon and a huntress. Posidon's province was the sea and also earthquakes and horses. Hermes was the guardian of flocks and herds, of travellers and of thieves, and (like Iris) the messenger of Zeus. Dionysus (Bacchus), an old spirit of vegetation, is better remembered as

Plate 69
Plate 46
Plates 48, 56
Plates 48, 56
Plate 61
Plates 75, 84

the patron of wine and drama. Demeter remained a corn goddess; with her was worshipped her daughter Persephone or Kore (meaning 'maiden'). Hephaestus, the divine smith, naturally acted as the protector of craftsmen. Aphrodite was the goddess of love, sacred and profane; her son was Eros. Ares, though his province was war, had a lowish reputation. Hestia, the deity of the hearth, was important in cult, but not in myth. Hades (or Pluto) was the shadowy lord of the underworld. This divine family was official and universal. Though each state had its particular favourites and patron – as Athena at Athens and Hera at Argos – the others were recognised and Zeus's seniority was admitted.

Plate 60

Plate 87

These were the prime functions of the Olympians, but they acquired others too, sometimes contradictory and sometimes overlapping, from alien deities they absorbed or were equated with in one place or another. So Hera, Artemis, and the Eileithyiae might assist in childbirth. So, more remarkably, the virgin Artemis, because of her interest in wild beasts, became in Asia the heiress of a great mother goddess. The manifold character of these and other deities was often marked by special epithets. Apollo Hyacinthius at Sparta had replaced an earlier deity, Hyacinthus; Delian Apollo was Apollo as worshipped at Delos; Apollo Alexikakos was the god in his capacity as averter of pestilence. As ideas developed, this was a convenient way of expressing new aspects of an established god.

The lesser divinities, mostly local and specialised, included older gods who had been degraded, men who had been promoted, river spirits and the nymphs of springs and woods. But some had a wider fame – Castor and Pollux (the Dioscuri) whom sailors invoked in storms; Priapus, the rampant promoter of fertility; Pan, the herdsman's friend; and the Muses, who fostered the arts. The Satyrs, whom Hesiod called 'good for nothing', are well known as attendants of Dionysus; but

Plate 87

Plate 75

whatever their origins, they were not usually worshipped in the Iron Age.

The Greeks thought of their gods as anthropomorphic; that is, made in man's image. There were a few minor exceptions. Pan was half goat, the Satyrs half horse (but, unlike the Centaurs, two-legged), and river deities might be human-headed bulls. Occasionally a trace of another kind of concept adhered to a major god. So Apollo Lykios may be the supplanter of a wolf-god ('lykos' means 'wolf'), at Phigaleia an image of Demeter had a mare's head, Dionysus was sometimes invoked as a bull, and it could be argued that the familiar creatures of certain gods – the owl of Athena and the eagle of Zeus – were deposed deities of animal form. There were also sacred trees, stocks and stones, though we very rarely find them openly identified as gods.

Homer's gods quarrel with each other and show more selfishness than moral sense; but to Hesiod, who was little later, Zeus was the supreme and righteous ruler, and this trend towards a single just and omnipotent deity was continued by later thinkers. But at lower levels polytheism flourished and magic, of which some traces were embedded in official rituals, always had its adherents.

Behind the gods lurked the concept that man's lot was foreordained. In Homer, Fate governs even the Olympians; later thought tended to assimilate it to the will of Zeus. But though most Greeks would have admitted that no one could escape his destiny, they usually acted as if they had free will or at least some choice. What that choice was might be discovered by divination from dreams, the observation of birds and other chance omens, or the entrails of a sacrificed animal. There were also oracles, of which the most ancient was that of Zeus at Dodona in remote Epirus, though by the end of the Early Iron Age Delphi was more honoured. Other noted oracles were those of Trophonius at Lebadea, of Amphiaraus near Oropus, and of Apollo at Delos, at Claros, and at Didyma (or Branchidae) near Miletus. Most oracles required specialised interpreters to expound the god's answers.

The cult of the dead had no extravagant importance. The local heroes, whose tombs were officially venerated, ranked as beneficent demigods. But the ordinary Greek received only modest attention after burial. Some offerings, mostly pottery or personal possessions, were put with him in the ground, for a little while portions of drink and food were left at the grave, and its site was respected; but this was more from superstition and sentiment than any positive creed. Whatever the original purpose of their funeral customs, the Greeks of the Iron Age did not believe generally in any effective after-life, nor was there any significance in their changing preference for cremation or inhumation. The purpose of burial rites was to consign the dead man's spirit to Hades, and all that was necessary was that his remains should be covered with earth.

Figs. 3, 31

To reconcile this medley of religious beliefs and traditions was a principal task of mythology. It too had several sources – divine and human history, the explanation of rituals and of natural phenomena, national and family pride, etymology, and literary invention. Myths varied from one place to another and it is not a gross exaggeration to say that no two Greek writers told the same story in the same form. Greek myths became favourite subjects of poets and artists, and transmuted by their imagination are now more familiar to northern Europeans than the unimproved myths of their own pagan ancestors.

The forms of worship were more or less uniform. When praying to the gods above, the Greeks stood with arms raised and hands turned upwards. For the gods under the earth the arms were stretched down or a hand touched the ground. But kneeling was avoided as being a gesture of submission or servility; man might be the sport of the gods, but not their slave. In most ceremonies offerings were essential, whether of

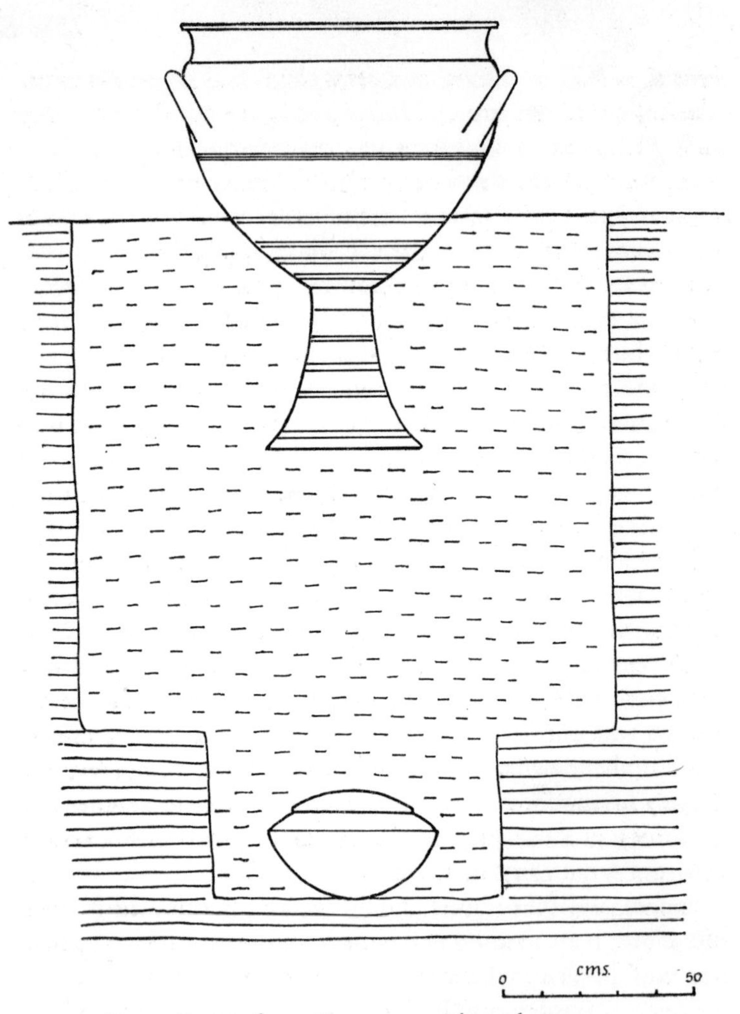

Fig. 3. Section of cremation grave at Athens, about 740 BC

the bloodless produce of the earth, such as wine, fruit, corn, milk and honey, or of a living creature. The choice of offering depended on the god, the donor and the purpose. At home, libations of a little wine were poured out regularly. Sacrifice in a sanctuary was made on special occasions, and when an

Plate 83

animal was to be offered a careful ritual had to be observed. The chosen victim was garlanded and led to the altar and, after such preliminaries as sprinkling the worshippers with holy water and the animal with grain, the priest or an attendant stunned it and cut its throat. In the ordinary sacrifice, in which the purpose was to thank the god for a favour or to secure his good will, the blood was poured on the altar and the carcase was skinned, cut up and cooked; the god received the thigh bones, fat and savour, the priest the hide, and most of the meat was eaten by the worshippers. But if the sacrifice was to expiate pollution or guilt, the whole of the victim was burnt or thrown away. Offerings of other kinds were frequent, some rich but most of them trivial; the great number of carelessly made toy pots that excavators find in sanctuaries show that the gods were satisfied with the intention of the giver. Besides private offerings official sacrifices were made at public festivals, the only regular holidays in the Greek year; these were, of course, more elaborate. There were also ceremonies, especially those of Demeter and Dionysus, which involved the mystical or ecstatic performances that are expected in cults of fertility. In a few rituals traces survived of the more primitive institution of human sacrifice; but though Homer has Achilles slaughtering Trojan prisoners at the funeral of Patroclus, the impression he gives is one of savage vengeance, not of religious duty.

Sanctuaries, that is open spaces consecrated to a deity, were numerous, both in town and country. The one necessary structure was an altar, which for obvious reasons usually stood in the open. Temples only housed the image and furniture of the god and valuable offerings, and in the Early Iron Age they were simple, small and, it seems, rare. Most sanctuaries had a reputation limited to their own locality or state, but a few were more important. To judge by finds, Delphi and Delos were already attracting visitors from further off; the popularity of Olympia came later. There were also some associations of states for common worship at a chosen place. In Ionia the twelve cities jointly celebrated the Panionian festival at the sanctuary of Posidon on Cape Mycale, and the Asiatic Dorians had a similar congress at Cape Triopion. In European Greece the Amphictyons, that is the neighbouring communities (from Thessaly as far as Western Locris and Athens), met at Anthela (and later at Delphi), and the Calaurian league came together at Calauria opposite Troezen. The first three of these groups had, or developed, some political functions. The fourth, which faded out in the Archaic period, may well have had political purposes too; otherwise it is hard to explain its scattered membership – Prasiae, Nauplia, Hermione, Epidaurus, Aegina, Athens and Orchomenos. But political leagues proved too much for Greek ideas of the sovereign city-state.

Greek orthodoxy was elastic. The individual was free to accept or reject as he liked, provided he did not openly offend established ritual. Religious persecution succeeded only in times of emergency or when harnessed to political hatred. There was tolerance too of foreign cults and deities, who were regularly identified with whichever Greek gods they seemed most to resemble. One reason for this easy-going attitude was that there was no organised professional clergy. In the state religion the king, if there was one, naturally represented the community; where kingship was abolished, his priesthood became a regular magistracy. For complicated rituals there were, of course, trained priests, sometimes hereditary. But priests, as such, were more officials of a cult than representatives of a god. Compared with other ancient peoples the Greeks were lucky in their religion.

WAR

The Greeks indulged in war surprisingly often for a people who recognised its evils so clearly. In Archaic and Classical times few Greek states were regularly on good terms with their neighbours, and it is not likely that the Early Iron Age was much more pacific. For the military practices of that time our evidence comes from weapons found in graves, from paintings on pots, figurines and models, and from Homer's descriptions. All this information must be used with discretion. Not every kind of equipment was buried with the dead, and not everything that was buried has survived; in the paintings and figurines, none of them much earlier than the eighth century, artists had their conventions, which are discussed in the next section; and the Homeric poems contain not only poetic exaggerations, but also some details that tradition had handed down from the Bronze Age in which their themes are set.

The first-class soldier was armed with two throwing spears, sword, dagger, plumed helmet, shield and (very probably) corselet. The sword, about two and a half feet long, could be used for slashing and stabbing. The helmet, which generally did not cover the face, and the corselet were presumably of leather, since no examples have been found. Paintings show three kinds of shield – the so-called hour-glass type, a small round targe, and, though rarely, a rectangular variety. The materials were pretty certainly leather on a wood or wicker frame or core. These shields could be carried or worn by a strap over the shoulder, leaving both arms free; or they could be wielded by a central grip held in the left hand. For auxiliaries there were archers, some using the simple and others the composite bow, and probably slingers too. The battle began with the long-range missiles. Next the fully-armed soldiers engaged the enemy in loose order, first throwing their spears and then, if necessary, closing with their swords; if Homer is describing the practice of his own time, this fighting often resolved into a series of duels, prefaced by boasting and followed by the despoiling or rescue of the body of the loser. The archers, no doubt, continued their skirmishing or sniping. Chariots appear regularly in Homer and occasionally in paintings, but only to convey their owners to and from or along the field of battle.

Fig. 4

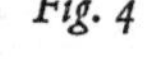

Fig. 4. Drawing of soldier, about 750 B.C. Scale about 1:3

For cavalry there is little or no direct evidence, hard though it may be to believe.

Remains of ships have not been found and, if found, may not give much information, but Homer knows of broad merchant vessels and on Geometric pots there are several pictures of what seem to be war-ships, designed for speed and attack. Both kinds of ship could be sailed or rowed. The war-ship had *Fig. 5* a narrow deck along each side above the rowers and from it archers and soldiers fought, sometimes using longer spears for thrusting or grappling. But if (as it appears) these ships had a serviceable ram, more refined tactics too were in use. Whether there were state navies or only privateers we do not know. It is a pity, since the question involves the organisation and financing of the Early Iron Age communities.

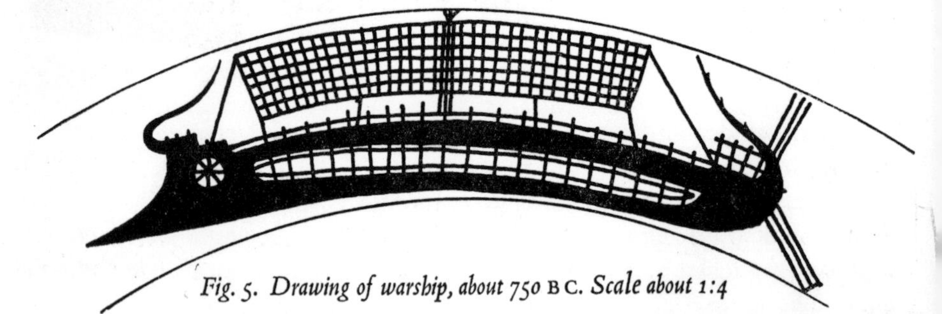

Fig. 5. Drawing of warship, about 750 B C. *Scale about 1:4*

ARCHITECTURE AND ART

The Greeks of the Early Iron Age practised fewer arts than either their Mycenaean predecessors or their Archaic descendants. Their architecture (if it can be called that) was unpretentious, their sculpture was negligible, the clay figurines were crude or careless, there is no evidence for large paintings on walls or panels, and textiles have vanished. Towards the end a neat style developed for small figures of bronze, and some well designed bronze tripods survive. But the most plentiful and characteristic of the finds are painted pots, so much so that archaeologists often use the stylistic terms Protogeometric and

Fig. 6. Model of temple from Perachora, late eighth century B C. *Height (as restored) 33 cm.*

Geometric to denote (more conveniently than correctly) cultural or historical periods.

The usual materials of building were simple. Walls were of rubble or of mud-brick preferably on a stone footing; roofs were either pitched and of thatch, or flat and of timber and mud. The normal choice of material probably depended on climate (or altitude) and local resources, and the choice of plan – rectangular or apsidal – on the material; it is difficult to make good corners of rubble, especially if mud and not cement is used for binding, and conversely rectangular bricks encourage (though they do not enforce) rectangular corners. So it is unnecessary to look for ethnic reasons for the planning of buildings in the Early Iron Age.

Plate 22

Fig. 6, Plate 24

Few sites of this period have been examined carefully, but there seem to be two main types of building – temples and houses. The standard temple on the Greek mainland is a

Fig. 7. Gold diadem, about 725 BC. Scale about 7:8

Fig. 6, Plate 22

narrow one-roomed structure with a door and a simple porch at one short end; the other end may be rectangular or apsidal. There is no compelling reason for deriving this kind of temple from the Bronze Age 'megaron'; the shape is an obvious one for a single-roomed building. Some houses, anyhow of the less poor, must have been more complex and may have been reasonably comfortable. But neither in temples nor houses is there any sign of architectural refinement.

Plate 39

Plates 37, 38

Fig. 7

No trace exists of monumental sculpture in stone or terracotta and, if (as seems certain) there were idols of wood, they were probably clumsy or formless. Certainly the artless clay figurines, infrequent as they are, do not suggest consciousness of any plastic tradition. During the eighth century some small bronze figures of animals and men show a spare abstract style, but it is a style designed for a miniature scale and does not bear enlargement to monumental size. A few thin gold bands, found in graves as early as 750 BC and probably used as diadems, were decorated by pressing into or on dies; their designs, which are

Fig. 8. Bronze spectacle brooch, eighth century BC. *Scale about 2:3*

often repeated, resemble but are rather more advanced than the designs on painted pottery.

Metalwork was competent, though because of its intrinsic value little has survived. The most impressive products are bronze tripods, consisting of a large bowl supported by three vertical legs. On the lip of the bowl two rings stand erect, and occasionally the legs have wheels. Tripods were used for cooking and the rings may have been intended to pass a pole through to lift the bowl off the fire. But the big decorated tripods, as much as 6 feet high, seem to have been objects of prestige rather than utility. They appear in Mycenaean inventories, in Homer,

Figs. 8, 9

Fig. 10

Fig. 9. Bronze brooch with square catch-plate, about 700 BC. *The pin is broken off. The inset shows the back of the plate. Scale about 2:3*

and on Geometric, Archaic and Classical pots, and their use was as prizes in athletic and musical contests, as dedications to the gods, and (it seems) as items in the elaborate system of gifts which according to Homer was a convention of noble society.

Fig. 17, Plate 39

Weaving was the most widely practised of the arts, but on a domestic and not a professional basis. Nothing has survived, but if clay figurines and drawings are reliable, the patterns re-sembled the abstract ornaments on Geometric pottery. For wall

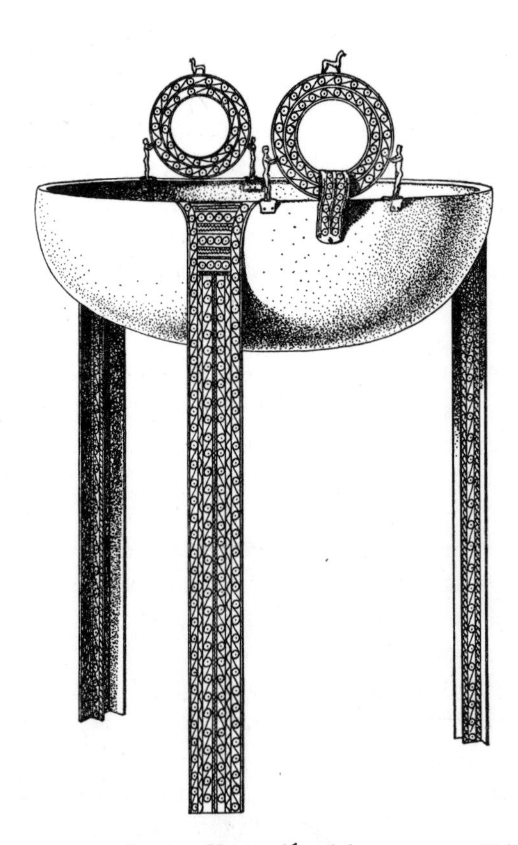

Fig. 10. Bronze tripod and cauldron, mid eighth century BC. *Height 1·87 m.*

paintings there is no evidence, and the paintings on pottery (like the figurines) do not suggest any larger style.

There remains the painted pottery. This was a form of art which the Greeks appreciated until the time of Alexander, and fortunately for archaeologists its style changed with convenient rapidity. The principal uses were for drinking and for the toilet, and though much pottery was put in graves or dedicated in sanctuaries, in general this was not specially designed. The commonest shapes, which vary within the limits set by utility, were the wine jar (*amphora*), the jug (*oinochoe*), two-handled cups, and – since the Greeks mixed their wine with water – the mixing bowl (*krater*) and water pot (*hydria*). Large jugs could, of course, serve as wine jars and water pots. Plates of fired clay did not become frequent till the fifth century; presumably the earlier Greeks had wooden platters. Small jugs or flasks with narrow mouths (*lekythos*, *aryballos*, *alabastron*) were made for oil, the equivalent of our toilet soap, and for perfume. A round lidded box (*pyxis*) seems to have been a container of powder or trinkets. The names in brackets are those used by archaeologists, partly because the modern range of shapes is not the same as the ancient, and partly (in origin) from pedantry; but it is not often that the ancient and modern meanings of those names coincide exactly.

Plates 62–67, 75
Figs. 21, 23
Plate 76
Fig. 22

Most of the processes used by the Greeks in making pots were ordinary enough, but the colour and sheen of the surface are more peculiar. The chemical reasons for these effects, which were not fully exploited till the sixth century BC, are still uncertain. The sheen is not a glaze of the kinds to which we are accustomed now, but results from the plate-like structure of the particles facing the surface or from sintering of that surface at the temperature reached in Greek kilns (up to 950° C) or from both structure and sintering. The contrast of reddish body and blackish paint (one a coarser, the other a finer preparation of a clay rich in iron oxides) comes in the firing; these oxides fire red in an oxidising atmosphere, black in a reducing (where oxygen is short); so contrast can be obtained by reduction followed by a partial reoxidation which penetrates the body but not the paint. Both oxidation and reduction can be produced easily, one by allowing a through draught, the other by damping the fire. These effects of sheen and contrast have been found as early as the fourth millennium BC in the Tell Halaf ware of northern Mesopotamia, appeared in Greece before the end of the Neolithic period, were greatly improved at Athens around 580 BC, and persisted in part till the final adoption of a true glaze in the seventh or eighth century AD.

In the thirteenth century Mycenaean pottery had been remarkably uniform in style, but towards the end of the Bronze Age local schools appear and in the Early Iron Age their differences increase. Even so, there were certain general changes, whether brought about by similar conditions or, as is easier to believe, through the influence of the progressive school of Athens. The so-called Protogeometric style, which develops from the latest phase of Mycenaean (the 'Submycenaean'), was dominant from about 1025 to 900 BC. The shapes, while plump, are firmly modelled, with some emphasis on the distinction of neck and body and foot. The decoration deliberately rejects free-hand informality; instead simple, regular ornaments are placed carefully and symmetrically in fields that emphasise the important areas of the shape. It is typical of the new style that the favourite sets of concentric circles and semicircles are drawn with compasses. The general evolution is shown best in the jars and jugs, where more and more of the unornamented surface is covered with dark paint, shapes become slimmer, and the principal decoration shifts from the narrowing shoulder to the neck and the belly.

Plates 62–64

The Geometric style follows around 900 BC. The anatomy of the shapes is still more sharply and tautly defined, the plotting of decorative fields is more exact, and the repertory of ornament

Plates 65–67

is revised. The semicircles vanish, the circles are rarer, and the continuous hatched meander (which seems to have evolved at Athens) becomes characteristic. This austere and almost mathematical ideal persisted through the ninth century. In the eighth century painters tended to multiply their decorative fields till they covered most of the surface of the pot, to break up continuous bands into narrow panels, and to enrich old or invent new abstract ornaments. A more important novelty was the introduction of figures, converted into half-abstract silhouettes. The animals mostly appear in unvaried rows, but the human figures are grouped in scenes of action, which in their way illustrate contemporary life. The favourite subjects are battles by land and sea, the lying in state of a noble's body, and his funeral procession. But before interpreting these scenes we must understand the conventions of the painters. The human figure is regularly shown nude – only towards the end do women acquire a skirt – and at first there was no anatomical distinction of sex; but on such occasions the Greeks were no more naked than neuter. Again, the pall that should cover the dead man is raised above him. Chariots, though presented in profile, often show both wheels side by side, and in ships the further bank of rowers is sometimes drawn above the nearer. Conventions of this sort can be explained partly by a desire for clarity of view, which is not easily attained in silhouette, partly by a more analytical than pictorial interest in the construction or mechanism of whatever is portrayed. The end of the Geometric style was protracted. New styles appeared in Corinth about 725 BC, at some places not till a generation or more later, and even then old and new might continue together for a while. It is important to recognise this overlap when interpreting material from sites of the late eighth and the seventh centuries; failure to do so has caused much misunderstanding, especially about early Greek contact with Italy.

Plate 68

The relations of the local Protogeometric and Geometric

schools of pottery were varied. In the southern Peloponnese, Protogeometric seems not to have developed fully. Thessaly was rather and Macedonia very backward, Aeolis specialised in a reduced grey ware and did not make painted pottery, Crete went its own way till the late ninth century, and Cyprus had passed out of the Greek orbit. But in general the Protogeometric and Geometric styles were accepted by the potters of the Greek states. There were some closer groupings. Corinth, Argos and Boeotia were usually fairly close to Athens; the Cyclades and perhaps Euboea share some peculiarities with Thessaly but are mainly dependent on Athens; Ionia, Rhodes and Cos appear to have followed Athens at first, but gradually diverged. What inferences should be made from these relationships I cannot say, but they do not correspond to the patterns of dialect or conquest.

HOMER AND HESIOD

The Greeks of the Early Iron Age (except in Cyprus) could not read or write. But illiteracy does not preclude literature, and the *Iliad* and the *Odyssey* remain two of the great achievements of epic poetry. Epics transmitted orally are liable to change and develop in the course of time, so that it is generally hard or impossible to know when any passage was first invented, how much it derived from earlier poems, and what alterations it underwent afterwards. But it is a fairly common opinion today that the *Iliad* was fixed in substantially its present form about 750 BC, and the *Odyssey* fifty years later. Since they show no definite awareness of the changes that marked the Archaic period, it would be surprising if they were much later, but they might well be earlier. From the sixth century onwards, if not before, most Greeks believed that both poems were by a single poet, Homer. The scholars of the last century, looking too closely at details, saw a patchwork of separate lays. Their successors have greater regard for the unity of each epic, but more often than not consider that *Iliad* and *Odyssey* are the products of two different men. Ancients and moderns agree that these epics were composed or completed in Ionia.

The *Iliad* describes in some 15,000 lines six weeks from the ten years of the siege of Troy (Ilium), beginning at Achilles' quarrel with Agamemnon and ending with the funeral of his friend Patroclus and the return of the body of Hector, who killed him. The poet offers an ideal of humanity, passionate and self-willed, but with an aristocratic code of personal honour. The gods in contrast are childishly irresponsible; they punish affronts to themselves, pride, and sometimes innocence. In this pitiless world life is short, without any happiness after it, and man must be resigned to his fate, but act above it. The *Odyssey*, a little shorter, recounts, not straightforwardly, the return of Odysseus (Ulysses) from Troy to his home in Ithaca. Its attitude to life is that of the *Iliad*, though less insistently.

Both of these Homeric poems were composed for recitation, and they contain many of the tags and repetitions that the oral poet needs to relieve his memory or invention. Since their subjects are set in Heroic times before the Dorian invasion, they presumably include much traditional material. But though some details seem to go back to the Mycenaean Age, much may be more recent: after all, the poet had to be intelligible to his hearers. The difficulty is in deciding which is which. But the historical services of Homer were more to the future than the past.

Hesiod was reckoned as the author of the *Theogony* and the *Works and Days*, and Homer's contemporary. Modern critics tend to assign the two poems to separate poets and to date them in the early seventh century, partly because the society they depict seems more advanced than that of Homer. But Hesiod had different aims and a different point of view, and besides he lived in Boeotia, where conditions may not have been the same as in Ionia. In the *Theogony* the history and generations of the gods are expounded systematically. The *Works and Days* is a farmer's calendar, mixed with ethical fables, magical hints and acid complaints about his lot. The poetical dialect is much as Homer's, the tone more earthy. Hesiod is a pessimist, though he asserts – not altogether with conviction – a belief that God is ultimately just.

Recitation at public festivals soon made the *Iliad* and the *Odyssey* widely known, and though never thought of as literally inspired or even as religious works, they came to be venerated as more than the great classics. Not only was Homer believed to be historically accurate, so much so that in the sixth century his text was accepted as decisive in an arbitration over the island of Salamis; but also in spite of being taught in schools he provided the Greeks with an ideal of human behaviour and helped to give them a sense of unity. Xenophanes, a radical thinker of the late sixth century, objected that 'Homer and Hesiod attributed to the gods everything that men censure and think shameful – thieving, adultery and deceiving one another.' Herodotus, a shrewd observer of the next century, considered that Homer and Hesiod settled the relationships and functions of the Greek gods. Xenophon in the early fourth century makes a character in his *Symposium*, an ordinary upper-class Athenian, say with conservative pride that as a boy he learnt the whole of the *Iliad* and *Odyssey* by heart and still remembered them. Alexander the Great was a passionate admirer of Homer's Achilles. In the first century AD the scholarly geographer Strabo maintained that Homer was a master of all branches of knowledge.

Some scholars, believing that art and literature alike reflect the spirit of their age, discern resemblances between Homer and Geometric vase-painting, though curiously they rarely or never test their assumptions on Hesiod, whose *Works and Days* describe contemporary life much more faithfully than do the *Iliad* and the *Odyssey*. Still, if Homer's artistic counterparts must be found, it is more agreeable to look at the works of the mature Classical period.

Plate 68, *Fig.* 9

Plates 56, 79–80, 83

HISTORICAL EVENTS

When in the fifth century BC the Greeks developed a historical interest, the legends of the Late Bronze Age were still extensive enough to allow a reconstruction of past events, picturesque if unreliable. But the doings of the Early Iron Age (after the upsets of the Dorian invasion) did not stir the imagination of later story-tellers, and we have little more than noble pedigrees and lists of officials, both for familiar reasons suspect in their early parts. The only date that is widely accepted is the founding of the Olympic games in 776 BC, and it is reasonable to doubt even that. There is nothing shameful in the honest admission of ignorance.

CHAPTER III

The Archaic Period

LATE EIGHTH CENTURY–480 BC

ABOUT THE MIDDLE of the eighth century a series of inventions and enterprises began which transformed the culture of Greece and gave it the character that deserves the name of Greek. Over-population led to colonisation and trade; from this some states were able to become richer and more urbanised, and new standards of urbanity were suggested by closer (but not too close) knowledge of the older and more sophisticated models of the East. In the political and social changes that followed, neither tradition nor authority was strong enough to repress individual freedom of thought and even – to some extent – of action. Though Greek individualism had fatal defects, it produced the first civilisation of modern type.

THE SURROUNDING WORLD

In the Archaic period the Greeks came into closer touch with the outside world. That world was changing. In the East the Assyrian empire was advancing and in the second half of the eighth century annexed the small principalities and city-states in Syria, Phoenicia, Palestine and Cyprus, and finally Egypt. But the supremacy of Assyria soon collapsed. In the mid seventh century Egypt under Psammetichus I recovered its independence, and in Iran the Medes were becoming strong and together with the Babylonians overthrew Assyria in 612 BC. Syria and Palestine went to Babylonia, while the Medes pressed on into Asia Minor as far as the frontier of the kingdom of Lydia, with which after a battle that was interrupted by an eclipse (probably 585 BC) they made an alliance. During the Early Iron Age the Greek settlers on the Anatolian coast had not been molested seriously, except by one another. The only considerable power in Western Asia Minor was the kingdom of Phrygia, and its interests did not reach the Aegean coast. But early in the seventh century the Cimmerians, pushed out of the Ukraine by the Scythians, came south through the Caucasus; some of them gave trouble to the Assyrians, others, turning west, destroyed the Phrygian kingdom. This gave Lydia its chance; and though its ruler Gyges was defeated and killed by the Cimmerians, his successor established the new state more strongly than before. The emergence of Lydia was important for the Greeks; the Lydians were the neighbours of the Ionians and Sardis, their capital, was only two days' march from Smyrna by an easy route. Once the Cimmerian danger was over, Lydia became aggressive and in the reign of Croesus (*c.* 560–*c.* 546 BC) all the Greek cities of western Asia (except Miletus, which had made a special treaty) were under Lydian suzerainty. They had been too jealous of their independence to combine effectively. The new order did not last long. In 550 BC the Persians took over the empire of the Medes and by military success and tolerant and reasonably competent administration soon enlarged it. In or about 546 BC Cyrus, the first Persian king, defeated Croesus, and Lydia and its Greek dependencies came under Persian rule. Further conquests added Babylonia (538 BC), Egypt (525 BC), and – crossing into Europe – Thrace (512 BC). All the Mediterranean lands east of Greece were now under Persian rule and so, with some ebb and flow, they remained till Alexander. But at first few of the Greeks of Europe showed much concern for their danger. At least, when in 499 BC the Ionians rebelled, only Athens and Eretria sent help and that very little. The Persians quickly put down the revolt, but other troubles kept them busy till 490 BC. Then an expedition crossed the Aegean to punish the interfering states.

Fig. 11

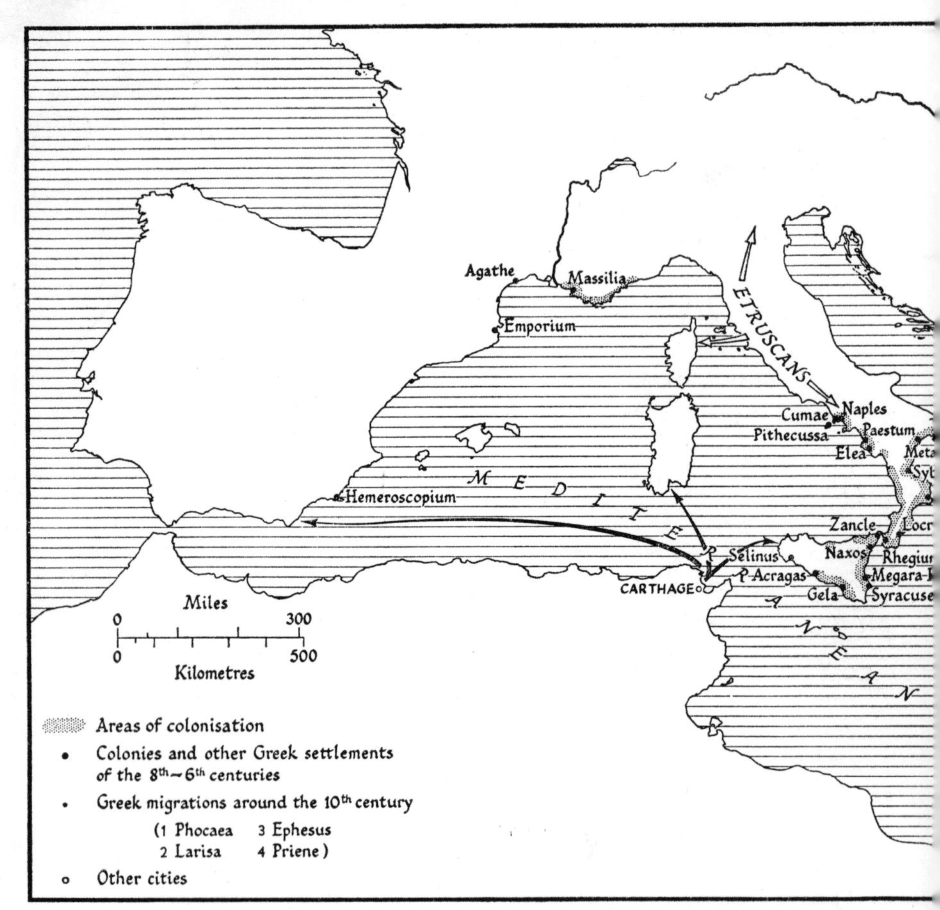

Fig. 11. Map of Greek colonisation

Eretria was duly sacked, but the Athenians surprisingly defeated the invaders at Marathon. Ten years later a full-scale invasion of Greece was led by the Persian king Xerxes. The army marched through Thrace and Macedonia and entered Greece from the north, and the fleet accompanied it. After a

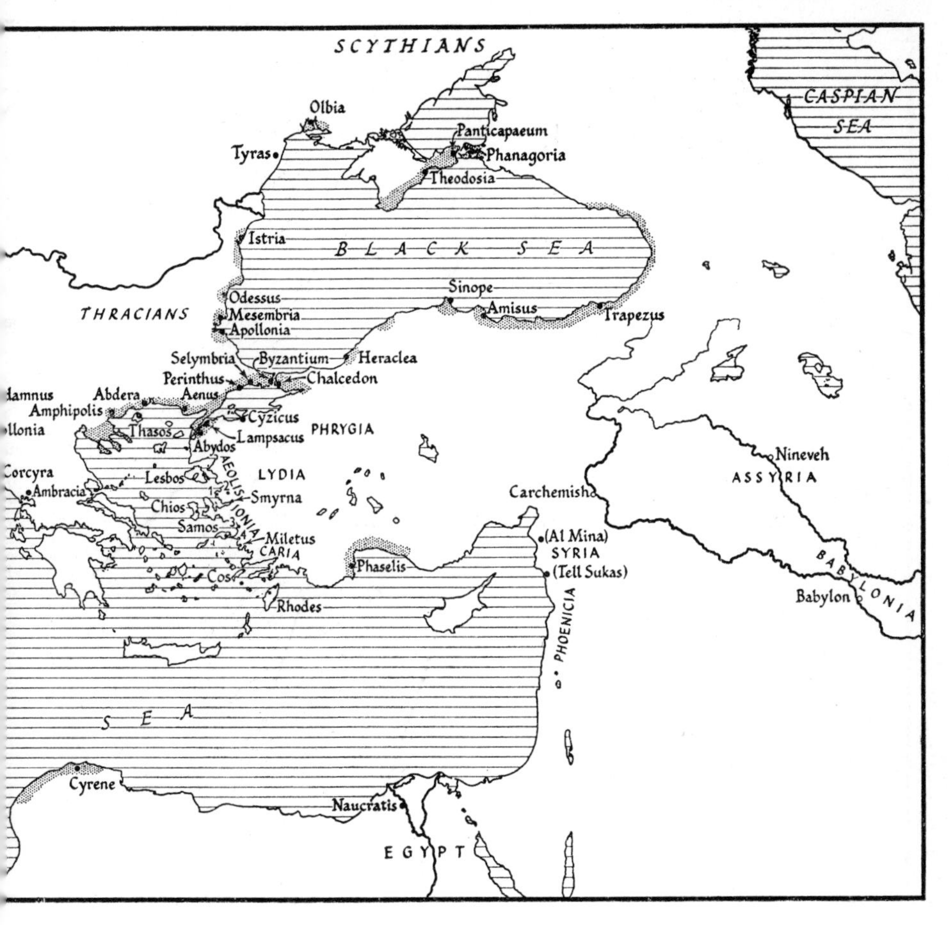

short delay at Thermopylae, where Leonidas and his three hundred Spartans held the pass for six days, the Persians reached Athens and controlled all the eastern part of continental Greece. Soon after the sea-battle off Salamis eliminated the Persian fleet and next year at Plataea their army too was defeated but retired in good order to Asia. It was a remarkable achievement of Greek unity, about fifty per cent complete.

To the north of the Black Sea the Cimmerians had been replaced by the Scythians about 700 BC. The Scythians were a nomadic people from the steppes, but some of them settled down and took to corn-growing. Though split into several kingdoms they remained powerful enough to hold off aggressors.

In the western Mediterranean the Greek pioneers of the eighth century met two strong competitors. The city of Carthage in what is now Tunisia was founded by Phoenicians not later than the eighth century. They soon set up dependencies in western Sicily, Sardinia and south-east Spain. In central Italy the Etruscans, whatever their origins, became prominent about the same time, and in the seventh and sixth centuries expanded northwards to the Po and southwards to Campania. Both the Etruscans and Carthaginians were well-organised and well-armed, and the Greek settlers in the west, who were no more willing to co-operate than Greeks elsewhere, lost rather than gained ground against them.

In other parts of the Mediterranean the local inhabitants were at a lower standard of culture and organisation and, though they might resist Greek encroachment, were rarely a danger to established settlements. The Thracians, for instance, if combined, would have been more than a match for the Greeks – or so Herodotus thought. But it was not till the middle of the fourth century that any such combination arose and succeeded.

The impact on the Greeks of the elaborate civilisations of the East was much less than might be supposed. There was no influence in politics, literature and technology. In religion the Ionians borrowed from their Asiatic neighbours; but though Hesiod's cosmogony appears connected with that of the

Hurrians and Hittites, the connection may be of Mycenaean date. In social life the rich developed a taste for luxury, and perhaps this led in some cities to a worsening of the status of their women. Probably rational thought was encouraged by a wider range of experience, and something was learnt directly in geometry and astronomy. Art was certainly stimulated, to an extent that might be misleading if we had no other record of this period. A more valuable acquisition was the alphabet. The clumsy Mycenaean syllabary had been forgotten, except in Cyprus, and now that some Greeks, very possibly merchants in Syria, were feeling again a need for writing they took over the Phoenician script and improved it, especially by a fuller notation for vowels. The first examples we have are of the later eighth century. From early on, if not from the beginning, there was a variety of Greek alphabets, and it was not till the fourth century that the Ionian version was accepted universally; the Roman alphabet, which is the basis of the modern alphabet of Western civilisation, comes by way of the Etruscans from the old alphabet of Chalcis. Why Greece was so immune against the more sophisticated East is most simply explained by remoteness, and when the Persians reached the Aegean the new Greek standards were established securely and indeed began to exert some influence eastwards. It was very different in Cyprus where the Greek descendants of Mycenaean settlers evolved a hybrid culture with a peculiarly repellent style of art; but they shared the island with Phoenicians and were within the range of the Eastern empires. Till Hellenistic times Cyprus was not essentially Greek.

Figs. 12, 13

In the West the Etruscans learnt much from the Greeks, but gave little or nothing in return. With the Phoenicians there seems to have been neither give nor take. The other Mediterranean peoples were lower in culture and though the Greeks may have been curious about them, they saw nothing to imitate.

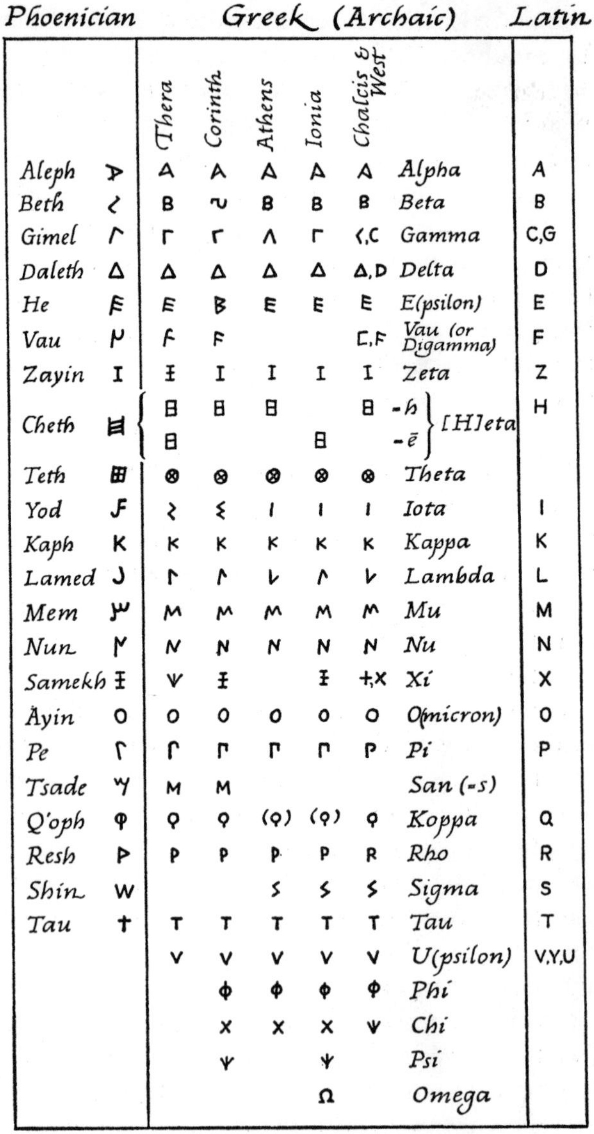

Phoenician		Greek (Archaic)						Latin
		Thera	Corinth	Athens	Ionia	Chalcis & West		
Aleph	𐤀	A	A	A	A	A	Alpha	A
Beth	𐤁	B	Ն	B	B	B	Beta	B
Gimel	𐤂	Γ	Γ	Λ	Γ	<,C	Gamma	C,G
Daleth	Δ	Δ	Δ	Δ	Δ	Δ,D	Delta	D
He	𐤄	E	B	E	E	E	E(psilon)	E
Vau	𐤅	F	F			C,F	Vau (or Digamma)	F
Zayin	I	Ɨ	I	I	I	I	Zeta	Z
Cheth	𐤇	⊟	⊟	⊟		⊟	-h [H]eta	H
		⊟			⊟		-ē [H]eta	
Teth	𐤈	⊗	⊗	⊗	⊗	⊗	Theta	
Yod	𐤉	ʒ	Σ	I	I	I	Iota	I
Kaph	K	K	K	K	K	K	Kappa	K
Lamed	𐤋	Γ	Λ	V	Λ	V	Lambda	L
Mem	𐤌	M	M	M	M	M	Mu	M
Nun	𐤍	N	N	N	N	N	Nu	N
Samekh	𐤎	Ψ	Ξ		Ξ	+,X	Xi	X
Ayin	O	O	O	O	O	O	O(micron)	O
Pe	𐤐	Γ	Π	Π	Π	P	Pi	P
Tsade	𐤑	M	M				San (=s)	
Q'oph	Φ	Ϙ	Ϙ	(Ϙ)	(Ϙ)	Ϙ	Koppa	Q
Resh	𐤓	P	P	P	P	R	Rho	R
Shin	W			Σ	Σ	Σ	Sigma	S
Tau	+	T	T	T	T	T	Tau	T
		V	V	V	V	V	U(psilon)	V,Y,U
			Φ	Φ	Φ	Φ	Phi	
			X	X	X	Ψ	Chi	
			Ψ		Ψ		Psi	
					Ω		Omega	

Fig. 12. Phoenician, Greek and Latin alphabets

COLONISATION

Fig. 11

About the middle of the eighth century the Greeks began again to spread overseas. The earliest settlements were in South Italy and Sicily; others occupied sites in the North Aegean, along the Sea of Marmara and, more sparsely, round the Black Sea; and there were outliers in Cyrenaica, Provence, Catalonia and up the Adriatic. By 600 BC, when colonisation was slackening, there were at least two hundred of these new cities of Greeks, ringing the Mediterranean and the inner seas except where some stronger power prevented them – Carthaginians and Etruscans in the West, Assyrians and their successors in the East, and Scythians to the North. The ruins of Paestum (which the Greeks called Posidonia) and of Selinus give an idea of what the richer colonies were like.

Over-population or land-hunger was the main incentive to emigrate. For though some colonies were well placed for trade, almost all had territory enough for their agricultural needs and often more fertile than that of their motherland. Indeed many of them soon had a surplus of foodstuffs and began to export it to Greece itself in return for manufactured goods and silver. So such cities as Corinth, Megara and Athens became able to support a larger population than local farming could feed and to develop industry and specialised agriculture. The decline in colonising may have been caused by this economic change more than by lack of suitable sites.

How a site was chosen in a new region is not often recorded. There must anyhow have been some exploration, whether deliberate or incidental to raiding or trading. Some scholars claim that a vigorous Greek commerce preceded colonisation, but in the colonial regions the exported Greek pottery on which they rely is very rarely earlier than the first Greek settlement. Presumably the organiser of a colony made what inquiries he could, if he had no first-hand knowledge himself. But we do not know how many colonial ventures failed. It is often asserted that the priests at Delphi regularly collected and passed on information about likely sites, but their prescient oracles may be later, self-interested inventions; in the eighth century Delphi had not yet any wide importance. The next stage was the preparing of the expedition. It was organised and commanded by a 'founder' and sponsored officially by a city, though the colonists were not necessarily all from that city. The original colonists, and occasionally later arrivals, received citizenship of the new city and an allotment of land there. Since colonies were self-supporting, it was natural by Greek standards that they should be independent too, though they kept some sentimental ties to their mother-city. The principal mother-cities were for the West Chalcis, Corinth, Megara and the Achaean states, for the North Chalcis, Eretria, Megara, Paros and Miletus. In the sixth century a few politically dependent colonies were founded by Corinth and Athens, but this form of imperialism did not become normal. A few settlements in Syria and Egypt were tolerated by the Eastern powers, but like Naucratis in the Nile Delta had no more than municipal self-government.

Generally the colonies were set among peoples who were not Greeks nor as civilised. When they could, the colonists enslaved them; when they could not, they showed more scrupulousness. In a few instances, notably in South Russia and Campania, there was some fusion of Greeks and natives, but most of the colonies that survived wars with each other remained properly, if provincially, Greek till Roman times or even later. Their influence on their free non-Greek neighbours was, though, less than might be expected; Greek art was imitated and occasionally methods of fortification, but Greek institutions were not suited to rural societies. On Greece itself the effect of the colonies was mainly economic. Locri in South Italy is said to have been the first Greek city to publish its laws, several important philosophers and some literary pioneers flourished in the West, the doctors of Croton were famous in the late sixth century, but on the whole the colonies did not maintain steady progress and when they were not imitative their novelties were too often provincial.

ECONOMICS

Ancient writers generally were not much concerned with economics and we have very little direct information for the Archaic period. So most of what is said in this section is inference or conjecture, except where the source is quoted. But it is obvious that from the eight to the sixth century much of Greek life was transformed decisively by economic changes which occurred in a relatively few maritime states. Yet even there peasant farming continued to be the biggest source of production, while the rest of Greece was affected only indirectly or not at all. States principally involved were Corinth (so conveniently situated on routes by land as well as by sea), Sicyon, Aegina, Megara, Athens, Eretria, Chalcis, Paros, Naxos and some of the settlements on and off the Anatolian coast.

About the time that colonisation began, in the middle of the eight century, Greek connections became closer with the venerable civilisations of the East. The Mycenaeans, as finds of pottery show, had traded with Syria and Egypt, as well as with South Italy and Sicily. But in the Early Iron Age contact was much less, though it was not broken altogether; Oriental objects are found occasionally in Geometric graves in Greece, and Homer had heard of Sidon and Egypt. But now, as excavation has shown, a settlement of Greeks grew up in Syria at Al Mina – the ancient name may have been Posideïon – and perhaps at other places – and soon afterwards Oriental motives which were domesticated in Syria became popular in Greek art. Egypt does not seem to have been open to the Greeks for another century or more. Contact with Syria and Egypt was by sea, for though there were land routes across Asia Minor, they were not important commercially; at least the Lydians, if not the Phrygians before them, were more influenced by Greek than Oriental art.

Greek trade with Syria was for luxury goods. In exchange they could offer wine, oil, slaves, silver, and perhaps raw materials and corn. The trade with Egypt, to judge by Greek objects there, was not established till near the end of the seventh century, though Greek mercenaries had arrived a generation earlier. Egypt was a great producer of corn and that presumably was what most attracted the Greeks. Payment was at least partly in silver, as caches of Greek coins show. According to Herodotus, the Greeks were not always popular with the Egyptians and by an official regulation the merchants, who came mostly from the East Aegean, were concentrated in the city of Naucratis up the western branch of the Nile. The excavation of this site, done sixty or seventy years ago, was not up to the standard expected (often fondly) today: it yielded a great deal of Greek pottery, but little else. Greek pottery has been found also at a few other settlements of Greek traders or mercenaries in the East, but till the later Archaic period none of the Eastern peoples (those of west and north Anatolia excepted) had acquired a taste for any works of Greek art.

Fig. 13

The earnings of the Greek mercenaries, who are attested by literature and inscriptions, were another item in the balance of trade. They came mostly from Asiatic Greece and the adjacent native communities of Caria, and from the middle of the seventh century onwards had a high reputation as heavy

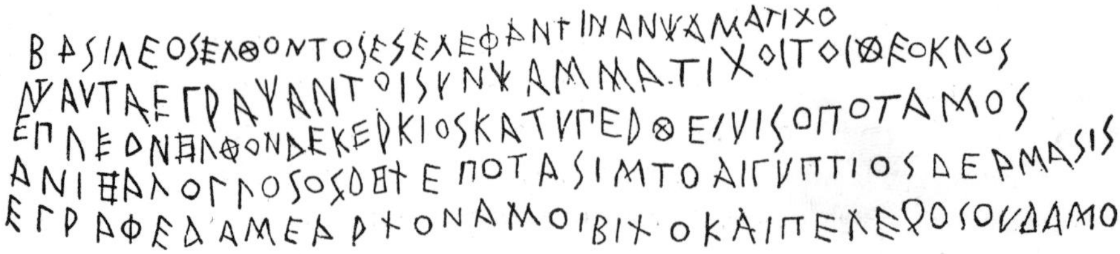

Fig. 13. Greek inscription at Abu Simbel, 591–580 B C. *Length 2·80 m.*

infantry with the Egyptians and Babylonians, and later still with the Persians.

But the bulk of the overseas trade of Greece was with the colonies. This trade, largely for foodstuffs and primary products, must have been established fairly early in the seventh century and it had far-reaching consequences. It was almost inevitable that the importing cities grew larger, that in their own territory industry and specialised agriculture developed to provide saleable exports, and that these economic and social changes had their effects in politics. Indeed it is partly from the political effects that the economic causes are inferred.

A mistake that is easily made is the assumption that in the early Archaic period economic development was deliberately initiated or sponsored by the state. Athens in the fifth and perhaps already in the sixth century took action to protect its supply of corn from the Black Sea. But as a rule shippers were regarded officially as a source of revenue; at Athens again in the fifth century, the customs tax was normally two per cent on both imports and exports, and in the first half of the seventh century the Bacchiad government of Corinth, the leading commercial city of Greece, was – so Strabo says – accused particularly of exploiting the market dues. But some official actions, especially those of the 'tyrants' of the sixth century, did much to help trade, even though the ultimate aim may have been sometimes increased revenue. Such helps were the suppression of piracy, the construction of harbours (though Athens used the open beach of Phaleron till the beginning of the fifth century) and the encouragement of skilled immigrants. Another public work, which may have been used for merchant ships as well as ships of war, was the 'diolkos' across the Isthmus of Corinth: this was a track four miles long designed for bogies on which ships could be transported from one sea to the other. The 'diolkos' was cut, so excavation suggests, about 600 BC, and it was usable as late as the ninth century AD.

Fig. 29

In the Early Iron Age, if Homer is to be believed, the status of the trader was despised. So it was again generally in the fifth century. But during the Archaic period there are hints in literature that some reputable men engaged in trade, or anyhow that some men who engaged in trade were considered reputable. Solon, the Athenian lawgiver, is said to have travelled commercially to Egypt, and Sappho objected to her brother's spending his profits on a prostitute in Naucratis. In any case the capital needed to fit out a long trading voyage must have been considerable and so in the early Archaic period it is likely that the landed aristocrats often had a stake in such adventures. Still, some commoners became wealthy, as Theognis in the sixth century complained with bitter jealousy. But though such commoners were a new factor in political life, they did not form a mercantile party: the most respectable and the safest form of wealth was in land, and the new rich preferred to settle down as gentlemen. But there must also have been a growing number of traders who acquired moderate means.

Industry suffered from similar handicaps of lack of capital and low repute. It was practised at the craftsman rather than the factory level, and the ordinary workshop remained a family concern with perhaps one or two hired assistants or slaves. The industry we know most about is that making fine pottery, since intensive study of the painted decoration has reached the stage of recognising the handiwork of individual painters, and this with the occasional signatures allows some conclusions about mobility of labour, the size of the industry, and methods of marketing. As might be expected, potters normally had no contact with overseas markets, but sold to customers or traders in the workshop. What is perhaps more surprising is that in the finer grades of pottery it continued to be profitable to export over long distances in spite of local competition. Some Attic (that is Athenian) potters of the late sixth century prospered enough to make expensive dedications on the Acropolis at Athens.

The wealth of information about fine Greek pottery of the Archaic period is most useful for dating sites. For economic studies it is, in spite of some modern historians, disappointing. The principal facts for the Archaic period are that there were many local schools of fine Greek pottery, that till the early sixth century Corinthian pottery was imported more than any other (especially in the West), and that afterwards Attic more than took its place. From these facts it does not necessarily follow that at first Corinth conducted the greater part of all overseas trade or even of the Western trade and that later Athens captured this trade from Corinth. For most Greek states that were active in trade made little or no fine pottery, goods from any state were not always carried in ships of that state, and fine pottery (as can be shown statistically) was a minor item in Greek industry and trade. The obvious reason for the dominance first of Corinthian and then of Attic pottery – a dominance evident not only in export, but also in their artistic influence on other schools – is that Greek customers preferred Corinthian and Attic wares whether for their technical or their artistic superiority. It must be remembered too that fine pots (as many of the shapes prove) were usually exported as fine pots and not as containers for some more valuable commodity.

The development of trade and industry tipped the economic balance of many Greek states against self-sufficiency. But even there agriculture usually provided the biggest part of the national income, and there were good returns for those who had enough land and the reserves to tide over a bad year. While the methods of farming did not change, there was some increase in production or productivity by the specialised culture in suitable places of such crops as grapes and olives (though the olive tree needed some seven years before it began to bear and at least twenty before it reached its maturity) and some ground that was by Greek standards arable was turned over to sheep. So the rich continued to invest in land and there were enough substantial peasants to keep up the number of heavy infantry in the militia. Agrarian trouble was certainly serious – in Attica around 600 BC many peasants were falling into debt and being sold as slaves by their creditors; but since the cancelling of such debts seems to have proved a fairly effective cure, it looks as if the causes of the trouble were harsh laws, excessive rates of interest, or abnormally bad harvests rather than an economic revolution (resulting, according to some historians, from the introduction of coined money). Another factor was the small size of many plots, especially where a man's land was divided between several heirs – Hesiod advises the farmer to have only one son – and this shortage of land was aggravated by the growth of large estates. The reallotment of privately owned land became a regular demand of democratic revolutionaries.

A curious phenomenon of the late seventh century was the invention of coinage. To judge by the earliest types and by the testimony of Xenophanes in the next century, this happened in Lydia. Coinage is to us so necessary a convenience that its original purpose seems self-evident. But the governments and trading cities of the East, whose economic structure had been for a long time more advanced than that of seventh-century Lydians and Greeks, had managed without coinage and after it appeared were very slow to adopt it. Further, the earliest coins (which were of electrum, an alloy probably at first natural of gold and silver) were of high values; what may be reckoned the standard denomination, the so-called 'third', had a value of about ten Attic drachmas and in Solon's laws, promulgated in the 590's, an Attic drachma was the value of a sheep. So the early coinage was not intended for small transactions, while for large transactions it was prudent and most likely usual to weigh coins as bullion. Perhaps, then, the original purpose of coinage was not commercial, but a convenient method of paying fixed weights of bullion to mercenaries. In later times the payment of mercenaries was often enough an occasion for new issues of coins. But in any case it was a long time before the Greeks took to using coins for ordinary everyday transactions.

POLITICS

Greek writers had a strong interest in politics, both practical and theoretical, and a fair amount of information survives about developments in the Archaic period. Unfortunately this information is not always accurate, since records were defective and there was a tendency to reconstruct the past in the spirit of the present or to support political propaganda. So, for example, several Athenian pamphleteers of the late fifth and fourth centuries BC wrote accounts of the Archaic constitution of their state, with judicious alterations to justify their own party programmes. But in general the dominant prejudice of our authorities is oligarchical, since the richer classes (whose interests were protected by oligarchy – that is, their own rule) were also the most literate.

At the end of the Early Iron Age kings still reigned in Argos, Messenia, Epirus and Macedonia, and at Sparta there was the curious system of two co-regnant kings. But most Greek states were governed by aristocracies with annual magistrates of limited functions and a permanent council, whether hereditary or chosen; the assembly of the commoners might vote for candidates or proposals put forward by the council, but had little or no positive power. This ancestral constitution, happy enough for the privileged group, was now exposed, anyhow in the maritime states, to the effects of the economic and social changes of the early Archaic period. The ruling nobles may have become greedier and more oppressive, as Hesiod suggests. A new rich class, drawn partly from the lesser nobility and partly from the commoners, was likely to demand a share in government. The more modestly successful farmers, craftsmen and traders had their complaints, and of these the farmers at least, who provided most of the heavy infantry in the new armies, were becoming a necessary and potentially formidable part of the state. In the lowest stratum the pressure of poverty was increasing. Besides the new distribution of wealth other changes were disturbing the balance of the constitution. The growth of cities naturally encouraged political discussions and combinations, but it required besides a more complex system of administration; the development of temple architecture after the middle of the seventh century implies a certain level not only of civic feeling, but also of public financing. Further, as population grew, the aristocratic government with its fixed number of councillors and magistrates became less and less representative even of the nobles, and (as usually happens) it was the dissatisfied rich whose aspirations were most dangerous, although to some extent they were admitted to a share of power and privilege. The middle and lower orders, ineffective by themselves, were not necessarily inarticulate and it was they, presumably, who now enriched the political vocabulary of the Greeks. The old term 'aristocracy' means the rule of the 'best', and even much later the upper-class parties liked to call themselves by similar complimentary names. The new 'oligarchy' is the rule of the 'few', whom their opponents also called the 'rich' or more simply the 'fat'. But though in advanced states oligarchies tended to have a larger membership than aristocracies and to be based on strict property qualifications which allowed individuals to be promoted or expelled, yet in general the nobles remained rich and especially where there was not much urban development the 'best' and the 'few' remained much the same.

In agricultural states the aristocracy or oligarchy kept its hold, even if it had to make concessions. But in most of the maritime and commercial states more radical solutions were necessary. The first victory of the malcontents was sometimes the improvement of justice. Previously the laws had not been written down and the aristocrats who administered them had tempting opportunities to twist their decisions. Now lawgivers clarified or revised the legal codes and published them. Later Greek writers thought the first such publication was at Epizephyrian Locri in South Italy about 660 BC, and that at Athens a similar reform was completed around 625. But both these early codes were grudgingly harsh. It usually needed a 'tyrant' to make the break with tradition.

The word 'tyrant', which is of unknown origin, is recorded for the first time not long before the middle of the seventh century. It meant or came to mean an unconstitutional absolute monarch; the connotation of cruelty and oppressiveness was added later by the opponents of such monarchs. Though circumstances differed from one state to another, some general statements are valid. It was in the maritime, trading cities that tyrants occurred. They were of noble birth and often had distinguished themselves in war. They came into power by force. They were hostile to the power of the nobility and so could not afford the hostility of the commoners. Their policies aimed at peace and prosperity, and they spent freely (partly at the expense of the old ruling class) on useful public works, civic amenities and the arts. They hardly ever succeeded in establishing family dynasties. They were overthrown in the end by oligarchs or by foreign intervention on behalf of oligarchs, but the restored oligarchies did not dare to abolish many of their innovations or reforms. In summary these early tyrants were enlightened despots or rather dictators, impelled often by ambition or personal spite, but sometimes perhaps by idealism; and later Greek tradition, for all its hostility to tyranny as such, admits that some of them were mild and just and popular. Cypselus, for instance, who was the first tyrant of Corinth, managed without a bodyguard, his son and successor Periander won a place among the Seven Sages, and in democratic Athens the sons of Pisistratus were vilified but Pisistratus himself was remembered with affection.

The first tyrants appeared at Sicyon and Corinth about the middle of the seventh century. But it is the Athenian tyranny of which we know the most, since so many of the Greek historians and political theorists lived or worked in Athens. Here about 630 BC a noble called Cylon, who had won the chariot race at the Olympic Games and also was married to the daughter of the tyrant of Megara, attempted to set up a tyranny of his own, but failed. A few years later, the government, presumably under pressure, allowed the publication of a code of laws. But internal troubles grew worse and in the 590's Solon, a well-to-do citizen who may have been engaged in trade, was appointed as mediator with full powers. Among much else he cancelled debts, freed enslaved debtors, made the law more humane, organised the citizens in four classes based on annual income, and allotted to each class graduated civic privileges and duties. But Solon's political reforms, like those of most other such mediators, did not produce a lasting solution, and indeed civil struggles became worse. Thirty years later Pisistratus, a noble who had been a successful commander in the war with Megara, made himself tyrant while the other clans were quarrelling, was ejected, restored and ejected again, and at last after some years returned and established his power firmly. The commoners, even of the hoplite class, appear to have had little influence in these events, which were determined by the personal feuds and followings of the great aristocratic houses. Pisistratus drew his revenue partly from his own estates in Attica and Thrace (where he had been busy mining before his successful return), partly from a tax of five per cent (or perhaps at first ten) on agricultural produce, and partly – it may be guessed – from customs duties. He maintained peace at home and with neighbouring states, made loans to small farmers and sent judges round Attica to try cases locally, established Attic strongholds in the Hellespont – so presumably Athens was already importing corn from the Black Sea – improved the water supply, built elaborate temples and added to the splendour of civic festivals (including the Dionysiac performances from which tragedy grew). His sons were even more active patrons of the arts, welcomed famous poets to their court, and embellished the roads of Attica with milestones in the form of herms inscribed with distances and good proverbial advice. In the conduct of government Pisistratus used his absolute power moderately and humanely and within the framework of the constitution; the annual officers were appointed, and presumably the council and assembly continued to exist. He died in 528 BC. His son and successor Hippias continued his policy with success. He survived the murder of his brother in 514 BC, a rising of some nobles the next year, and a Spartan invasion to restore oligarchy. When he fell in 510, it was because of another Spartan expedition and the unlucky capture of his family. This, of course, was not emphasised in the civic tradition of Athens; before 480 the murderers of Hippias's brother were commemorated by public statues, and the private grievance which prompted them became a selfless patriotism.

For mainland Greece and the nearer islands the tyranny of Pisistratus and his sons may be reckoned broadly typical. But in the Greek states of the East Aegean the imminence first of Lydia and then of Persia encouraged the rise of military autocrats, of whom Polycrates of Samos, a daring and unscrupulous adventurer, was the most notable. Perhaps similar conditions in Sicily, where the Carthaginians were dangerous, led to similar tyrannies towards the end of the sixth century. Yet another type of tyranny was established by the Lydians and Persians in Greek cities they conquered; they allowed these cities a considerable autonomy, and for convenience preferred a local man as governor.

In Greece itself tyranny had disappeared before 500 BC, in some states by oligarchic revolts, in others by the intervention of Sparta on behalf of the oligarchs. Generally the tyrants, like the strong monarchs of late Medieval Europe, were public benefactors whatever their private motives. The nobles were oppressed to some degree, the common people suffered less oppression. More positively important was the encouragement of peace, employment, and efficient administration. At the end of the Archaic period the Greek states were more prosperous, better organised and more powerful than ever before.

Tyranny was succeeded regularly by oligarchy. But now a rival form of government was emerging. This was what the Greeks called 'democracy', though it was very different from modern democracy, whether of Western or Eastern type. Both oligarchy and democracy conserved the traditional organs of Greek government – officials (elected usually for a year), council, and assembly; they were distinguished by their attitude to class structure, the classes being normally determined by wealth. In an oligarchy office and membership of the council, which held effective control, were reserved for the upper class or classes, and the poorest class might be excluded even from the assembly, although that assembly had only limited powers of election and discussion. The complete democratic theory was that all citizens had equal rights in the government; offices (where practicable) were filled by lot, the council only prepared business for the assembly, and the assembly itself was sovereign. Between the extreme forms of oligarchy and democracy there was a range of intermediate constitutions shading into each other so that some might be called with equal reason either broad oligarchies or moderate democracies. The struggle between oligarchs and democrats reached more spectacular heights of bitterness, but belongs rather to the Classical period. In Athens, where democracy flourished most securely, its establishment seems to have been largely accidental. When the Spartans deposed the tyrant Hippias, two noble factions competed for dominance of the state and Cleisthenes, the loser, took the people into partnership. Before long other nobles saw that family prestige and wealth were useful assets even in a democracy, and later developments made reaction futile and dangerous. Of other early democracies we know very little.

In Sparta things were different. There as far back as tradition went the constitution consisted of two joint kings, a small council, and a weak assembly. To this at some early date was added a committee of five annually elected officers, the 'ephors', who took over from the kings the executive power in civil affairs though not the conduct of war. All full citizens might in due course be elected as councillors or ephors. The impression is of a system very advanced at the time that it was established and then arrested in its development. The reason must have been Sparta's peculiar institution: the citizens had a common interest in exploiting a much greater number of subjects and serfs, whom they kept down by force, and so in a sense they were all aristocrats and under army discipline.

In all these constitutions there was no clear notion of representative government, but every citizen was entitled to attend the assembly and, unless he did, could not record his vote. This meant, of course, that in democracies – as anti-democrats justly argued – the farmers tended to have less influence relatively to the city-dwellers. Women, of course, had no franchise and slaves no civic rights, but it is more surprising that from the sixth century on, and perhaps earlier, there was no normal provision for naturalising freed slaves or even the resident aliens ('metics') who in Athens at least came to take an important part in commerce and industry and showed enough loyalty to the state of their adoption.

Indeed the democratic government of Athens pushed exclusiveness further by requiring as a test of citizenship that both parents should themselves be of citizen families. The fully developed Greek city-state was in one way a sort of profit-sharing institution, and no one likes to share his profits.

RELATIONS BETWEEN THE GREEK STATES

During the Archaic period the Greeks developed some feeling of racial unity. Such a feeling requires, of course, contact with peoples of foreign speech and foreign, preferably inferior, culture. These conditions had been met already in the Asiatic settlements, but now colonisation and trade made more Greeks acquainted with 'barbarians', a term that at first was not contemptuous but simply described the sound of an unintelligible language. A more positive aid to unity was the acceptance of a common stock of poetry; the Homeric epics soon became widely known, and the lyric poets who followed were recited even where their dialect was unfamiliar. Another cause, as well as effect, of Panhellenism may be seen in the great sanctuaries and festivals, notably those at Delphi and Olympia, which during the seventh century gained respect and visitors from the whole Greek world. Apollo of Delphi became the premier prophet of the Greeks, consulted regularly on questions of private and public religion and policy, and Croesus of Lydia was not the first foreign king to make rich offerings to him, whether from piety or as a bid (belatedly successful) for general Greek goodwill. At Olympia competitors in the games came from all Greek states, but this consciousness of unity was most typically expressed in the ban on non-Greek entries: the Macedonians, for instance, were excluded sedulously, except for their kings who might make useful allies or patrons. Greek national feeling was only skin deep, and solidarity even against foreign aggression was hard to arouse and to keep. So in the mid sixth century the Ionians let themselves be conquered piecemeal by the Lydians, though to be fair they revolted together in 499 BC; and when in 480 the Persians invaded Greece, the oracle at Delphi advised submission and Argos refused to co-operate with its neighbour and enemy Sparta.

In fact the Greek states were very jealous of their own independence, and though they did not respect the independence of others no one of them became powerful enough to achieve complete domination. But some states were or became dominant over their neighbours. The northern kingdoms, though extensive, were only potentially dangerous till the fourth century. Thessaly too was usually disorganised, but in the seventh and early sixth centuries seems to have used its cavalry and the Amphictyonic league to impose itself on districts to the south. In more civilised parts Thebes slowly subdued the other states of Boeotia; and Chalcis and Eretria, two adjacent cities of Euboea, conquered some of the nearer island states and fought the mysterious Lelantine war, in which Thucydides says that most Greek states took sides. Among the Cyclades the largest island, Naxos, had some sort of control over its neighbours around the middle of the sixth century.

Athens was fortunate in being the only proper city in an area the size of a county, and so had more breathing space than most Greek states. Even so, it took some territory from Megara, as did Corinth on the other side. But Corinth had no such success against its Peloponnesian neighbours, and more than any other Greek city built its considerable naval and even military importance on trade. To the south of Corinth, over the watershed, was the Argive plain. Here in the Early Iron Age there were several independent cities, of which Argos, the strongest, patiently subjugated or destroyed the rest – Asine already in the eighth century, Nauplia in the seventh, and finally Tiryns and Mycenae in the 460's. Argos also for a time possessed the coastal districts to its south and under king Phidon, probably around 670 BC, had a short-lived hegemony over much of the Peloponnese. After that Sparta was too powerful.

The Spartans in the south-east were a ruling minority which developed into a military caste. Around 730 BC they conquered Messenia on the other side of Mount Taygetus and in spite of a vigorous revolt a century later kept its inhabitants in serfdom. Later they took some border districts from other neighbours. But further expansion was difficult and unnecessary, and about 550 BC the Spartans tried a new policy: other Greek states were invited to make military alliances with them. All the Peloponnese was enrolled except of course Argos, Sparta's most dangerous enemy, and the cities of Achaea; and beyond the Isthmus Megara joined too. Since it was a Spartan principle to favour oligarchy, there was a campaign against tyrants and incipient democracy. This 'Peloponnesian league' was very formidable in its infantry, and though its organisation was cumbrous, it could defeat any rivals in continental Greece. But all members had a say in the decisions of the league and Sparta, while its leader and the most powerful single Greek state, could not always browbeat them. For example, in 506 BC the opposition of Corinth and other allies prevented Sparta from coercing Athens. But when the Persians invaded Greece in 480 BC, it was only natural that the command of the armies and fleets from those Greek states which resisted belonged to Sparta.

WAR

The battles of the Early Iron Age seem to have exploited the individual skill of warriors, on foot or horseback, armed with light shields, throwing-spears and swords. But around 700 BC an infantry equipment was introduced which had a remarkable effect on Greek warfare and history. The innovation consisted primarily of a round, heavier shield, which was worn on the left forearm and reached from the neck to the thighs, and a six-foot spear for thrusting. The other armament was helmet,

Fig. 14

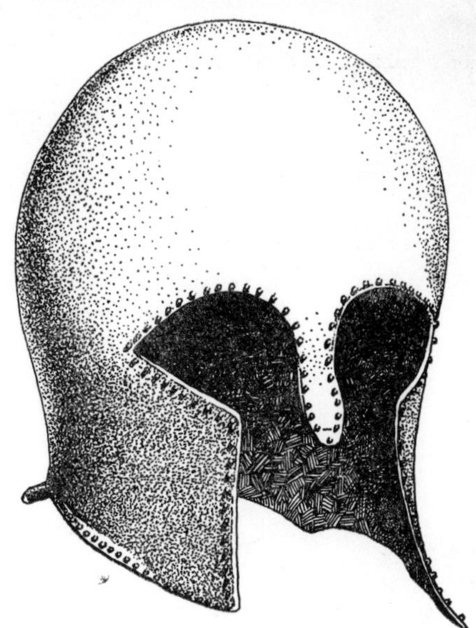

Fig. 14. Bronze helmet, late seventh or early sixth century BC. *Scale about 2:7*

corselet (of leather or metal), greaves (that is, shin-guards), and a short sword that could be used for hacking or stabbing. With or for the novel equipment novel tactics were developed. The 'hoplite', as the new infantryman was called, was well protected in front but too heavy to move quickly and for defence as well as attack needed co-operation. The new tactics placed the hoplites in a long line, with shields overlapping so that each man covered the next man's right side. This formation, the 'phalanx', was normally eight lines deep, the second line perhaps thrusting its spears over the shields of the first: sometimes for extra weight the phalanx was deepened in decisive parts, but unless the line was long enough there was the serious danger of being outflanked. In the normal hoplite battle between equal forces the two armies were drawn up facing each other across fairly level ground, with cavalry and skirmishers to protect the flanks. When the charge was sounded, the phalanx moved forward and pushed and jabbed at the enemy till one side or the other broke. Since the individual hoplite relied on his right-hand neighbour's shield to

Fig. 15
Plates 48, 83
Plate 70

cover him, there was a tendency during the charge for the whole line to edge to the right and so for the right-wing to overlap, outflank and defeat the opposing left wing: victory often depended on the ability of a successful right wing to break off pursuit and round on the rear of the enemy centre. In the

Fig. 15. Back of bronze corselet, about 650 BC. *Scale about 1:4*

battle itself casualties were usually light, as long as the lines held firm; they were much greater when a contingent was attacked in the rear or during flight, though if he threw away his heavy shield and spear a hoplite could run much faster than a pursuing hoplite who was fully armed.

After the signal to charge there was little scope for manoeuvre and when battle had been engaged even less. So the principal requirement of the hoplite was steadiness, and that and the necessary arms drill could be learnt by a citizen militia. The officers too could be amateurs and, since successful generalship at the tactical level consisted mainly of choosing the ground, positioning the forces, and keeping up morale, even commanding officers were expected to fight in the ranks. Professional soldiers, like the Spartans, were of course more efficient, but the occasional levies of other Greek states were formidable enough. Cavalry, mounted on ponies without stirrups and armed with thrusting spear and sword, could not break the solid front of the phalanx and, though light-armed troops might harass hoplites with arrows, sling-shots and javelins while staying out of range of reprisal, this form of warfare was not organised in any advanced Archaic state: the invention of the hoplite made the middle class indispensable, the development of light troops would have emboldened those who were too poor to provide themselves with the hoplite's equipment. The phalanx was certainly not the most flexible of formations, but in an age of set battles it was the most effective. The proof was in the eagerness of the Oriental states to engage Greek and Carian mercenaries and in the defeat of the best Persian infantry at Marathon and Plataea at the end of this period.

On this heavy infantry we are well informed, since Archaic and later writers regarded war as an important part of history and civic duty, artists found battle a convenient subject, and many pieces of equipment have survived. For though the fashion of burying men with their armour was dropped about

700 BC, it became customary to dedicate spoils taken from an enemy, with the addition, very often, of a suitable inscription. So we have helmets of various types, metal blazons and bands from shields (which were made of thick leather), greaves, the heads and butts of spears, swords, and occasionally parts of plate or scale corselets. It is worth noting that bronze and not iron was the usual metal for defensive armour and common for weapons. Archaic vase-paintings, reliefs and figurines, much more detailed and lifelike than Geometric, are helpful if their conventions are kept in mind; in particular for reasons of composition or legend hoplites are usually pictured as if fighting duels, and from an interest in anatomy they may be shown naked or later with the cheek-pieces of their helmets hinged up. Sometimes mounted hoplites appear, but these are well-to-do soldiers riding to battle and not cavalry.

Fig. 14
Fig. 15
Plate 73
Plate 57

Mycenaean castles had been fortified and, though at the end of the Bronze Age their inner buildings were destroyed, the outer walls were presumably still kept in repair. At Mycenae itself, for instance, much of what remains is Hellenistic renewal, after the town had been destroyed by the Argives in the 460's. It is also likely enough that even in the Early Iron Age any new acropolis was strengthened by a rough wall. But we do not know when the walling of towns became general, and indeed knowledge of this must usually be difficult to unearth because of later expansion or rebuilding. At Smyrna the small city of the Greek settlers was fortified in the ninth century; at Corinth there may be remains of a very extensive city wall of the seventh century; and in the sixth century it is certain that most important cities had walls, whether of stone or mud brick (recommended later as less vulnerable to battering rams). Sparta, of course, with its invincible infantry felt no need to fortify itself, but could make little impression on the fortifications of others. This was because methods of assault were rudimentary and siege artillery did not exist. If, then, a walled city was not taken by surprise or treachery, there remained only blockade. But the provisioning of besiegers was poorly organised and the ordinary soldier (who was unpaid) objected to being away for long from his civilian livelihood, so that a protracted siege was usually not feasible and the invading army contented itself with burning farms and crops and then returned home.

At the beginning of the Archaic period the standard war-ship was the penteconter, so called from its fifty oars. There is no evidence that the Greeks copied from the Phoenicians; and, according to Thucydides, Corinth was the pioneer in improved ship-building. The bireme with its two banks of oars appeared probably in the sixth century and was followed by the trireme. This was a low ship about 140 feet long, 20 feet wide amidships, and drawing perhaps four feet of water. It had up to a hundred and fifty oars, arranged in three banks with one man to each oar; scholars dispute about the exact arrangement of the three rowers of each group, but anyhow they did not sit on the same bench nor directly over each other. There were platforms for marines above the rowers, a mast which could be unshipped, and a strong ram which was in effect an extension of the keel. The trireme sacrificed sea-worthiness in rough water to speed and manoeuvrability. In battle the aim of the commander was to ram the side of an enemy ship or to sheer through its oars. Where conditions were suitable the trireme was remarkably effective, but it needed a skilful captain and a well-trained crew. The tactical principles of land and sea fighting were becoming very different.

Fig. 16

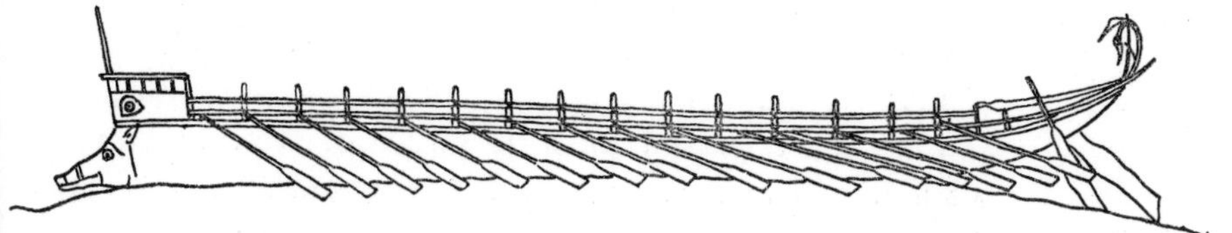

Fig. 16. Drawing of warship, about 570 BC. *Scale about 2:5*

The earliest sea battle still remembered in the fifth century was fought about 660 BC between Corinth and Corcyra (Corfu), a colony founded by Corinth some seventy years before. But there is little information about Greek navies before the end of the sixth century. The buccaneering Samian tyrant Polycrates had a hundred penteconters and forty triremes in the 520's. Athens, it seems, had only fifty warships of all sorts in 487 BC, but seven years later was able to put nearly two hundred triremes to sea for the battle of Salamis. Some of the Greeks were perceiving the uses of sea-power.

SOCIETY

Fig. 17

Plate 47

The changes that introduced the Archaic period brought with them more opportunity for the rich to be luxurious. The lyric poets speak of perfume and expensive clothes, the later Archaic statues (for instance those from the Acropolis at Athens) show women with intricate dress and coiffure, and from literature and archaeological finds we know of elaborately worked jewellery and furniture. This luxury was exhibited particularly in personal wear; houses remained simple in materials and design, though to judge by vase-paintings the main front inside the courtyard acquired sometimes a columned porch. But by the end of the sixth century there was a reaction, whether from severer principles or political tact: the change is illustrated clearly in art.

In cities it is pretty certain that the condition of women worsened. Economic advances enabled more citizens to keep their wives at home, and social prestige and respectability encouraged them to do so. There was variety in this development, and one permanent exception. In Lesbos, for instance, in the early sixth century Sappho had some liberty and spirit, and the Spartan ladies were always expected to have a morale and physique worthy of their husbands. But throughout Archaic and Classical history reputable Greek women very rarely are credited with more than matrimonial importance.

Fig. 17. Drawing of Athenian gentleman, about 690 BC. *Scale about 3:2*

One consequence of this restriction was that the profession of the superior prostitute ('hetaera') developed. Another was the acceptance of male homosexuality as a social custom, often sanctified by moral and educational clap-trap.

Before the end of the sixth century some private schools for boys are mentioned, and to judge by artists' inscriptions on pots there were a few artisans who could write and presumably read. But we have no details of early curricula: evidently the three R's were taught (if indeed the Greeks needed to be taught arithmetic), some poetry, singing and playing the lyre. Athletics had special trainers, and later there was military service. Formal schooling was simple, and teachers and tutors were, as often, despised. Girls needed only domestic skills, though naturally some indulgent parents allowed their daughters education at home.

Men with the wealth to be leisured might hunt in the country. In town they could watch athletes practising, when they were disinclined or too old to practise themselves, or chat and look on in other public places, which were becoming larger and more convenient during the sixth century. Of such public places the most important was the 'agora', in origin an open space for meetings but, as government and economy became more complex and popular, the seat also of public offices and a regular market. A kind of backgammon and dice were the favourite games of skill and chance. Dinner was the important meal of the day, to which guests might be invited; the diners

Plate 45

Plate 36

Figs. 38, 39

Fig. 18

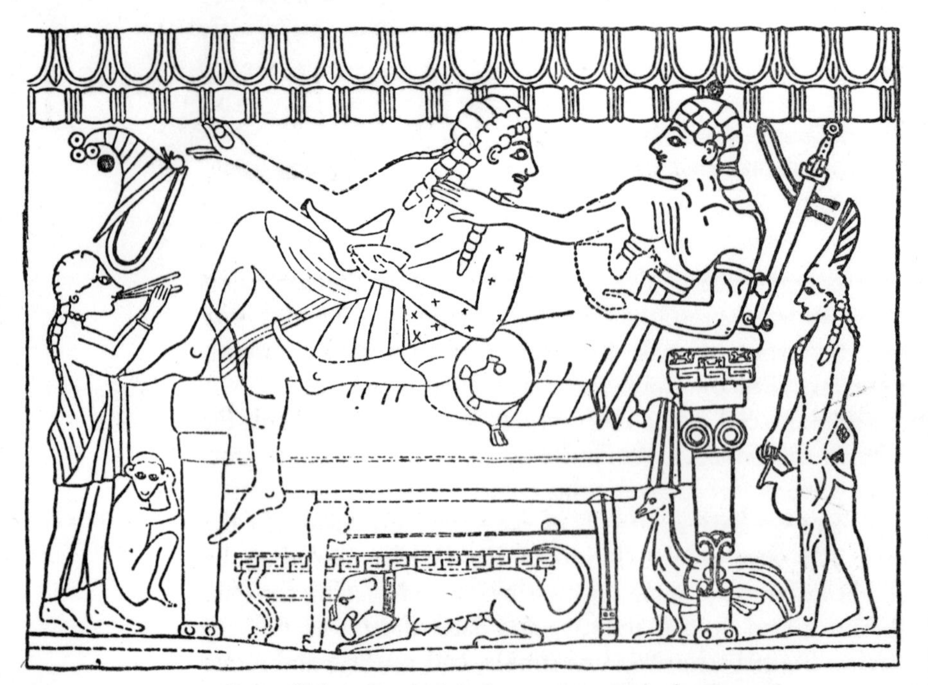

Fig. 18. Moulded terracotta relief, about 530 BC. Scale about 1:4

lay on couches, propped on their left elbows. Where the new standards of respectability were enforced, gentlewomen were excluded from the company of any man except close relatives. Later in the evening men with the taste and means could enjoy drinking parties; those described later by Plato and Xenophon were distinguished by the conversation, but poets and vase-painters record singing, wenching and the convivial game of 'kottabos', in which the dregs in the wine-cup were flicked into or at some chosen target. The amusements of the poor were necessarily more ordinary.

Plate 78

As birth ceased to be the only social criterion, society became more fluid. The old élite prided itself on better breeding, but once political concessions had been made there was no barrier of education or social habits to keep out the new rich. So, for example, in the later sixth century Pythagoras, the son of a gem-cutter in Samos, was able to become a distinguished philosopher and the originator of exclusive political societies in the oligarchical cities of South Italy.

There was one important state which developed differently. In Sparta, at some unknown time but possibly within the Archaic period, a militaristic organisation was enforced on the citizens. At the age of seven boys were taken from home to live in barracks and learn to become good and contented soldiers. The girls too had their training. But the austerities of Spartan life are probably exaggerated: our evidence comes mostly from political admirers of Sparta or else from its opponents, but there is no account by a Spartan.

ATHLETIC FESTIVALS

Athletic contests have been common everywhere at local festivals and fairs and probably existed in Greece long before the Archaic period; Homer indeed describes with gusto the games at the funeral of Patroclus. But by the early sixth century the Olympic festival (founded traditionally in 776 BC) was drawing competitors from distant parts of Greece, even the colonies, and though it remained pre-eminent three new festivals were soon ranked with it in the first class – the Pythian, held like the Olympic every four years, and the Nemean and the Isthmian, held every two. The rota in any four years was Olympic, Nemean, Pythian, and Nemean again; the Isthmians were probably in the first and third years. The time chosen was summer, convenient to everyone except perhaps the competitors. The Olympic, Pythian and Nemean festivals belonged to Pisa, Delphi and Cleonae, small cities of no military importance, and one reason for the success of the festivals may be that other Greek cities were not jealous of them. Admittedly the Isthmian sanctuary was in Corinthian territory, but it lay by the junction of two very important routes.

Plates 12, 13, 16, 18

The Olympic games may be taken as typical. Competitors had to be Greek citizens. They competed naked, after some very early date. The events were running a stade (rather more than two hundred yards), running two stades, running two stades in armour, a long-distance race, boxing, wrestling, all-in wrestling, the pentathlon (consisting of a foot race, long jump, throwing the javelin, throwing the discus, and wrestling) – in all except the race in armour there were competitions for boys as well – and various forms of horse racing and chariot racing. There were also musical contests. Entries, which were made individually, were limited (it seems) not by official standards of performance, but by expense and fear of ridicule. The prizes at Olympia were wreaths of wild olive, but at some lesser festivals they had more value; in the Panathenaic games at Athens winners received jars of fine oil.

Plate 49

The Greek attitude to these games was not unworldly. If by an amateur is meant someone who pursues a sport without pay but is ready to make on it in other ways, Greek athletes of the Archaic and Classical periods were pure amateurs. The cost of training and travelling might be high, so that a competitor had to be rich or have rich backers, but if he won his event, his prestige in his own city was great and in Athens from the early sixth century on – so Plato implies – he could count on free meals in the Town Hall for the rest of his life. For the ambitious politician who was not a prize athlete there was the four-horse chariot race, in which professional drivers were allowed; this was the premier event of the games, and the glory went to the owner. On the whole the games were a preserve of the aristocracy, but most Greeks had an admiration for aristocrats.

The great games drew not only competitors from all Greek lands, but also crowds of spectators and hucksters and, anyhow by the Classical period, propagandists or others who wished to advertise their views or themselves. Most of the visitors must have slept out. It would be naïve to suppose that competition between entrants from different states did much for Panhellenic harmony, but at least we do not hear of riots in the stadium and the Olympic truce, a month's cessation of hostilities in the neighbourhood from before till after the festival, was usually honoured.

RELIGION AND THOUGHT

The sketch of orthodox Greek religion in the Early Iron Age (pp. 30 – 36) holds good for the Archaic period too, from which indeed much of the evidence is derived. But there were some new developments. The worship of Dionysus (or Bacchus) became more popular, probably because it offered the pleasure of ecstasy (or, as the Greeks called it, 'enthusiasm'), though artists then and later were more interested in its comic scope for drunken postures. Other rituals catered for the human appetite for immortality. Of these the mystic cult of Demeter at Eleusis had little effect beyond Attica till the fifth century, and the similar ceremonies of the Great Gods at Samothrace were perhaps not yet organised. Orphism was a new and more calculated commodity, complete with theology, itinerant priests and spiritual regimen: the soul was judged after death, reincarnated, and when finally purged emerged as divine. The philosopher Pythagoras adopted much of the Orphic teaching for the rule he founded in the later sixth century. More normal was the trend to insinuate justice into the Olympian religion: a man's misdeeds are punished in this life and, since there is in effect no other, on his descendants if he himself has escaped by dying. Another general belief, rooted in the jealousy of the gods, held that great prosperity leads to excess (the Greek word 'hybris' is stronger) and excess to doom ('atê'). These two doctrines – of justice and moderation – had the support of the priests at Delphi, who were now accepted widely as arbiters in religious matters. In general they used their influence humanely, but with discretion; so, for example, when the cult of Dionysus was spreading, they gave it Apollo's blessing, although Bacchic enthusiasm was anything but moderate.

Philosophy was one of the great discoveries of the Greeks. The term includes many pursuits, from physical speculation and mathematics to theories of education and to mysticism, but its chief contribution to Western civilisation was the development of rational thought and logical method. Its weakness was in an unwillingness to experiment and to consider limited scientific advances and applications – a weakness due much less to the lack of suitable instruments and apparatus than to the preoccupation with ultimate principles reached intellectually. So the most lastingly successful results of Greek mathematics were in geometry. So too Thales, according to a tradition – whether true or false does not matter – made a corner in olive presses, but never thought of turning scientific theories to economic profit. The earliest philosophers – Thales, Anaximander and Anaximenes, active in the sixth century in Miletus in Ionia – looked for a single constituent from which all material things are formed and chose in turn water, the 'unlimited' and air. Their successor Heraclitus, Ionian too, saw a unity of arrangement and behaviour, produced by fire, which operated in a world of constant but regular change. Pythagoras, who left Samos for South Italy about 530 BC, besides his geometrical theorem and other mathematical discoveries examined the intervals of the musical scale; and since the soul is affected by music and music is dependent on numerical intervals, he thought that everything – from moral qualities to the physical constituents of the universe – could be resolved into numbers. Xenophanes, another Ionian who migrated to the West, was a radical who attacked in neat verses the conventions and prejudices of his contemporaries – from the nature of their gods to the honours heaped on successful athletes: his own deity, unlike man in form or mind, was identified with the universe.

It is to the credit of the Greeks that they tolerated such different opinions on religious and sacred subjects. But official orthodoxy was satisfied by formal observance, and willingness to assimilate was strong. Xenophanes may have given offence, but he lived to be ninety; and though the Pythagoreans were persecuted in South Italy, it was because they turned into a repressive political party and not for their religious or philosophical beliefs.

LITERATURE

Homer and Hesiod, whatever those names may mean, had set a standard for Greek poetry, but their successors did more than imitate them. The so-called Cyclic poets supplemented the *Iliad* with the rest of the tale of Troy and covered other heroic themes; the 'Homeric hymns' offer us 'epyllia', that is, descriptions in epic style of single episodes; and the Hesiodic school also continued with genealogies. More characteristic of the Archaic period were the 'lyric' poets, whose title implies that they composed for singing to the lyre and not that they were lyrical in any modern sense of that term. These Greek lyrics were short or shortish pieces varying in metre, dialect, diction and treatment, and their themes ranged from choral anthems to personal invective and from moral or political propaganda to delicate love poetry. For example Archilochus of Paros, who lived in the first half of the seventh century and is the earliest to survive as a personality, was a cynical realist; a little later, Tyrtaeus wrote patriotic appeals to inspire the ancient Spartans (and modern historians) to combat; and in the early sixth century Sappho in Lesbos made poetry of her loves and hates, while at Athens Solon pamphleteered in verse. Socially the most remarkable characteristic of the new style is its unashamed indulgence in individual feeling, an attitude foreign to Homer though not entirely to the poet of the *Works and Days*. Prose as a literary form did not yet exist, not that prose style can have been neglected in public speeches; but books were very few and expensive, and so political and even some philosophical ideas and programmes were composed in verse to be memorised and circulated more easily. Such fragments of written prose as survive – from laws or from treatises like Hecataeus's geographical compilation – were plain and artless.

Little of this literature has survived. Though the great Hellenistic libraries, especially that at Alexandria, collected all the manuscripts they could of earlier authors, the short list of school classics, picked partly for literary merit, partly for good moral tone and easy reading, did not include much lyric poetry. Few people read literature after their schooldays, and in later antiquity and the Byzantine period what educated taste remained was largely for useful information, curious miscellanies, and digests, so that new copies of most of the unlisted books were not required or made. Since in ordinary conditions papyrus rolls, which were usual till about the fourth century AD, perish with age and parchment books, which succeeded them, are not everlasting, many of the old authors became lost, especially in the seventh and eighth centuries when interest in the classics was very small and the iconoclastic troubles led to much destruction. All the same, till Constantinople, the last refuge of native Greek culture, was sacked by the Crusaders in AD 1204 and again by the Turks in 1453, the repertory of ancient literature must have been larger than now. We have gained a little (and, as publication proceeds, are gaining a little more) from finds of papyri in the rubbish tips of Roman and Hellenistic Egypt; but even so, many Greek writers will probably never be known to us by more than their names and a few brief quotations.

MUSIC

Not only was much lyric poetry composed to be sung, but throughout antiquity music was composed only as an accompaniment to singing. For this music we have some not very informative observations by ancient writers and a few more or less fragmentary scores, of which the most famous are the two hymns inscribed on stone at Delphi in the second century BC. It appears that the only instruments so used were the lyre or its relatives and some kind of pipe, that intervals of a quarter or a third of a whole tone were admitted, and that no complicated harmonies were attempted. But simple though their music was, the Greeks considered it an essential part of education and some of them were convinced that certain kinds of tune were morally and others immorally stimulating.

Plate 78, *Fig.* 15
Fig. 18

POTTERY AND PAINTING

Pottery of the Archaic period is very plentiful and much of it has painted decoration. This painted pottery has been studied in detail for its artistic qualities and they are often high, since many skilled and progressive artists were employed in vasepainting (a term, incidentally, which reveals an attitude prevalent in Greek archaeology). But purists need not grumble: close analysis of style allows close dating, and much Archaic painted pottery can be placed with a margin of from ten to twenty years in the chronological system or systems of the period. The conversion into calendar years is less sure. The Persian sack of Athens in 480 BC gives an excellent fixed point and there are two others, less good, about 525. Earlier fixed dates are the institution in 566 BC of prizes of special jars of oil at the games in Athens and the foundation of four colonies in Sicily – Selinus in 628 (or 650) BC, Gela in 688, Megara Hyblaea in 728, and Syracuse in 733; but these traditional dates may not be accurate nor indeed are the literary traditions agreed about all of them, and also the earliest Greek finds from the Sicilian sites may not belong to the moment of their foundation. So the absolute chronology of Archaic pottery should not be trusted implicitly. At the beginning of the period it might be as much as thirty or forty years out, though the range of error diminishes to negligibility at the end. Other classes of archaeological remains are fairly well related to pottery, either by style or contexts. But the dates given by ancient writers are certainly not all on the same system, and the student must be careful about equating Greek archaeological dates with those of Greek literature, and further with the dates of Syrian, Mesopotamian and Egyptian history. Even so, the excavators of Archaic Greek sites are fortunate.

In the second half of the eighth century Greek art, or at least Greek vase-painting, was ready for a change. The new patterns came principally from Syria and Phoenicia, where Egyptian, Assyrian and local elements were juxtaposed in slick routine. From this repertory the Greeks took some animals, plants and abstract ornaments and quickly remodelled them. At the same time they experimented with outline drawing and with incision (that is engraving) of detail on a full silhouette. This last technique may have been adopted from metalwork and in the early days of archaeological study was dubbed 'black-figure'. The Orientalising movement began at Corinth, where the so-called Protocorinthian style emerged about 725 BC or, to be more exact, at the time of our first Greek deposits at Syracuse and Megara Hyblaea. Other states followed sooner or later,

Fig. 19
Figs. 15, 20
Plates 71, 72
Plates 69, 71

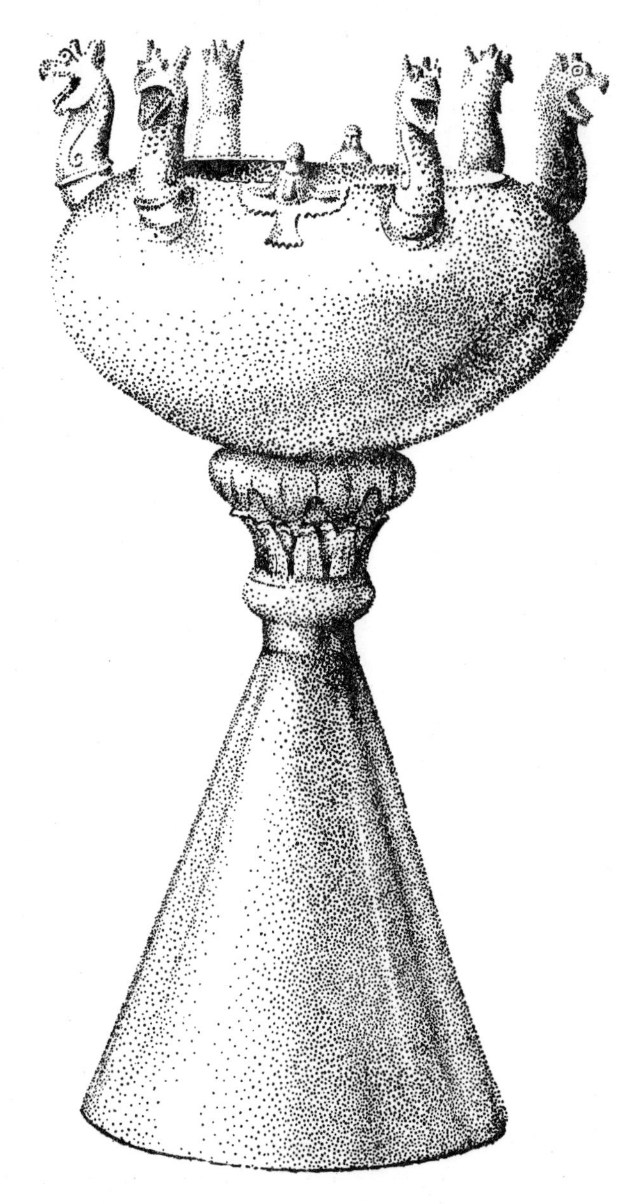

Fig. 19. Bronze cauldron and stand, about 700 BC. Height 80 cm.

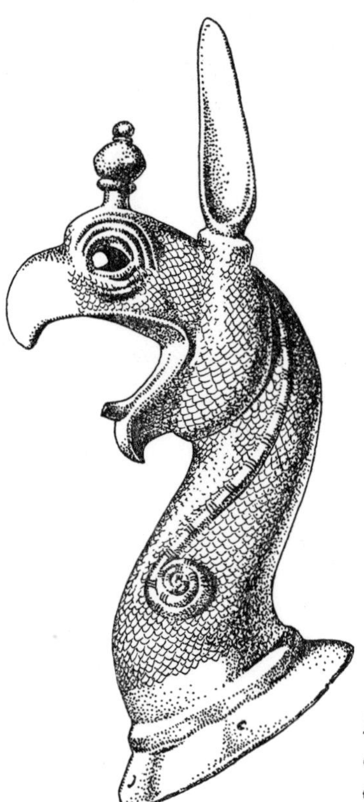

Fig. 20. Bronze head of griffin from a cauldron, mid seventh century BC. *Scale about 2:7*

though without close dependence on Corinth. The variety of local schools has perhaps taken up too much of the energies of Greek specialists in the last forty years.

In Corinth the new art rebelled vigorously against the Geometric tradition, but after a generation of experiment settled down to a well-mannered black-figure style with neat and effective little animals, brightened with small patches of purply paint. Animals in Greek vase-painting are set out in groups or processions, and since their purpose was usually no more than decorative, they very rarely engage in action. But the majority of Corinthian pots were decorated with simple Geometric or linear ornament until the Protocorinthian phase ended about

Plate 71

Fig. 21

625 BC. There followed the Ripe Corinthian (or, as it is usually called, the Corinthian) phase, which concentrated on a hastier and more gaudy use of animals. This style, which was imitated widely, soon degenerated and became extinct in the second quarter of the sixth century. A few painters indulged in human figures, especially towards the end when gay and crowded compositions were attempted. It does not take long to recognise Corinthian pottery, since its pale clay as well as its style is distinctive. This is fortunate, since from the late eighth till the early sixth century it was exported very widely, much more so than the products of any other school. The Corinthian series provides the framework of the relative chronology of its period.

Plates 69, 70
Plate 74
Fig. 22

In Athens the new, Protoattic style is reckoned as beginning just before 700 BC and lasting for about a hundred years. It too had its Orientalising fauna, flora and ornaments, but always paid more attention to human figures. While at Corinth vase-painters concentrated on precision of drawing and small pots, their Attic contemporaries experimented on the grand scale with results more often surprising than successful. In the last third of the seventh century observation of Corinthian virtues established the black-figure technique instead of partial drawing in outline and the style became more harmonious, but this was followed by the imitation of Corinthian vices. Still, the

Fig. 17
Plate 73

Fig. 21. Corinthian cup ('kotyle'), first half of seventh century BC. *Scale about 4:7*

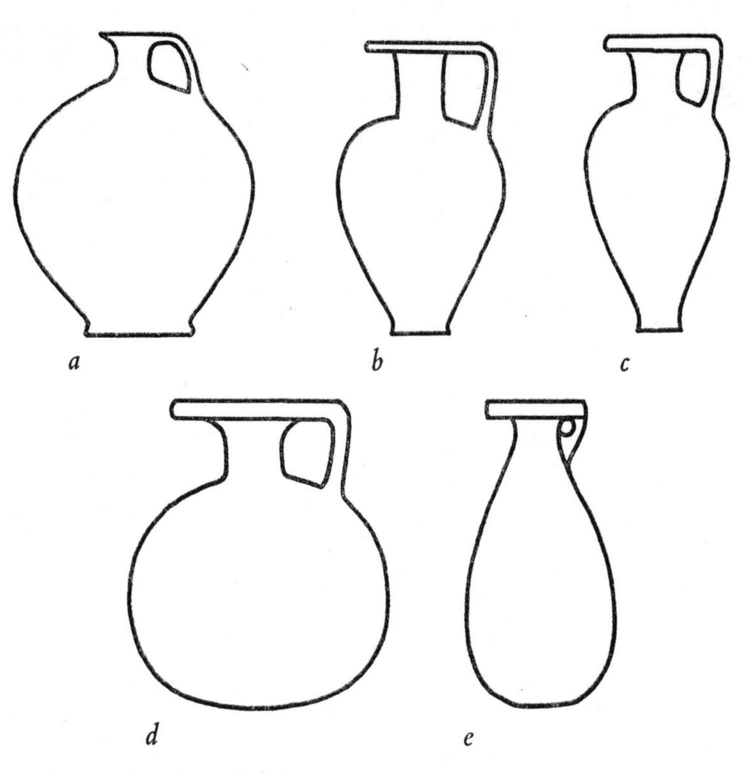

Fig. 22. Corinthian oil flasks, late eighth to late seventh centuries BC.
Scales from 3:4 to 1:2

Plates 75, 76

Attic Black-figure style, as it is now called, soon recovered. About 580 BC some technical innovator produced a redder clay, a blacker paint and a shinier surface, which suited Greek taste, and by 570 Attic painters were becoming independent of Corinth. Instead of many narrow bands the next generation preferred large panels with a few human figures and in the works of Exekias action begins to give way to mood. The new and more exacting aims needed a subtler medium and so the red-figure technique was adopted. Here the background is filled in with black paint and the figures, left (or 'reserved') in the reddish colour of the unpainted surface, have inner details

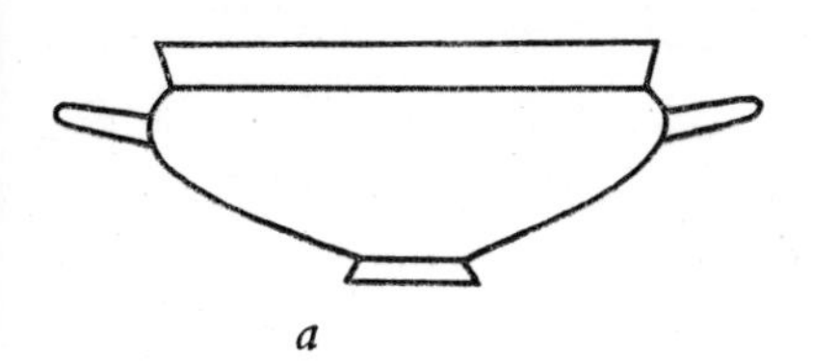

a

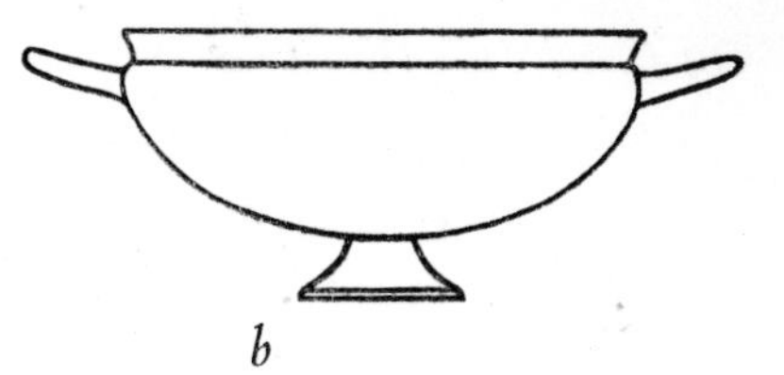

b

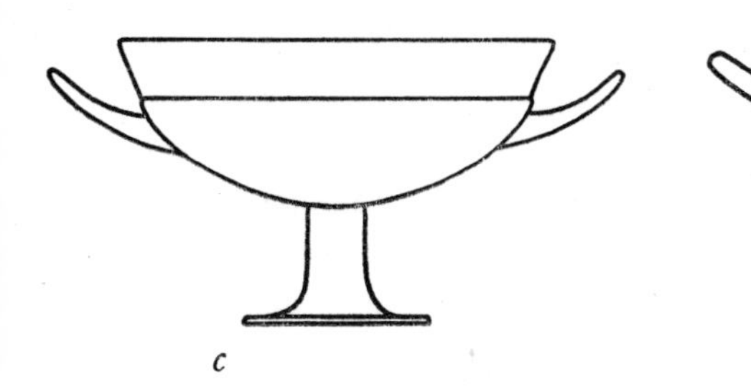

c

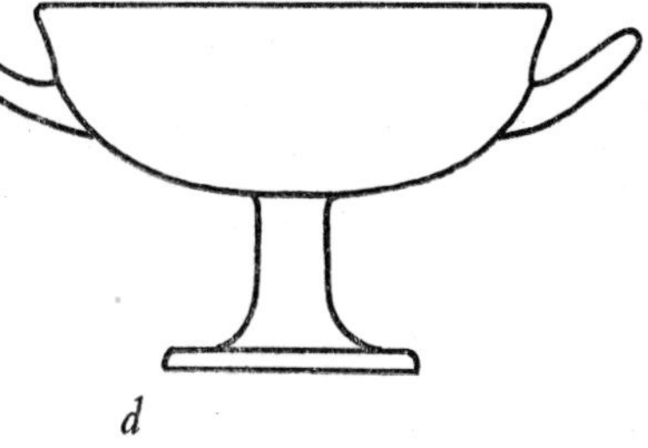

d

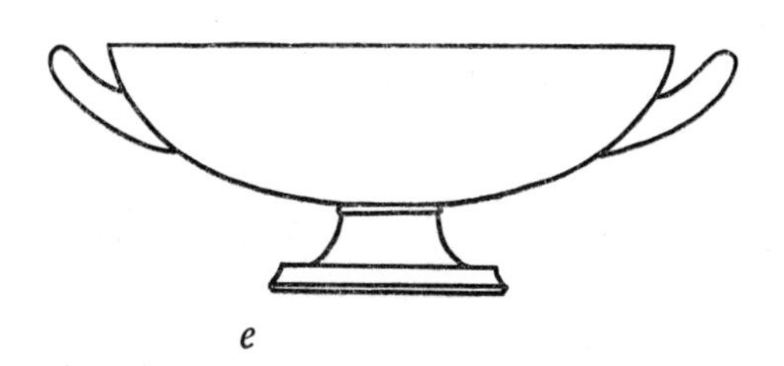

e

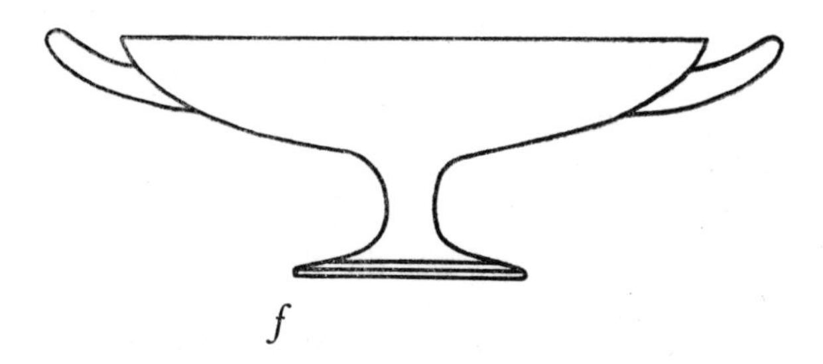

f

Fig. 23. Archaic cups, seventh to fifth centuries BC. *Scale about 1:4*

drawn in sparse lines of paint, some flush and others – by use of a viscous solution of paint – in perceptible relief. Though much black-figure work was done well into the first half of the fifth century, the abler artists preferred red-figure: the best of them were draughtsmen of the first rank, and during the last years of the sixth century they succeeded in breaking the venerable rules of constructing the human figure. Till then all views had been profile or (for the chest) frontal. Now the parts of the body (except the head) were shown in different views and even foreshortened. But, sensibly enough, movement was kept along the surface of the pot, depth of grouping was avoided, and settings were no more than suggested. Before the beginning of the sixth century Attic pottery was not exported much, but in the second quarter it replaced Corinthian as the leading school, both in exports and influence, and after 550 BC acquired almost a monopoly in the production of fine painted pottery for Greek consumers.

Plates 77, 78

Other states in European Greece were not important. Argos continued into the seventh century with an overblown Geometric and never established an advanced school. At Sparta a humble Orientalising developed into a vigorous, if not overfine, black-figure, which sold abroad in the first half of the sixth century. Boeotia made clumsy imitations of neighbouring schools as well as some specialities of its own. Chalcis and Eretria in Euboea did not do much better. Crete was thought at one time to have been the pioneer of the Orientalising style; but though Orientalising motives appeared there very early, Cretan vase-painters used them erratically and sparingly. In the islands of the Aegean several workshops produced pleasant though mannered work in the early and middle seventh century and later there was the larger and showier school called 'Melian'.

The East Greeks – that is the Ionians and other Greeks of the East Aegean – went a different way. The Wild Goat style, often called Rhodian but made in other places too, is tamely decorative with its rows of animals drawn with outline heads and a few roughly outlined details on their bodies. The clay of these pots is coarse and has on its outer surface a thickish coat of pale slip, but a finer brownish clay and a sort of Geometric decoration continued in use for cups (the so-called 'bird bowls'). The Wild Goat style cannot have begun much before the middle of the seventh century and by its end was being still more deformed by imitation of the Corinthian black-figure technique. In the second quarter of the sixth century Attic influence came in. In the region from Rhodes to Samos the Fikellura style, which kept to reserved detail, tried to combine old techniques with new effects, and further north the black-figure technique was accepted but not very well understood. East Greek pottery was exported to Greek settlements in Egypt and round the Black Sea. Till recently its importance was exaggerated, and so it was dated too early and credited with a determining influence on the art of the West. Students should still beware of claims about East Greek or Ionian effects in Italy.

Plate 72

The Greek colonists in Sicily and South Italy, as has been shown in the last few years, had a large output of imitations and adaptations mostly of simple Corinthian types, and there were a few more ambitious pieces. This output was greatest in the late eighth and seventh centuries, but continued in the sixth. The Etruscans went further. They too imitated Corinthian but with more ambition, and from the mid sixth century onwards turned to Attic black-figure as their model. There were also at this time a few workshops in Etruria where Greek immigrants produced for a while a purer style. 'Chalcidian' is a disputed case: some have its home in Chalcis in Euboea, others – I think with more reason – in South Italy or Etruria. There is no help from the painted inscriptions on 'Chalcidian' pots: the alphabet of Chalcis was by then general in the West.

In choosing subjects Greek vase-painters turned regularly to mythology, sometimes to aristocratic life. But their choice is not a simple index of the popularity of any particular myth. Some myths were beyond their powers of representation, which in the Archaic period were more or less limited to scenes of clear and vigorous action, and others were not suited to the shape of the field to be decorated. Whether the mythological subjects came from epic or lyric poetry or from popular tradition usually cannot be decided. The rendering, of course, is most often contemporary, but with artistic licence: in spite of vase-paintings Greeks did not go into battle with naked bodies, nor did they admire purple faces (as might be supposed from some works of the early sixth century). But the principal value of this pottery is artistic. It has survived more fully than other forms of Greek art and throughout the Archaic period was among the most important. We can see in it more clearly than elsewhere the development of the Greek style and how eventually it advanced its conception of the human body beyond anything achieved by the older cultures of the East.

Plate 73

Greek pottery, especially Corinthian and Attic, is invaluable for dating sites and phases of sites. Its use as evidence for trade is more hazardous, since (as has been remarked already) Greek trade was not organised by governments and pottery was not one of its major items. In the first half of the sixth century Laconian pottery travelled widely over the Greek world, but it is not likely that the direct trade of Laconia was extensive; on the other hand Aegina was a maritime power, but it made no fine pottery to leave as evidence.

Painting on flat surfaces, panels or walls, can be traced back as far as the middle of the seventh century and may have existed earlier. What little remains shows that the style was much like that of vase-painting, though usually figures were drawn in outline filled with flat washes of various simple colours and details were painted on in dark lines, but not more effectively than in vase-painting. The composition may sometimes have been elaborate or crowded, but perhaps not more so than on some pots. Relief sculpture too followed the same general rules of two-dimensional art.

SCULPTURE

Greek sculpture, as an art, began in the second quarter of the seventh century, almost at the same time as architecture; or rather that is the date of our earliest remains, and they do not look as if they had much tradition behind them. Until the Hellenistic period the course of development was straightforward, from simple abstraction to a completer though idealised representation of natural anatomy and mood. The normal medium was whitish marble or, after the mid sixth century, bronze. Terracotta had its uses, especially with architecture, but limestone was not thought suitable for good work after the seventh century, and wood even less so. The Greeks liked their sculpture coloured, at first in crude contrast, but gradually for natural effects: even on bronze the lips and nipples might be inlaid with gold or silver, and eyes were filled with paste. Though Greek religion was too loosely organised to be restrictive, it usually provided some sort of excuse for sculpture. Statues were used for images of gods, monuments on graves, or public memorials of athletic or other achievement, but before Alexander no serious thought was given to individual portraiture. Reliefs, normally of mythological scenes, decorated some Doric metopes and Ionic friezes, and a single figure or later a small group was permitted on a gravestone ('stele'). In the pediments of important buildings sculpture appears from the early sixth century, at first sometimes in relief, but soon regularly in the round, though the laws of relief still governed the composition. Animals had only a subordinate place in Greek life and art.

Plate 41

Plate 28

During the Archaic period there were two main types of statue – the naked standing man and the draped standing woman. They have been christened with the names of 'kouros'

Plates 42, 43

Plates 41, 47

and 'kore'. Both types are strictly frontal and in anatomy axially symmetrical, except that the male has the left foot forward and the female may move an arm across the body. The ultimate origin of the 'kouros' may be in Egypt, though there are significant differences. But the immediate models for the first sculptors are more likely to have come from Syria and to have been small figurines, since there seems to be no foreign source for the forms and execution of details, hair excepted. Reliefs were less troubled by the third dimension, so that (as in painting) there was no special difficulty in representing groups. But (as in vase-painting) there were strict conventions. Head, arms, belly and legs must be in strict profile, the chest might be frontal or profile. All movement was in the plane of the surface, figures were not arranged in depth and there was no suggestion of scenery. At their best Archaic reliefs have a simple clarity of action, without any shades of thought.

Plate 48

The first phase of Archaic sculpture, which lasts till the late seventh century, has been named Daedalic. The face is triangular, with big eyes set high and a horizontally waved coiffure. The body is summary and drapery a flattened case. The figure, roughly rectangular in section, has little depth. Progress is towards rounder forms and more human proportions. Daedalic figurines of clay were common only in the southernmost Greek lands – Corinth, Laconia, Crete and Rhodes. Statues are rare, but one has been found also in Delos (dedicated, so an inscription on it says, by a Naxian) and another in Samos, so that the Daedalic style of sculpture may have been general. Anyhow it seems to have had no rivals in its period.

Plates 41, 42

The sculpture of the sixth century is more plentiful, especially from the Acropolis of Athens, where after the Persian sack of 480 BC the Athenians with practical piety used broken statuary as ballast to reterrace the surface. Two main schools developed or diverged. In European Greece the emphasis was on the mechanism of the body, particularly in the naked male type, and the main structure was mastered gradually. Plate 43 In female figures there was more concern over dress and hair: at first drapery was enlivened by simple, mostly vertical folds and then, about the middle of the century, more complicated transverse systems were borrowed from East Greek and elaborated. Plate 47 East Greek sculptors were more superficial, preferring plump flesh (to which they had not the skill to do justice) and soft varied drapery. Not surprisingly they added the draped male to their repertory.

Around 500 BC the leading sculptors of European Greece had progressed so far in their understanding of the framework and musculature of the human body that the Archaic pose appeared by comparison stiff. Their solution, revolutionary in the history of statues, was to relax the pose. Plate 44 One leg is represented as bearing the weight of the figure and the other as idle; consequently the hips are at different levels and the median line of the trunk is slightly curved. The shoulders too may be tilted, and the head is turned a little to one side. At the same time a new severity comes in. Hair becomes less finicky, in drapery strong vertical folds are preferred, and the face loses its broad Archaic smile and other cheerful details with the result sometimes that the expression is surly or oafish. Plate 46 Relief sculpture (and painting) had made another innovation a little earlier, that of oblique and twisted views of the human body. Plate 45 But though these views were adapted to pedimental figures, free standing statues were as a rule still planned frontally. East Greek sculpture contributed little or nothing to this transition to the Classical style.

In the Archaic period there is a broad distinction between European and East Greek sculpture, but there is not yet the evidence to distinguish many local schools. We have a fair notion of Attic from about 600 BC, when the eccentric Sunium master produced his gigantic 'kouroi', and the provincial efforts of Sparta and Boeotia can often be recognised. But it needs divination to fix the local characteristics of, for example, Corinth or Argos. Besides the scarcity of finds from many Greek states there is the difficulty that sculptors (or their products) travelled, or so we are told by later writers who had no reason to lie; in any case most names of Archaic sculptors must have been preserved through the signatures, already common, on the bases of their statues.

The first home or homes of Greek sculpture cannot be ascertained. In the seventh century Corinth appears the most progressive of Greek states and led in the painting of pottery and perhaps in architecture. Crete has its backers, but though there is some support in the muddled traditions recorded by later writers the artistic finds from that island are disappointing. Naxos has left the earliest large statue – that dedicated by Nikandre at Delos – and had quarries of a coarsish marble much used in early work. Nor are those the only claimants.

Small plastic works are very common. Most are of fired clay, many of bronze, and some of ivory or bone or precious metal. Relatively few are of good quality, and some of these have a freedom of pose that is not found in large works. But it is dangerous to judge of sculpture from figurines: difference in scale allows or encourages different treatment, and especially where moulds were in use old types survived for an unconscionable time.

ARCHITECTURE

About the middle of the seventh century, or so the archaeological finds suggest, both new building materials and architecture began to appear in Greece. Of the materials the most revolutionary in immediate effects was the heavy, large tile of terracotta which demanded a roof of low pitch, in contrast to the high pitch of thatch and the flat surface of packed mud. The second important innovation was in masonry; for the first time since the Mycenaean period the Greeks took regularly to hewing and trimming accurately large blocks of stone. The consciously architectural style which accompanied these more imposing and expensive materials formed itself, for good or bad, on a single type of building, the temple. Essentially the temple consisted of a single room intended for storage and needing a door, but no window, skylight or vent, so that the early architects had no special problems of planning and could concentrate on aesthetic appearance. The style that evolved was, as it happened, fairly flexible; but when compared with the subsequent achievements of the Roman empire, Greek architecture is restricted and unambitious.

The planning of the new temple was simple. The essential room, the 'cella', which usually had a door in its east end, was now regularly rectangular. An extra room might be added or partitioned off behind it. Usually the cella had a porch in front and, if the building was large, a second porch balanced it at the other end, whether or not there was a back room for it to open into. Such porches might be composed of columns standing

Fig. 24

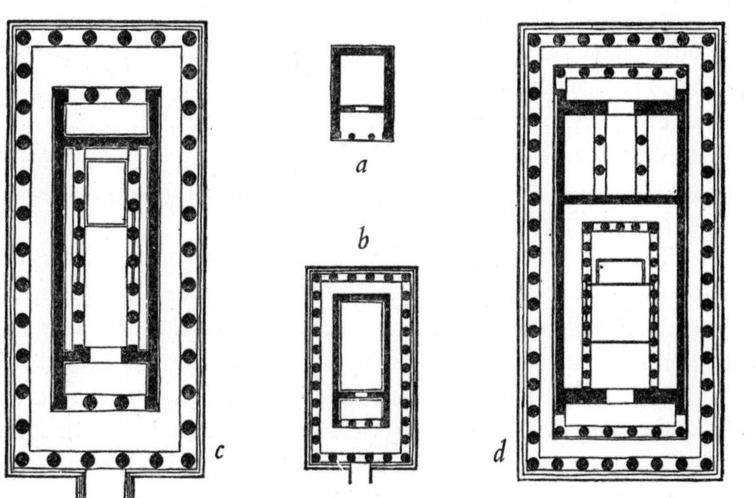

Fig. 24. Plans of temples

between prolongations of the walls of the cella – the decorated ends of these walls are called 'antae' and the porch itself 'in antis' – or there might be a clear row of columns (the 'prostyle' porch). For further elaboration this whole block might be enclosed by a colonnade ('peristyle'). The platform on which the temple stood showed steps on all sides. The columns had capitals which supported an architrave, and above the architrave was the frieze or its equivalent. This in turn was crowned by a cornice, running horizontally round the building and serving on the sides as the edge of the roof; to throw rainwater clear of the lower parts of the building it projected some way outwards. Where there was no surrounding colonnade, the outer wall – to be properly decorated – still required an entablature (that is architrave, frieze and cornice) though in appearance a plain architrave and a course of wall blocks might be very much alike. Finally, the roof was of low pitch with a gable ('pediment') at front and back; a raking cornice supported the ends of the roof. Each part tended to have its characteristic ornaments, and the proportions for its size in relation to other parts were fixed closely, but without much regard to use. So, for example, in a large Doric temple the steps of the platform became much too high for human comfort. In fact the architecture of Greek temples was much more decorative than functional, and when fully developed it could be classed instead as a sort of abstract sculpture.

Fig. 25

Though temples remained the principal form of Greek architecture some other types of public buildings too might be embellished, if only with a façade. The 'propylon' was a porch, normally double, which dignified the entrance to a sanctuary. The so-called 'treasury' was in effect a small cella with a porch at the front alone: treasuries were put up in sanctuaries to store offerings or equipment and sometimes, as at Delphi, they were executed with great lavishness to advertise the states that built them. There was more utility in the 'stoa', a long building with

Plate 20, *Fig. 36*

Plate 18

Plates 27, 35

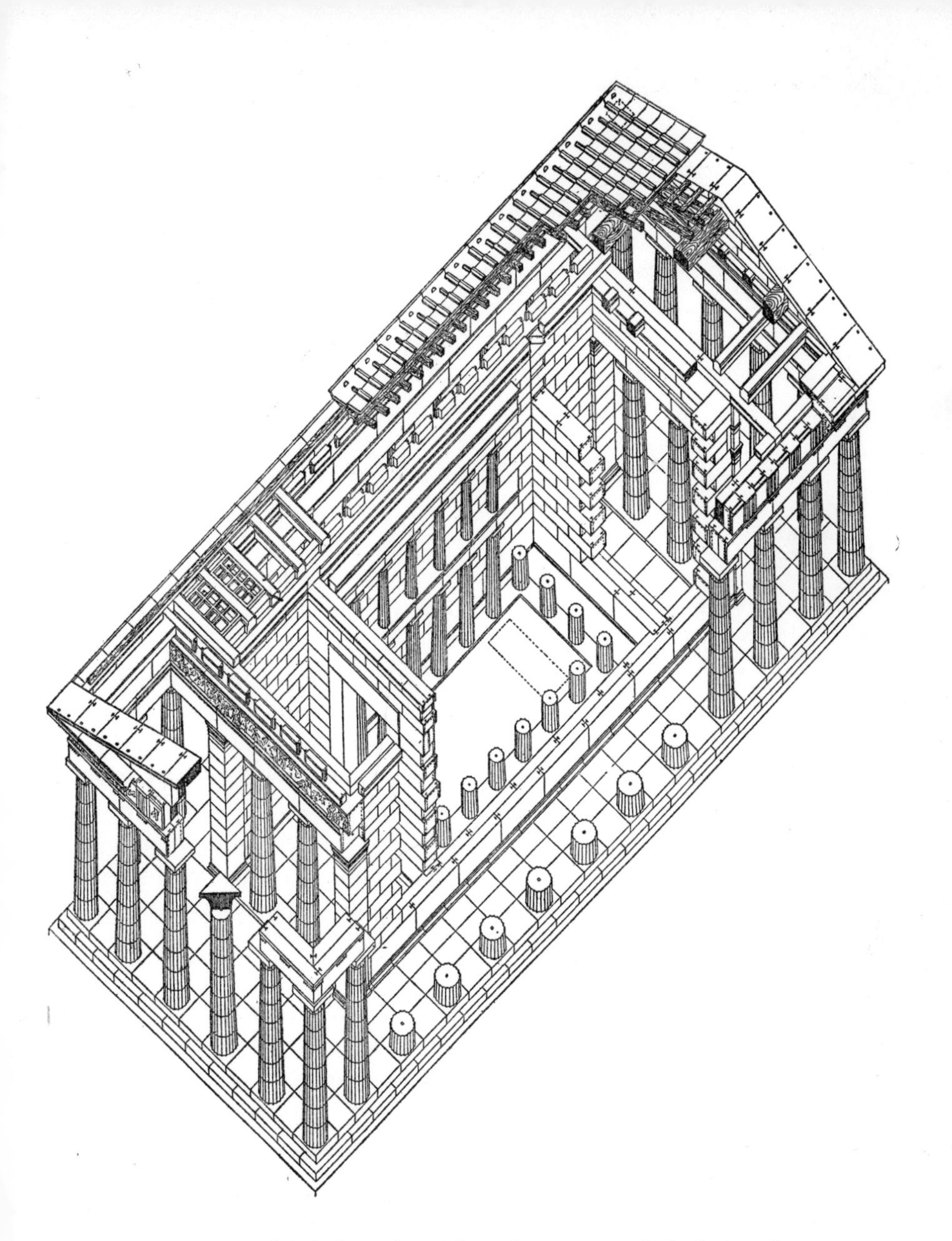

Fig. 25. Reconstruction of the 'Theseum' at Athens, about 445 BC. *Scale about 1:280*

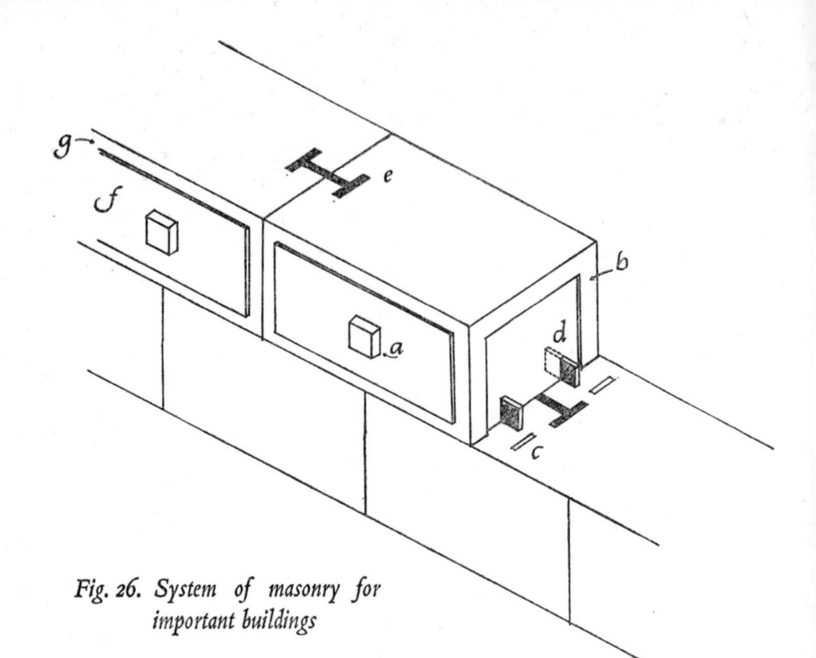

Fig. 26. System of masonry for important buildings

an open colonnade in front and (in many later examples) shops within. The 'fountain house' was a simple porch which covered the spouts and basins of a public water supply. Altars too were treated architecturally, though here columns were not wanted. If vase-paintings are to be believed, a few private houses had a columned porch to the main room. All these structures used architectural forms familiar in temples, though usually in secular buildings the workmanship and materials were less careful and costly.

Plate 76

Structural principles were and remained simple, however sophisticated the execution might be. Though cement and mortar were known (for instance in cisterns), architects worked with very large blocks of stone, kept in position by gravity and, to avoid slight shifting, by small inset clamps of metal. To span open spaces (even when the arch was known) longer blocks were laid horizontally, in what is often called the 'post and lintel' method. The jointing of blocks was meticulous: in good

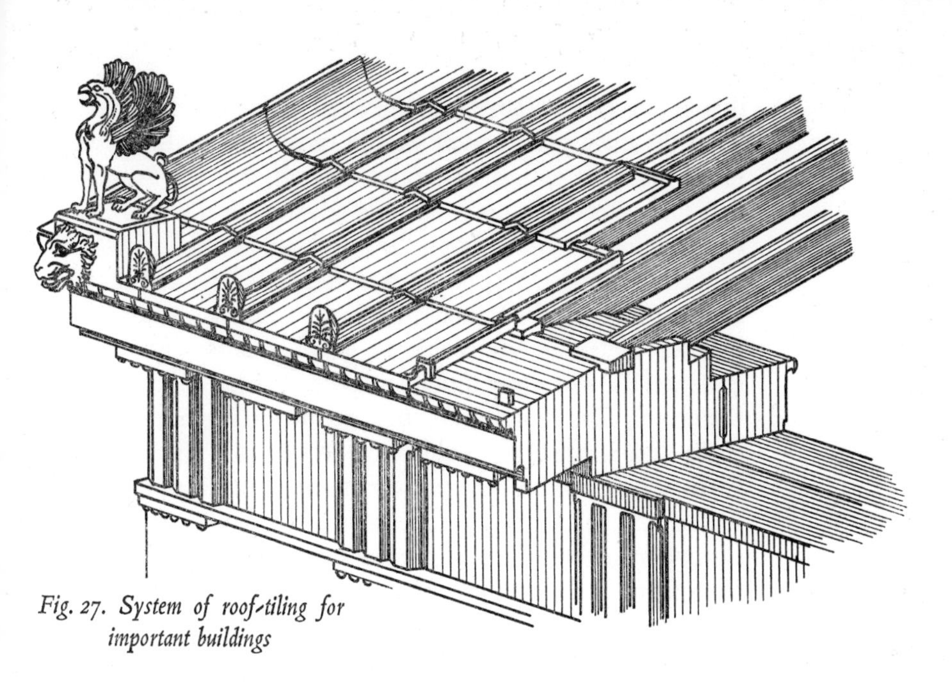

Fig. 27. System of roof-tiling for important buildings

examples adjacent faces were trimmed back except for a two- or three-inch band along the edges, and when they were fitted together and the surfaces smoothed down the join was so neat as to be almost or quite imperceptible. If inferior stone was used, this monolithic effect was improved by a coat of fine stucco on the superstructure. In less pretentious buildings walls above the lowest course were often of mud-brick, plastered over, and columns and entablature might be of wood; these economies were less frequent in temples. For the framework of roofs timber was regular, and again the main weight was borne by horizontal beams, unaided by any form of truss. Lastly the tiles, too heavy to be pegged, were made with ledges to fit on to their neighbours so that they could not slip of their own accord. The stone parts of buildings constructed in this way were extremely durable, though the timbers were liable to rot with time or neglect, and it speaks well for the stability of good Greek architecture (though less well for its structural economy)

Fig. 26

Fig. 27

that much of the Parthenon survived an explosion inside it. That the early practitioners should have been timid in using novel materials is understandable enough, but it is surprising that their successors made so little advance in the methods of construction. Presumably public opinion was satisfied with the aesthetic results, the new architectural buildings served their simple purposes, the demand for them was not great, and the practice of letting out work in small and closely specified contracts did not allow much variation. When, as occasionally happened, Greek architects were set to roofing a large open space – for instance the Hall of the Mysteries ('Telesterion') at Eleusis, near Athens – they did not attempt to span that space with trusses or vaulting, but made do with various arrangements of supporting columns. In private work, of course, clients and contractors had a stronger incentive to structural economy, but this led to jerrybuilding rather than new devices.

This architectural style had two principal schools. In Greece itself and the western colonies the Doric order was normal, but across the Aegean the Asiatic Greeks and some of the islanders preferred the Ionic, which (on our present evidence) appeared rather later and took longer to settle down. Though Doric and Ionic differ obviously in decorative treatment, their general principles are remarkably alike.

Plates 28–30

The Doric order can be understood generally from the illustrations. The platform has three visible steps above the level top of the foundation. On it stand the columns, without bases since good stone does not rot: normally the shafts have twenty vertical flutes, separated by a sharp edge ('arris'), and they taper upwards and should also have a slightly curved profile ('entasis'). The capital consists of two members: below is the 'echinus', round in plan and swelling towards the top, where it recedes a little to mark it off visually from a square low block (the 'abacus'). The architrave is plain, except for a band (with groups of 'guttae' or drops) at the top; decoratively this band attaches to the frieze. The frieze is composed of projecting trifurcated members (the 'triglyphs') and recessed flat surfaces (the 'metopes'); simple bands mark the tops of the triglyphs and the metopes. The cornice, which overhangs the frieze, has plates ('mutules') with guttae suspended below its overhang, and in its standard form is crowned with a hawksbeak drip-moulding. At the ends of the cover-tiles there were antefixes, commonly in the form of palmettes, or a continuous gutter ('sima'). Large ornaments or figures ('acroteria') were placed on the corners and peak of the gables of elaborate buildings. Very soon, if not from the beginning, this architecture was coloured. The platform, columns, architrave and tiles were plain, but triglyphs were blue and the metopes (or their background) red, and the various mouldings and ornaments were coloured or picked out with patterns. In addition, if costs allowed, there might be sculpture in the pediments or painting or sculpture on the metopes.

Plate 28

The earliest Doric temple of which we know anything is that of Apollo at Thermum in Aetolia, built in the 630's; it had metopes of terracotta with paintings on them, and since nothing of the columns and triglyphs survive they were most likely of wood. The earliest temple of which we know much is that of Hera at Olympia, some forty years later in date; here stone was used for the platform (which had only two steps) and the lowest course of the walls of the cella, but the upper part of the walls was of sun-dried brick; the entablature and many (if not all) columns were of wood, and the cornice was sheathed in coloured terracotta. But ten years or so later the temple of Artemis at Corcyra (or Corfu) was all stone below the roof and had sculpture in its pediments and probably on some metopes. Though a Doric canon had been established by the early sixth century, that did not prevent some evolution. In the plan of the temple there was an unsteady widening: the temple of Hera at Olympia had six columns at each end and

Plate 26

sixteen on each side, but a hundred years later a temple at Sunium had six by thirteen. Inside the cella the roof often needed or was felt to need support between the walls, if the span was more than some twenty feet: at first a central row of columns was used, but since this spoilt either the view or the placing of the cult image it soon became regular to have two rows, set nearer the sides than the middle. For reasons obvious on reflection each internal colonnade, if Doric, normally was in two tiers; the best surviving example is in the so-called temple of Posidon at Paestum, and in Greece itself part of the double tier has been re-erected in the temple of Aphaea in Aegina. The columns too alter: in the early sixth century the height might be only four times the lower diameter, but in the early fifth the proportion was nearer one to five. The echinus in sympathy became less spreading and less curved. The spacing of the columns shows neatly how much Greek architects were occupied with aesthetics. The Doric frieze consists of narrow triglyphs and squarish metopes, and it was a rule that there were triglyphs at the corners (or ends) of the frieze and over every column (as well as between each pair of columns). But the frieze had, for appearances, to project about as far as the architrave and columns and, for stability, to be centred over the columns. So, unless the width of the triglyph was equal to the depth of the frieze – and the Doric canon of proportions did not allow so wide a triglyph – the corner triglyph must be set beyond the axis of the corner column. The Greeks accepted this eccentricity of corner triglyphs, but felt that in other parts of the colonnade triglyphs should be centred accurately on the columns. A simple solution was to widen the metopes between the corner column and its neighbour, but this makes the frieze look uneven. More subtle was the device of setting the two columns nearer together, while also slightly widening the metopes between them. Later, mathematically minded critics have asserted that the problem of the corner triglyph was the

Fig. 25

death of the Doric order. If so, it was a slow and painless disease, much less serious than that of the re-entrant angle (where, as in some stoas, the façade had projecting wings). Besides such general developments there were many minor variations between one Doric building and another, especially in the Western colonies; they are lovingly catalogued in the favourite handbooks.

Plate 27

Many students believe that the Doric order as we know it in stone was the result of a long and lost evolution in timber; the guttae evidently mimicked wooden pegs, the triglyphs represent the ends of wooden roof beams, and there were always many small Doric buildings which used wood and not stone. But first, down to the early seventh century the surviving remains of buildings seem very crude and imprecise, and the terracotta models have no suggestion of Doric decorative forms. Secondly, even in our earliest Doric the forms that supposedly imitate wood do not make sense structurally – in particular the guttae below the triglyphs are set too far forward to peg into them, and the triglyphs themselves are not level with but below the roof beams. Thirdly, the use of wood in later Doric buildings (and even in the temple of Hera at Olympia) can be explained as a cheap substitution for stone rather than as a survival from earlier usage. Fourthly, if Doric evolved gradually throughout Greece, it should not be so uniform in its more decorative features. If these arguments are sound, the Doric order and the whole Greek style of architecture were not so much evolved as invented or else imported. Import is not likely, since nothing generally similar is known from other parts of the ancient world in the seventh century. The idea of precise architecture may well have been picked up in the East; the use of carefully dressed large blocks may have been copied from the East or from Mycenaean ruins; Mycenaean remains again may have had an influence on the forms of capitals and columns; and such details as the guttae were very probably inspired by wooden

Plate 22
Fig. 6

pegs, although the inspiration may have been decorative rather than structural. But the character of the Doric style is profoundly original and it is hard to doubt that it was formed very quickly and diffused from a single centre. Where that centre was may be guessed from an allusive statement of Pindar's (made about 464 BC) that the characteristic low gable of the new architecture was invented at Corinth, and by the coincidence (perhaps chancy) that the earliest and most experimental tiles found so far come from Corinthian territory.

We know much less of the beginnings of the Ionic style and indeed of architecture generally in the Greek settlements of the East Aegean. But since another volume in this series is allotted to the East Greeks, only a summary account is wanted here. In Samos a temple 100 feet long was erected in the eighth century and fairly soon (like a contemporary temple at Thermum in European Greece) it had a wooden colonnade (or verandah) added round it; but this big shed can hardly rank as architecture. In the late seventh century an elaborate temple was being built in Smyrna, with a stone platform and stone columns and capitals: one of these capitals survives, circular in plan and decorated with closely fitting long leaves, but with a profile as yet unique. In the earlier sixth century a few less careful temples in Lesbos and mainland Aeolis provide both leaf capitals and capitals in the form of spirals spinging from a deep V. It may, though, be chance that we have no strictly Ionic capitals or other members which are quite as early.

Fig. 28

The early Ionic style, in the middle and later sixth century, is much less uniform than the Doric. The typical temple stood on a stepped platform, but the steps were of a convenient height and of no fixed number and, while in Doric the superstructure began almost at the edge of the platform, in Ionic there could be clear space all round. The cella tended to have very deep porches. The columns stood on high bases of two or more members, which were often busily decorated by turnery. The

Plate 31

Fig. 28. Aeolic capital, second half of sixth century B C. *Width 1·36 m.*

shafts were more slender than Doric, with more numerous flutes (the eventual canon was twenty-four); the division between the flutes was at first a sharp arris but by the fifth century usually a flat fillet. The capital comprised a low echinus with egg and dart moulding, a pair of volutes spreading sideways, and (though perhaps not at first) a low abacus. So the front and side views of the capital were very different, and there was a problem at the corners of a colonnade: if the columns of the side row were to display their front (and better) view, the corner capital needed two adjacent fronts. What solutions were attempted in the sixth century we do not know yet, but in the fifth (when the volute member became square in plan) the corner capital was given two adjacent fronts with the volutes between them twisted out against each other at an angle of 45°. Above the capital came the architrave, usually divided into three bands protruding one over the other; above the architrave was a row of narrow rectangular projections called 'dentils'; and above the dentils came the cornice and roof, shallower in pitch than the Doric. Admittedly there are hardly any remains of entablatures from Archaic Ionic buildings in East Greek lands, and it is likely enough that there was much more variety. For minor decoration Ionic was profuse with its mouldings, not always happily placed; the favourite form was the egg and dart. Colour was used much as in Doric. Sculpture had no obvious place: the showy temple of Artemis (Diana) at

Plate 33

Ephesus had reliefs above the bases of some columns and perhaps on a dado round the cella; carved or moulded gutters or parapets occur, but the shallow pediment was not filled.

Soon after the middle of the sixth century, that is less than a generation after our earliest East Greek relics, Ionic appeared occasionally in Greece itself. Here it took a different form, in part presumably through the influence of Doric. A continuous frieze, sometimes carved, more than took the place of the dentils, the pitch of the roof was raised, the columns were made slimmer and perhaps spaced farther apart, mouldings were revised, and gradually a neater two-tiered base became regular. This European or (as it is usually called) Attic Ionic, lighter below and heavier above, was altogether more elegant than the Asiatic, and in the fourth century it came to be accepted by the East Greeks themselves.

Plates 31, 32

In Ionic during the sixth and part of the fifth century there were wide variations. But the most notable general change was in the capital, which grew squarer and more compact, till the volutes no longer sprawled wide of the column: the position of the eyes of the volute is still the easiest stylistic guide to the date of an early building.

The origins of Ionic are as elusive as those of Doric, since its characteristic forms too have no good parallels in architecture elsewhere. The volutes of the capital and some minor ornaments were familiar in other arts and may have been enlarged and adapted from them. The dentils look like projecting wooden beams or planks, though the position they are in would be suitable only in a flat-roofed building, as would the parapet too. Dadoes, if in fact they occurred, could have been borrowed from further east. As for the turned bases of columns, the invention of a large lathe should be excuse enough. Where Ionic began is also uncertain. A very early column (with base and capital) came from Naxos: it was erected at Delphi about 570 BC to support a sphinx. About as early, according to current notions, was the so-called 'Rhoecus' temple at Samos (though probably Rhoecus was the architect of its successor). This vast edifice, more than 300 feet long and half as wide, was rivalled a few years later – or so it is said – by the temple of Artemis at Ephesus, to the building of which (as Herodotus and an inscription record) Croesus, king of Lydia, contributed. The treasuries of Cnidos and Clazomenae at Delphi are the earliest examples of European Ionic.

The Doric and Ionic styles remained distinct till the Hellenistic period, though from the fifth century at least a building might have a Doric exterior and an Ionic interior. The styles have different merits, not easily compared. But Doric is the more compact and tries to be more subtle. For example, in the plan of the temple the walls of the Ionic cella are aligned with columns of the façade, the Doric cella lies slightly within the axes of the corresponding columns; and the entasis of columns and later refinements of good Doric are abnormal in Ionic. But both styles had one curious quality: their effect does not depend on scale. This decorative adaptability is perhaps another argument that the origins too were decorative.

The dating of Greek architecture has its difficulties, especially since some large buildings took long to complete. Occasionally there is a mention in literature or a useful deposit of pottery or some architectural sculpture. But too often the student must judge by style and hope that he is not misled by provincial or individual oddities.

No surviving Archaic building retains its roof, and few have much more than the platform in position. Among these are, for Doric, the temple of Hera at Olympia (*c.* 590 BC), the temple of Apollo at Corinth (*c.* 540 BC), the 'Basilica' at Paestum (*c.* 530 BC), the re-erected Athenian treasury at Delphi (*c.* 505 BC) and in the early fifth century the temple of Aphaea at Aegina and the temple of Athena at Syracuse (instructively converted into a Christian church); there are also

Plate 26

Plate 28, *Fig.* 36

various temples at Selinus now undergoing restoration. The Asiatic variety of Ionic is less easy to view: the British Museum has some fragments of the Archaic temple of Artemis at Ephesus and the Naxian column with its sphinx is at Delphi. Delphi too has a reconstruction of the Siphnian treasury (*c.* 525 BC) and the stoa of the Athenians (early fifth century). But Greek ruins, picturesque enough where two or three columns are linked by a piece of entablature, tend to be misleading; the loss of the cella walls, almost always robbed for re-use or the lime-kiln, leaves an airy voidness that Greek architecture never intended.

HISTORICAL EVENTS

Most modern manuals of ancient Greek history have impressive lists of dates and events. These should be accepted with caution. Some come from Herodotus and Thucydides, who were working in the second half of the fifth century BC, but most are from later writers and the principal collection that survives is that chosen by Eusebius, a scholarly bishop of the fourth century AD. The sources from which all these authorities discovered their dates are scarcely ever known. But since in the Archaic period history (in our sense of the word) had hardly been conceived, there is no evidence that annals were kept in any Greek state, records of all kinds seem to have been rare, and the dates that have come down to us often vary, it is probable that Classical and later investigators (if they were scrupulous) relied on oral tradition, genealogies and some casual references in lyric poetry. How the archaeological chronology is constructed was mentioned on pp. 89–90. For the eighth and seventh centuries it depends on Thucydides, but Thucydides' dates for the relevant events are not the same as those of Eusebius, who remains the favourite authority for other Archaic dates. Still, the conventional lists do well enough, provided belief in them is elastic.

CHAPTER IV

The Classical Period

(480–338 BC)

HISTORICAL SKETCH

THE CLASSICAL PERIOD lies between the Persian and the Macedonian assaults on Greece, one repulsed and the other victorious. In this period Greek originality expressed itself for good and for bad most completely and characteristically, even though some of its later achievements were more durable. The name 'Classical' is just.

In 480 BC the Persians advanced by land and sea along the east coast of Greece. The Spartans, who, of course, commanded the Greek forces, did not intend any serious resistance beyond the Isthmus of Corinth, which was narrow enough to be fortified, and after a short and expensive delay at the pass of Thermopylae the Persian army proceeded to Attica, receiving the submission of all the Greek states along the route to the Peloponnese, except Megara, Plataea and – significantly – Athens. Although the Athenians ever afterwards prided themselves on this devotion to Greek independence, there was, as they knew, little to lose by it: they had already provoked the Persians too far by joining in the Ionian revolt and then (with the Plataeans) beating a punitive force at Marathon. So they evacuated Attica and, as the first naval and second military power among the confederates, pressed for an offensive strategy and contrived to force a naval battle off Salamis. The victory was complete enough to give the Greeks command of the sea provided the Athenians did not desert. This proviso helped the Spartans to decide next summer to risk the campaign beyond the Isthmus which resulted somehow in the decisive battle of Plataea. The defeated Persians started on their long march home, unmolested by the victors, who preferred to liberate their fellow Greeks across the Aegean. The Spartans were still in command, but their conduct was lukewarm, if no worse, and in 478 BC many of the eastern Greeks and islanders invited Athens to lead them in the struggle for freedom and protection from Persia. So Athenian imperialism was founded. The allies provided fixed contingents to the league's forces or, as most of them preferred, equivalent payments in money, but Athens was soon in complete control of policy and action and gradually came to treat the allies as subjects. The effect was that Greece and the Aegean, with some important exceptions such as Thessaly, was divided into two blocs. The Peloponnesian League, led by Sparta, was strong on land, preoccupied with agriculture, and oligarchical; the Athenian alliance was based on naval power, more commercial, and democratic. The division had its hazards. In particular Corinth, a principal trading city, stayed on the Spartan side; though Athens was connected by walls with its port, Attica lay open to invasion by land; and the Athenians had found that imperialism could pay (as their Acropolis shows still).

Plates 20, 21

Whether or not war had to come, it came. In the 450's Athens by various means enrolled as allies Megara, Boeotia and even Achaea, but by 445 this land empire was lost. The second and more open conflict, the Peloponnesian War, began in 431, after Athens had attacked the overseas interests of Corinth and Megara. Few wars are better known than this, thanks to the penetrating and vivid analysis left by the contemporary statesman and historian, Thucydides. Generally the Spartans were too cautious and the Athenians too bold, but at first neither side could do vital damage to the other and in 421 terms of peace were agreed and not honoured. Two years later Athens in league with Argos tried an offensive in the Peloponnese. When this failed, their next grand scheme was the extension of the empire in the West by conquering Syracuse and Sicily

(415–3 BC): the attempt nearly succeeded, but its final failure cost Athens the best part of its fleet and army. This seemed the end: the Spartans already had a permanent base in Attica, now they collected ships and encouraged the subject allies of Athens to revolt. But the Athenians recovered, and the Spartans had to accept Persian support and conditions before they surprised the last Athenian navy on shore and could starve Athens into surrender. So in 404 BC Sparta found itself victorious.

The Spartans were determined on peace among the Greeks, but trusted only themselves to enforce it. So they did not (as the customs of war permitted) destroy Athens and kill or enslave the Athenians, for fear perhaps that without an unfriendly neighbour the Boeotians might become too independent; they took over the Athenian empire, installing their own governors and garrisons in the cities they liberated and increasing the tribute to be paid; and noting the march of Xenophon's Ten Thousand through the Persian empire, they crusaded in Asia Minor for the freedom of the Greek cities (formerly protected by Athens) and for easy pickings. The Persians retaliated by recruiting Greek mercenaries into their own armies and subsidising Greek states to attack elsewhere. So in 387 BC the Spartans ceded to Persia all the Asiatic mainland and concentrated on restoring order in Greece. Finally, in 371 they sent an army to Boeotia to humble Thebes, the last recalcitrant. But the Thebans, who had been practising new tactics, won a conclusive victory at Leuctra, and then invaded the Peloponnese to free the Messenians and establish a stronger federation in Arcadia. By this sudden catastrophe the power of Sparta was broken; the legend of invincibility had gone, and new and hostile neighbours were created. The dominance of Thebes lasted some ten years. Next, the Phocians asserted themselves by seizing the treasures of Delphi and hiring mercenaries, till the money ran out. After that, Greece settled down to jockeying between second-class powers. It was not that the total military potential was less than in the fifth century, but there was no large concentration of force and more professional methods of warfare were making the old city militias insufficient.

Meanwhile in the north Macedonia was growing dangerous. The Macedonians, a fairly homogeneous people, had been too loosely organised for their numbers to be effective. But in 359 BC Philip II succeeded to the royal power. Philip was an organiser, general and diplomatist of unusual dexterity and patience. First he secured his own kingdom; then, as opportunities appeared, firmly annexed Thessaly (352 BC) and Thrace (342 BC) and any adjacent Greek colonies he could. The Athenians, whose supply of corn required the control of the straits leading to the Black Sea, were the first distant Greek state to be alarmed, but in spite of occasional action even they did not believe that Macedonia was becoming, except perhaps temporarily, the dominant power. It might not have mattered much if they had: Philip maintained supporters in most Greek states and, unless there had been some miraculous change of heart, sooner or later Greece was likely to be subdued piecemeal. The end came in 338 BC, when Philip with the young Alexander crushed the Thebans and Athenians at the battle of Chaeronea. The rest of Greece accepted the verdict and at the Congress of Corinth received the Macedonian dispensation of peace and unity. Two years later Philip was murdered and his son Alexander the Great succeeded him. But the old order (or disorder) had passed. The city states of Greece (or some of them) rebelled at once but uselessly, remained sullenly impotent during the conquest of the East, and then found themselves militarily and politically obsolete in a world of great empires.

Knowledge of the Classical period comes first from literature, secondly from inscriptions, a field of archaeology that has its special caste of students, the epigraphists. These sources are fullest for Athens. Ordinary archaeological evidence is not of major importance, except of course for art, architecture and

Plate 88

technology, and for some details of domestic life. Dates are reliable and numerous.

POLITICS

The guiding principles of politics in the fifth and fourth centuries were security and material profit, sometimes disguised and sometimes cynically admitted, but too often opportunist and short-sighted. Among the forms of government tyranny was no longer important, except in Sicily, and the choice lay in the range of oligarchy and democracy, represented most effectively by Sparta and Athens. As a rule, big property-owners believed in oligarchy; farmers and manufacturers of hoplite status preferred a moderate democracy, that is one that excluded their inferiors; and the poor, especially in cities, were radical democrats. The political influence of these groups corresponded normally with their military importance. In Thessaly, where cavalry remained the principal arm, and in Sparta, where the full citizens were few but unusually proficient infantrymen, narrow oligarchy persisted. But Athens depended on its navy and so its urban poor, who rowed the warships, could justify their claim to political equality.

The struggle for power within a state was often unscrupulous and savage, with massacring of political opponents and traitorous intrigues with the governments of other states. Even in Sparta several dangerous conspiracies came to light, and at Athens there were a few assassinations and at the end of the fifth century two bloody interludes of oligarchy. This was not due altogether to a decline in public morality since the period of the tyrants; the number of politicians had increased.

A desire to be independent was inherent in Greek city-states and led, notably in the fourth century, to rapid and scarcely predictable changes of friends and enemies. But as the greater powers continued to be aggressive, some threatened communities realised that full autonomy was impossible. So in a few instances independent states amalgamated peaceably, as in the new city of Rhodes in 408 BC, and a few attempts were made at federal unions. Very often, too, partisan or personal interest outweighed patriotism. Since Sparta favoured oligarchical governments and Athens democracies, it was regular – while those states were strong – for democratic parties to collaborate with Athens and their opponents with Sparta. This sympathy, more calculating than ideological, was an important factor in the stability of the Athenian empire: all revolts, so far as we know, were engineered by oligarchs and the democrats stayed loyal even after the disaster of Syracuse. Later on, Philip of Macedon had a growing number of supporters in Greece, some bribed but others seeing in him the only hope of peace. As for exiles, it was almost discreditable for them not to offer their services to the enemies of their native state. There were of course other Greeks whose political opinions were broader and more unselfish – a dangerous attitude when extremists are about – but they too usually acted parochially. So a voluntary confederacy of all Greek states was impracticable and a national state beyond the reach of imagination. Even the granting of citizenship to aliens and freed slaves, whatever their services, was very exceptional, more so perhaps than in the Archaic period.

In home and foreign policy oligarchies and moderate democracies were conservative and principally concerned with self-preservation; but radical democracies, whose supporters were poorer and had less to lose, encouraged projects of expansion and employment. This was recognised by ancient writers, though their own social position made most of them hostile or unsympathetic; a similar attitude is to be found in much current literature in references to the Welfare state. But it is perverse to deny any connection between the extraordinary cultural achievement of Athens and its radically democratic constitution. To its efficiency and material success there is a bitterly candid testimonial in a *Constitution of Athens* written about

430 BC by some nameless oligarch and preserved among the works of Xenophon: after all there were now more citizens with a stake in the profits of government.

POPULATION

From the Early Iron Age till the Classical period the population of Greece grew in spite of its high death rate. Adult mortality, so a little evidence from the fourth century suggests, was rapid by modern standards. Of 100 males twenty years old 70 might live to thirty, 25 to sixty and 7 or so to eighty. In wartime the loss of young men might be greater; but for young women childbirth was a constant and much more serious risk, so much so that though the proper age of first marriage was in the thirties for men and in the teens for women (which means that prospective brides should have outnumbered marriageable bachelors by at least three to two) we do not hear of many old maids. With women marrying so early the birth rate was high and population tended to rise. The surplus had somehow to be absorbed or removed. Denser settlement of the countryside was beyond a certain point impracticable, since the methods of agriculture remained the same. Emigration was frequent after the middle of the eighth century: admittedly, in the early sixth colonising slacked off, but in the East mercenary soldiers were always welcome and by now the growing cities were attracting settlers from other states. This urban expansion, promoted by trade and industry, can be plotted only very roughly; the most obvious evidence is in the location of cemeteries, since burial was regularly outside the city limits, but often early graves lie inside the circuit of later walls. There was also the exposure of infants to die like kittens, a practice that was legal and the theme of many plays and myths, though we have no notion how common it was in any place or period. But generally population responded quickly to prosperity, as is shown by the numbers of Athenian citizens in the fifth and fourth centuries, when citizenship was limited strictly to the children of citizens.

The Greeks had no belief in the crude theories of demographic nationalism.

It was not till very modern times that the population of Greece was once more as big as that of the city states of the fifth and fourth centuries. Yet those states were small. Some very rough calculations can be made from military levies and other hints. Athens with its countryside had about 30,000 male citizens in 480 BC and to these may be added roughly three times as many women and children; resident aliens and slaves were relatively few. Fifty years later the male citizens numbered around 40,000, resident aliens perhaps half that figure, and slaves – to risk a guess – 60,000: this makes a total of some 300,000 persons and most of the increase must have been in the city districts – the aliens, in particular, were not allowed to own land. This was the peak. In 321 BC the count of male citizens had fallen to 21,000, of aliens to 10,000. But the fluctuations of Athens are not typical, since in the fifth century its prosperity was increased unduly by successful imperialism. The population of Corinth (which had much less territory) was hardly over 90,000, of Thebes perhaps 50,000. At Sparta the full citizens were always a statistically insignificant minority; they numbered about 8,000 in 480 BC, but a century later only 1,500. Most states, of course, were much smaller: Priene, to judge by the size of the new city laid out soon after the middle of the fourth century, housed only some 4,000 people, but had all the regular public buildings and institutions of an independent community. A comparison of the census figures of the nineteenth and early twentieth centuries, when agricultural settlement and efficiency had not improved on antiquity, suggests that the total population of European Greece, slaves included, may have been around 3,000,000, with perhaps as many again in the settlements overseas. This should be remembered when considering the political systems, administration, warfare and even the cultural achievements of the Greeks.

Fig. 38

PUBLIC FINANCE AND ADMINISTRATION

The need for revenue varied from one state to another according to its economic development, size, military ambitions and political system. Ordinary expenditure was on defence, the maintenance of public buildings, festivals, such services as the water supply, and – especially in democracies – payments for official duties and even poor relief. The main sources of revenue were market and harbour duties, public lands, fines, and voluntary or enforced benefactions by the rich. It was not usual to build up a reserve for emergencies, of which war was the commonest, but extra revenue was raised by increasing existing rates or a capital tax on property: an income tax was probably thought too difficult to assess and perhaps inequitable.

In the more self-sufficing agricultural states public commitments were few and citizens were required to undertake military and other services at their own expense. But where there was a big city, and especially if it had overseas interests, such rustic simplicity was impossible. Athens with its imperial policy was the extreme example, and thanks to inscriptions and the statements of ancient writers we know most about it. Here around 430 BC the public revenue was about 1,000 talents a year (a talent was 6,000 drachmas and at that time a drachma was the day-rate of a skilled craftsman): of this sum about three-fifths came from the 'allies' in tribute and miscellaneous payments, the rest from harbour dues of 2 per cent on imports and exports, a market due of 1 per cent, rents of state property, including the silver mines at Laurion, and various minor items such as taxes on resident aliens. Peace-time expenditure amounted to 250 talents on the navy for pay and new shipbuilding; the cavalry cost 40 talents, the army less; and other items included the upkeep of public buildings, allowances (mostly occasional) to some 8,000 citizens for time lost while doing public duties, the purchase and maintenance of some hundreds of slaves as police, and poor relief. But this still left a large surplus, part of which went to new buildings (notably on the Acropolis), and part to a war reserve. In addition, the cost of maintaining the warships (but not the crews) and much of the cost of public festivals (such as the production of tragedies) was allotted to rich men on some sort of rota. During the fourth century allowances and share-outs became much greater, although the tribute had vanished. But in spite of the complaints of the rich, the state remained solvent, and some of the sufferers bore their burdens cheerfully. War, of course, sent expenditure up, partly because Athenian troops were paid, partly because of campaigning overseas: the siege of Potidaea in Chalcidice, which lasted two years (432–430 BC), cost 2,000 talents.

Plate 34

Administrative needs depended on the size, interests and political system of the state, though it was normal to have annual officials, whose accounts were audited when they had finished their term. In oligarchies these were normally men of influence and experience. But the theory of radical democracy, that all citizens were equal, had as its corollary that all or as many as possible should hold office. At Athens the ten generals, the highest magistrates in civilian as well as military affairs, were elected; but there were more than 1,000 officials, grouped generally in committees of ten, who were chosen by lot, as were the 6,000 jurymen available for public and private lawsuits and the 500 councillors who in rota prepared the business for the supreme assembly of the citizens, supervised administration and finance, and made preliminary decisions on urgent problems. The system worked.

Public services too varied from state to state. Defence and justice came first – at Athens there were even official arbitrators, though no public prosecutor. Sanctuaries were often endowed, but some festivals had to be subsidised. In cities markets were necessary, and at Athens in particular the corn trade was regulated. Not much was done about roads or police, and less about drains. By the sixth century towns were providing conduits for water, supplied to public fountain houses, but

Plate 76

many householders sank their own wells. Public baths were appearing in the fifth century, though their equipment was simple. Gymnasiums, for exercise in the open, were also provided by the state, and stealing clothes there was, in Athens, one of the more serious criminal offences. But schools were few and usually private, though the procedure of the Athenian democracy implies that the citizens were literate. Many states engaged public doctors, who treated citizens, slaves and visitors without charge. Insurance was unknown, though war orphans were usually cared for officially and sometimes relief was given to the poor; but the family remained the usual instrument of charity.

Plate 18

SOCIETY

Social life did not change essentially in the Classical period, though in many cities prosperity increased and spread. But we know more of its details. The houses of substantial citizens, to judge by excavations at Olynthus in Chalcidice and Priene in Ionia, became neater and more regular, but not ostentatious. The furnishing consisted of little more than some small tables, chairs and stools, beds and couches, chests, a large basin for washing, and kitchen equipment. Dress was fairly uniform for all classes and even for slaves. Generally youths and workmen wore a short dress, women and older men long ones, and for extra protection there were cloaks and shawls. The materials were wool and linen. Men no longer wore jewellery. The normal diet now was simple and light, even in the upper classes. Its staples were bread, porridge, cheese, olives, vegetables, soups, eggs, fruit, honey, and fish (often salted) where it could be got, but meat was eaten only at festivals. The regular drink was wine, mixed with water in the ratio of two to three. The position of women, if anything, grew worse. The best woman, said Pericles, is the one of whom the men say least, whether bad or good: yet Pericles was an unusually enlightened Athenian and lived happily with that brilliant courtesan,

Fig. 35
Fig. 18, Plate 58
Plate 77
Plates 56, 58

Aspasia. In Athens and probably generally a single woman (whatever her age) and any property she might have inherited were under the guardianship of her nearest male relative by blood, and when she was married off her property passed into her husband's control but not ownership: this provision for keeping property in the family also gave some security against divorce, which was easy for women as well as for men. Xenophon's *Oeconomicus* gives some illuminating advice from a decent conservative on how to train a young wife in her household duties.

So far any higher education had been picked up informally. But about the middle of the fifth century the philosophers, especially in the West, had produced enough teachable knowledge, and soon experts – known admiringly as 'sophists' – began to visit other cities where they could earn a living by lectures and instruction on grammar, semantics, style, and as the end of these pursuits the art of effective public speaking, an invaluable accomplishment in Greek political life. Other important subjects were politics and the nature of right and wrong, whether they existed absolutely or were conventional. Old-fashioned people complained that such studies were subversive (as education is liable to be) and certainly the new generation sometimes showed itself frankly unscrupulous; but it may have been hypocrisy that was undermined as much as morality. In the fourth century, as the shock of the new learning passed, more academic schools of philosophy grew up conducted rather like a seminar, though without competitive examinations or degrees, and these continued throughout antiquity as the equivalent of our universities. It needed money and leisure to be trained in these advanced doctrines, but something seeped down to the poorer classes.

Though the radical poor might attack the rich, they did not attack their way of life, since they hoped to reach it themselves. The ideal of leisure pervaded Greek political thought, and for that reason democrats urged that citizens should be paid for performing political and civic duties, the principal object of leisure. The man who willingly neglected those duties (or pleasures) was not merely retiring, but useless.

In a society so governed by the aristocratic concept, slavery seemed only natural. Slaves, as opposed to serfs, did not become numerous till the Classical period, and then only in the more commercial cities. Though there were some Greeks captured in war or kidnapped, the main supply came from backward foreign peoples, such as the Thracians. Slaves were used in private households, industry, agriculture, some public services, and – in Attica – for the heavy work in the silver mines. Apart from the miners, slaves were treated humanely; in Athens at least, though they had no rights, they were protected by law from gross cruelty, suffered few restrictions in public, and had some chance of being freed or earning their freedom. But as the number of slaves increased and they competed more with free labour in a market that did not expand, the status of both free and slave workers was forced downwards.

ECONOMICS

During the sixth and fifth centuries the intensity of trade was increasing and some cities came to depend on it not only for their standard of living but for their existence. Athens fortified the harbours of Piraeus about 490 BC and through its empire made this the greatest port of the Aegean. The chief import was corn, shipped from the Ukraine. Salt fish came from the Black Sea and the Sea of Marmara, hides from the Black Sea, timber (especially for ship-building) from Macedonia, slaves from Thrace and the Black Sea. The biggest port for the western trade was Corinth; here corn and slaves were probably the principal items. Exports were wine, oil, such manufactures as woollens and metalwork, and – invisibly – the savings of mercenaries. A few states, including Athens, had mines which sometimes produced a surplus.

Fig. 29

For overseas trade there were three kinds of specialist – the shipper, the wholesaler and the retailer. The shipper, whether he owned his ship or not, usually did not have the capital to buy a cargo for himself but hired out space to wholesalers, who often travelled with him. Since voyages were slow and there was little sailing in winter, it was even more important to take on new freight as the old was discharged: so wholesalers did not usually limit themselves to one type of commodity. These wholesalers too were generally short of capital, and by the fourth century there was special legislation for marine loans. Money could be borrowed from some of the big sanctuaries, but the main lenders were private speculators or, increasingly, professional bankers, who used the funds deposited with them for safekeeping or investment. Some of these bankers allowed their clients facilities for depositing or withdrawing money in other cities, but too much depended on the integrity of individuals for this system to develop. There were bankers, but no banks. Rates of interest were high, partly because borrowers were more anxious to borrow than lenders to lend. For ordinary loans and rents 12 per cent a year was normal, with interest paid monthly. Maritime rates were $33\frac{1}{3}$ per cent for four months to compensate for the risk of shipwreck and of defaulting; there was no separate underwriting or insurance. Those who are interested in shipping frauds should read some of the private speeches of Demosthenes, written for litigants in the law-courts of Athens.

Industry must have grown even more than shipping, since not all trade was overseas. The small workshop was still normal, but there were some sizeable factories. Stylistic study shows that in the mid fifth century one pottery had working in it as many as fifteen painters – they had the unusual but convenient habit of collaborating with one another in the decoration of the same pot – and though these fifteen painters may not all have been active at the same time, they can hardly have been the only operatives in this factory. Towards the end of the same century two aliens were running a shield-works with a hundred and twenty slaves – this is the largest unit of which we know. A generation later the father of Demosthenes owned two establishments (one making knives, the other beds) and employed in them thirty-two and twenty slaves: even these factories seem to have been above the usual size. For mining there were special circumstances; and at Laurium in Attica exploitation was often by syndicates and large gangs of slaves. But to judge by figures cited in court cases, most owners of industrial establishments cautiously kept as much or more of their capital in real estate or loans.

Agriculture prospered, by Greek standards, in spite of the burning of crops and buildings in war. But in cities there was usually much unemployment, anyhow in peace time. This condition was made worse by the growing use of slaves in industry, whether working in their owner's workshops or hired out to others. Domestic slaves, of course, did not compete directly with free labour, since no citizen was willing to be a servant and to a large extent servants create the needs they satisfy.

Those states which relied on imported food naturally safeguarded their corn supply by laws and even by force. But though it was widely recognised that trade and industry were useful, not only for the revenue from custom duties and other taxes but also because they diffused some general prosperity, little direct help was given them. Some special laws about contracts were introduced, aliens of means were allowed to become resident (except at Sparta), and in the fourth century we hear of treaties that incidentally gave citizens of the states concerned equal rights in each other's harbours. But official support or protection of industry was not suggested, nor would any detailed scheme have been practicable; no normal state had a permanent civil service and the annual officers and committees in charge of administration did not often have the time to become experts. For the same reason states could not manage property, though willing enough to own it: public lands and mines were normally leased out, and even the collection of customs. But big contractors did not exist either: in large projects of public building, as inscriptions record, the work was usually let and paid for piecemeal.

Snobbery added another obstacle to economic development. The moneyed classes regarded commerce and industry as degrading and, though willing enough to make profits by well secured loans, would not become merchants or manufacturers themselves. Some big fortunes were made by speculation, but there was little or no attempt to increase productivity. In the same way a producer's ambition was to make enough to retire and live like a gentleman. In the Archaic period the political and social changes seem to have had mainly economic causes, but in the Classical period social and political beliefs had their own effects on the Greek economy. Even so, Greece reached its greatest prosperity in these two centuries; foreign competition was negligible in the trade with the Black Sea and the Adriatic, and the terms of that trade were very favourable.

TECHNOLOGY

In politics, thought, literature and art the Greeks showed an extraordinary and effective originality. But in spite of a high level of craftsmanship their technology was almost stagnant. The working of iron had come in during the eleventh century, the next industrial invention was the screw, thought out by Archimedes in the later third century BC and applied first to raising water and windlasses and later to presses. Between these two came the adoption of the alphabet in the eighth century, improvements in shipbuilding which culminated with the trireme in the later sixth century, the development of clinical medicine in the later fifth century and of the catapult in the fourth. The likely reasons for this backwardness were first, that there was no regular shortage of labour; secondly, that those with the leisure and means to be inventive were usually contemptuous of manual workers and not directly concerned with industrial production. Greek scientific thought preferred pure theory and abstract argument; it had little interest in experimental evidence, still less in practical applications. War, of course, was different and excused the development of more powerful machines. Medicine also was too useful to be discouraged. As for alphabetic writing, this was at first presumably borrowed by traders in the East for their own purposes, but writing is almost a necessity of urban administration.

With the exceptions mentioned – and of these the use of iron was much the most important, since it provided cheaper (if not always more efficient) tools and weapons – Greek technology remained basically that established in the more advanced civilisations of the Near Eastern Bronze Age. At home the grinding of corn was done by hand with querns, usually of the saddle type; for spinning there was the spindle and for weaving the upright, warp-weighted loom – spindle whorls and loom weights, mostly of fired clay, survive in excessive quantity. Dyeing and tanning were specialised trades; the processing agents were largely organic. Carpenters had of course adzes, planes, chisels and augers; more elaborate tools were bow-drill, saw and lathe, which were used also by stone-masons. In building and for some other purposes simple cranes were available to lift heavy weights. Potters had their wheel, always (so far as we know) spun directly by hand. Kilns and furnaces were simple closed structures, fired by wood or charcoal; the normal maximum temperature in kilns was about 950° C, perhaps from choice rather than incapability, since we have many examples of pots and even structures that were heated so far that they vitrified and buckled. Agriculture followed the two-field system – that is, ploughed land was left fallow every other year. Besides the obvious hand implements, it used a shallow plough and carts with solid or cross-barred wheels; both ploughs and carts were drawn by oxen. Where there were passable tracks, oxen could also be put to haul such heavy loads as building stone. But most transport on land was by pack horses, mules and donkeys, if not on human backs. Sometimes these animals too, pulled light carts (with spoked wheels like the racing chariots); but their harness, designed for the ox, was throttling and so allowed only partial use of their strength. Here, incidentally, is an example of how archaeological evidence may be deceptive – in Greek art horses are common, oxen rare: the same snobbery appears in the art of the present century, if one compares the frequency of the horse and the automobile. Sea transport was better served: merchant ships were roomy, though slow, with a single square sail and auxiliary oars, and from the sixth century onwards ports were equipped with breakwaters and quays. About the same time tunnelling improved, for aqueducts and mines; and at Laurion in eastern Attica there survive well-designed washing tanks for silver. But methods of extraction from ores were not efficient. Nor was the production of good iron, let alone steel. Though there was empirical knowledge of some properties of particular ores, nothing seems to have been done to discover the reasons for their differences. But ancient technology deserves more detailed study.

WAR

The Greek states of the Classical period formed closer groupings than before. But though some of these leagues had defence as their purpose, wars still broke out and were indeed fought more intensely.

On land the heavy infantry, the hoplites, continued to be the principal arm and in the fourth century standards of efficiency improved. The Spartans had always been well disciplined and trained. Now there were large numbers of experienced mercenaries and in the 370's the Theban militia reached a professional competence. With reliable troops more difficult tactics became practicable; in particular the Thebans succeeded in charging in echelon, so that the battle could be decided by one specially strengthened division before the others engaged. A more radical innovation was made by Philip of Macedon in the 350's. He equipped his own infantry with a twelve-foot spear (the 'sarissa') and made the line ten men deep; so long as the flanks were protected, the front was almost impenetrable. At the same time Philip made his cavalry into an effective striking force; it was more numerous and more thoroughly trained than the cavalry of the city states, and perhaps better horsed and equipped.

Lack of mobility and the short range of their weapons had always been a defect of hoplites, so much so that at some unknown date Chalcis and Eretria (according to Strabo) made a pact not to use long-range missiles against each other. From time to time light-armed skirmishers, with throwing spears, bows or slings, made havoc of a hoplite force. In 426 BC the Aetolians harassed an Athenian expedition in this way, and the next year the Athenians with the same commanding officer applied the lesson against the invincible Spartans. But it was not till the fourth century, when professional corps of mercenaries were employed regularly in Greece, that light-armed infantry were organised and trained systematically. They had some spectacular successes, but when used by both sides their effect was neutralised. It would have been different if a powerful hand bow had been invented which could pierce armour.

Fortifications became more elaborate and extensive. The regular scheme was a curtain wall with a parapet and at intervals projecting towers to enfilade an assault; where the ground was open, a ditch was dug in front of the wall. Athens, Megara and Corinth (and some other cities) were connected to their ports by long walls, which also gave refuge to farmers

Plates 23, 25

Fig. 29

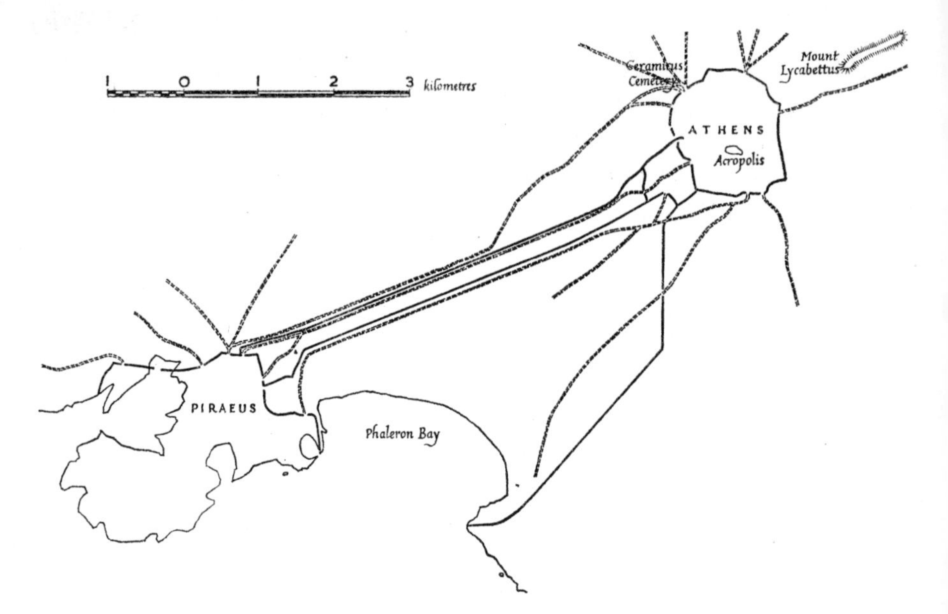

Fig. 29. Plan of fortifications of Athens and Piraeus, constructed 479–450 BC. *The double dotted lines represent roads, and the thick continuous lines walls*

and their animals in wartime, and Athens built a series of forts along its northern frontier. But siege-craft continued to be rudimentary till the fourth century. In 429 BC a strong force of Peloponnesians and Boeotians attacked Plataea, a small walled city of little natural strength and garrisoned by only 480 men and 110 women in attendance. The enemy built a siege mound and used rams, but the Plataeans resisted with tunnels, counterwalls and hooks. Fire too was tried. Eventually the city had to be blockaded, and it took two years to starve it into surrender. The Athenians were reckoned more expert besiegers, but proved little brisker. The first significant advances were made in Sicily in the wars between Greeks and Carthaginians around 400 BC. In the East, armies were already familiar with wheeled towers from which to shoot down or drop bridges on to the city wall, but the catapult was a new invention. At first it was used for small missiles against personnel, later larger versions were made for attacking walls. Of course catapults and mining were adapted for defence too, and fortifications could be improved by wider ditches and out-works. So treachery remained the quickest and the cheapest way of carrying a strong city.

Progress at sea came sooner. In 480 BC the Athenians had about 200 triremes at Salamis and during the next eighty years their navy was always in commission. This navy was manned by the poorest class of citizens, who benefited most by the Athenian empire, and – to the mortification of the conservatives – they acquired an efficiency and morale equal to that of the Spartan infantry. The trireme had been invented in the sixth century, but it was now decked throughout and the Athenian professionals perfected its tactics. In the fourth century there was some reversion, especially in Sicily, to heavier, clumsier ships and boarding tactics.

The scale and scope of operations became bigger. For example in 415 BC, while at war in Greece, Athens despatched to Sicily an expedition of more than 6,000 soldiers and 90 triremes, and was able to maintain and reinforce it heavily for two years; and in 413 BC the Spartans built and garrisoned for ten years a permanent fortress at Decelea in the hostile territory of Attica. The strategy of campaigns too became bolder, though often grand schemes were upset by bad intelligence and communications and amateurish generals. But higher planning and policy became more comprehensive and logical. In 432 BC Athens used economic sanctions against Megara, by excluding Megarians from all the harbours and markets of Attica and its empire. When the war with Sparta began in 431 BC, the over-riding strategy of the Athenians was to control the sea and avoid any land battle, however often and much Attica was invaded and devastated. Prisoners were massacred without compunction, if it would terrorise subjects, opponents or neutrals. Guarantees and treaties were made to be broken as either party found it paid. Similar principles inspired the wars of the fourth century, though till Philip came no state or league was powerful enough to have a reasonable chance of enforcing a lasting dominion over all of Greece.

From the seventh century onwards many Greeks had turned for employment or enrichment to mercenary service, usually with Oriental potentates, and when the Peloponnesian War ended in 404 BC, many more trained soldiers came on to the market. Some were hired by Greek states, others by the Persians. The total number of these mercenaries is unknown, but when Alexander invaded the East in 334 BC there were more than 50,000 Greeks in the armies that opposed him.

Our knowledge of Classical warfare comes mostly from the ancient writers and, since they took an interest in it, they were often well informed. The archaeological evidence is mainly in inscriptions, which give some useful details, and in the remains of fortifications, often impressive but not yet fully studied, especially in regard to the kind of attack they were designed to withstand.

RELIGION

Of the philosophers of the Classical period some looked for a supreme intelligent force which governed the whole universe, allowed the orthodox gods no more than an allegorical existence, and believed in absolute standards of good and evil. Others were agnostic or materialist, doubting or denying the existence of deities and arguing that standards of morality were invented by human beings to suit their needs at the time. In the later fifth century these views were publicised by the sophists, and became well enough known to be subjects of popular jokes. But there was very little conflict with the official religion, which was satisfied with conformity to rituals so familiar and unexacting that even the sterner philosophers accepted them as part of the routine decencies of life.

Yet in spite of the new teachings, old-fashioned piety continued. This is evident not only in the many new and expensive temples, not all of which can be explained by civic pride, but also from private dedications in minor sanctuaries and sacred caves. Of the orthodox gods Dionysus, Aphrodite and Eros became more popular, though not as much as might be inferred from counting their appearances on later red-figure pottery; the mystery religions gained adherents; and towards the end of the fifth century Asclepios was emerging as a Panhellenic god. Asclepios (in Latin Aesculapius) had little mythological background, his province was healing and his ethics were professional. His principal sanctuary was near Epidaurus, and there a long series of inscriptions by grateful visitors testify to the efficacy of faith and good medical advice. The oracles had lost most of their political influence – after all, Delphi had backed the Persians in 480 BC – but private custom flourished and even Socrates, who spent so much of his time exposing hypocrisy, seems to have been impressed by an oracular statement that he was the wisest of men. Some modern writers assert that plain superstition increased in the later Classical period – and even in 413 BC the superstitious observance of a lunar eclipse cost Athens 40,000 men in Sicily – but perhaps it is only that our information is fuller than for earlier times: there were more Greeks now and they were more literate.

Plates 84, 87

Plate 16

THOUGHT AND KNOWLEDGE

The earlier philosophers had been interested in the constitution of matter. Towards the middle of the fifth century Parmenides of Elea, a small remote colony on the west coast of Italy, considered the process of change and advanced the proposition 'what is is and cannot not be,' and conversely 'what is not is not and cannot be'; it followed, he argued, that change and empty space are impossible, and so his spherical universe was homogeneous and unchanging. Since this doctrine, set out in his poem *Truth*, did not fit the evidence of the senses, they must be unreliable; but he felt obliged to publish a second poem called *Opinion*, explaining the apparent universe as constituted of fire and dense darkness. The paradox of *Truth* impelled some thinkers to look for a fallacy and so to the study of logic. Others, contemptuous of philosophy, turned to factual inquiries, such as grammar, or the more marketable studies of political theory and public speaking: a frequent dogma was that there were no absolute standards – right was right because of custom, not of some natural law. A few physicists continued to ponder on the universe perceived by the senses. Empedocles decided on four elements – earth, water, air and fire – alternately attracted and repelled: between complete separation of elements and complete mixture various combinations occurred, the present universe being one such set of combinations. To Anaxagoras the elements were of infinite variety and combined through an initial impulse from a universal mind. The 'atomists', who followed after him, are more comprehensible. Leucippus thought of homogeneous particles, which differ significantly in shape, order and position, and of empty space (so that, after all, 'what is not' is); in the beginning these particles were separate and falling vertically, but since the heavier particles fell faster than the lighter they jostled and combined; sensations are what we should call chemical reactions and so subjective. Democritus added that the soul too is formed of particles and, applying his cosmological theory to human life, concluded that its aim should be pleasure – of the soul rather than the body, since the pleasure of the soul is greater. But this thorough-going materialism had few supporters till in the early Hellenistic period Epicurus adopted it for his gentle doctrine.

Till the late fifth century philosophers had worked more or less isolated from each other in various parts of the Greek world. Now Athens became the centre of thought. At the same time interest shifted from physical to metaphysical and ethical problems. The first Athenian philosopher was Socrates, a stonemason's son but not so poor, since he was registered as a hoplite. Socrates, who always maintained that he knew nothing, specialised in close argument and definition by question and answer, and he was singularly effective in exposing illogical opinions. His positive conclusions are less certain, and even his followers disagreed in interpreting them. But he believed in arguing from the concrete to the abstract, which was the pure form of truth; to understand this truth was useful, since a man did wrong only if he knew no better and to know what was right meant to do what was right; so only the good man was happy. With all this Socrates was a conscientious citizen, who did not shirk his official and military obligations. His execution in 399 BC won him a martyr's crown that he did not deserve. He was prosecuted for corrupting the youth – to be fair some of his pupils had been very criminal in their politics – and after condemnation the penalty had to be fixed: the prosecutor (a private citizen and not the state) asked for death, Socrates' counter-proposal was that he should have free meals in the town hall for the rest of his life.

The mantle of Socrates was worn with differences by his disciples. The Cynics, for instance, accepted the premise that knowing what is right is the only happiness; so they ignored the pleasures and sometimes even the proprieties of this life. The Cyrenaics took the opposite line that the happy man must be good, and impartially cultivated all the temperate pleasures. But the most influential of the followers of Socrates was Plato, a moralist of a religious turn of mind, whose school at the gymnasium of Academus in Athens gave us our word 'academy'. Plato has left a long series of philosophical works, from which it is clear that he gradually modified his theories. But to summarise crudely, he maintained that material objects and human concepts are reflections of eternal abstract 'ideas'.

When, for instance, we see a table, we recognise it as a table. So there must exist an 'ideal' archetype of a table, in which the tables we see share. So too since we recognise it – and truth is always elicited, not injected – the soul must previously have been acquainted with the 'ideas' and further through its kinship with them can be considered as being itself also immortal. Happiness, then, consists of contemplation of the 'idea' of good, and education should be directed to that aim. But man's aim should be missionary too, and Plato sketched in the *Republic* and *Laws* a model state, which (since his prejudices were for oligarchy and authority) shows some sympathy with the Spartan regime. This state was to be limited in size and agricultural; the citizens were to be classed by ability as workers, soldiers, and rulers, men and women having equal rights and duties; education, cultural activity and private behaviour were to be regulated and censored strictly. Though Plato became adviser to a tyrant, his political theory had no practical effect.

Aristotle studied under Plato, tutored Alexander the Great, and then set up his own school – the 'Peripatetics' – in Athens. Many of his works too survive, if only in the form of lecture notes. In intelligence Aristotle was shrewder and more academic than his master, and he relied more on argument from observed facts to general rules. His physical and metaphysical theories were still based on *a priori* reasoning, though he believed in the initial importance of individual objects: all material things, so he concluded, were the product of four causes – matter (divisible into the four elements of earth, water, air and fire), form (which unlike Plato's 'idea' did not exist by itself), agent (whether natural, deliberate or accidental) and purpose. Remotely superimposed was God, who gave the original impulse to creation. But logic was better served by Aristotle in his *Organon*, an exposition of admirable precision and clarity. He was concerned with ethics too and discovered a new position, that virtue was the mean between two vices;

courage, for instance, is the mean between the opposites of cowardice and foolhardiness. Similarly in politics, after examining the constitutions of more than a hundred and fifty Greek states, he decided that power was used best by the middle class and that civic education was impracticable. Here he has been criticised for confining his political thinking to the city state at a time when Alexander had shown that type of organisation to be obsolete, but it was the only type for which he had enough data and, as it turned out, the diminished city states of the Hellenistic period were usually controlled by the middle class. A literary treatise, the *Poetics*, examined among other topics the tragic dramas available and set out the apparent characteristics of the species. But, if not more valid, this method was certainly more successful in zoology, where accurate observation and systematic classification established Aristotle as a pioneer of science. A complementary study of plants was carried out by his pupil Theophrastus about the end of the fourth century.

There was steady progress in mathematics, particularly in geometry. Plato, it seems, established the method of analysis or proving a hypothesis by working backwards to ascertained facts, and he considered geometrical study an indispensable part of education. Euclid, who was working at the beginning of the Hellenistic period, largely sums up the achievements of his Classical predecessors. In arithmetic the Greeks were handicapped by not having any rational series of symbols or even (till, at the earliest, the third century BC) any notation for zero. Astronomy was concerned mainly with measurements in space and time, the latter having the practical value of improving the calendar. Some thinkers rejected the conclusion that the sun revolved round the earth. In mechanics a few principles appear to have been considered.

Even in Homer medicine was not tied to priestcraft, and in the Archaic period some doctors had a wide reputation. But systematic studies became properly established about the middle of the fifth century with Hippocrates of Cos. He relied on careful observation of symptoms and conditions and on treatment proved empirically; in this he preferred natural aids, such as diet and exercise, to the use of drugs. Treatises of Hippocrates and his school survive still.

History too began about the same time. Since the late sixth century some writers had collected and even criticised traditions about the past, but now Herodotus imposed a loose system and form on his very varied material. Towards the end of the fifth century Thucydides examined the Peloponnesian war, as it was proceeding, in a Hippocratic spirit, noting the symptoms and diagnosing the causes. None of his successors of the fourth century had his insight and few his honesty. History was declining so soon into political and even moral propaganda.

LITERATURE

In lyric poetry the exhibition of the poet's personal feelings was now outmoded, but choral pieces were still wanted at festivals or the celebrations for victorious athletes. The greatest choral composer was Pindar, a professional whose inspiration was none the poorer for being paid. This lyric form in turn declined soon after the middle of the fifth century, but its tradition was continued for another generation in the pieces sung by the chorus in tragedy.

Tragic drama had its origins in some unsophisticated ritual, but though still performed on sacred occasions it developed at Athens into an independent poetical form, which normally took its subjects from legend, treating them often as examples of the doctrine that excess leads to doom. Its curious conventions, established by historical accidents, allowed no more than three actors (who might, though, double their parts) and gave a large share in the drama, but not in the action, to a chorus which sang and danced. All the players were men or youths, though there were many women's parts, and the actors wore masks and heavy costumes, so that the movement, gestures and probably delivery were stately and formal, in complete contrast to the practice in modern revivals. This very restricted kind of drama occupied many Attic poets throughout the fifth century and (as with some problems of art) concentration led to success and exhaustion. Aeschylus, the first great tragic poet, was a pioneer whose rich and pregnant language makes his theological thought seem profounder than it was. In Sophocles, creative for more than sixty years, social interest and sympathy blend in with the tact and purity of his style. Euripides, a younger contemporary, was more colloquial and more strident; his problems have twists to them, and the tragic conventions creak. Their successors in the fourth century could not or at least did not make any progress in tragedy.

The antecedents of comedy were much like those of tragedy, and its development was equally arbitrary. What is called 'old comedy', which flourished in the later fifth century, had a structure comparable to tragedy, though looser, and the masks and costumes were less cramping. We know it from surviving plays of Aristophanes. Though produced at a religious festival and officially, they ridicule the gods and attack contemporary politicians and notables with a bawdy, partisan venom that speaks well for the tolerance of Athenian democracy. The style is racy, and in the songs of the chorus sometimes lyrical. The comedy of the fourth century is tamer, and prudently avoids personalities and politics. It developed into the 'new comedy', which has no chorus and is constructed in acts and scenes, with stock plots and stock characters of middle-class complexion. This new comedy remained popular, was translated into Latin by Plautus and Terence, and from them had some – fortunately not much – influence in the Renaissance.

Writing in prose form had, of course, existed before, though even in the mid fifth century Herodotus was conversational, while not casual, in his manner. But at the same time in Sicily the need of philosophy for precise expression was leading off some inquirers to examine style. The most celebrated of these was Gorgias, who in 427 BC as member of a visiting delegation captivated the Athenians with his neat balance of thoughts and clauses, catholic vocabulary, and assonances. This self-conscious prose was adapted and, to avoid monotony, roughened by Thucydides in set pieces of his history, though elsewhere he preferred a more narrative style. Thucydides died about 400 BC. His eminent successors – among them Lysias, Xenophon, Plato and Demosthenes – show an easy command of a lucid and disciplined prose, without affectation or dullness, and even the clumsier performers were aware of a standard. Ancient writers had, to be just, advantages over modern, in that they did not write so much and they expected their writings to be read aloud; even so, this rapid mastery of a new medium was not only new but also complete, and it should not be undervalued. The subjects of prose literature were as wide as might be expected – historical studies, political pamphlets, forensic and political speeches, philosophical dialogues and discourses, monographs, and even memoirs and miscellanies, though not the novel.

Books were still rare, even if by the end of the fifth century the bookseller had appeared in Athens. Publication was not yet organised: the usual practice was to borrow a copy and transcribe or have it transcribed for oneself, and those who enjoyed verse normally memorised it.

PAINTING

To the later Greeks painting ranked as high an art as sculpture, though it was tardier in reaching its acme. Nothing of merit survives, so that we depend on indirect evidence. From ancient writers we have names of the masters and some very general observations; wall-paintings in Etruscan tombs give a provincial and often cursory version of current standards;

some painted marble and terracotta slabs of Greek workmanship reflect the technique and types but not the composition of major works; in vase-painting and elsewhere a few ephemeral or permanent innovations are most easily explained as borrowings from more pictorial art; and Roman wall-paintings and mosaics sometimes imitate what seems to be a Classical style. From these secondary sources one may arrive at a very rough idea of the development and nature of monumental Greek painting on panels and walls.

Archaic painting had been very close to vase-painting, though its greater scale allowed more details (for instance eyelashes) and its technique more colours. But about the beginning of the Classical period some painters, of whom Polygnotus of Thasos was the most famous, created a new grand manner. Twisting and foreshortening had been introduced at the very end of the sixth century. Now, by a logical extension, the rule of profile stances was abandoned and spatial depth was admitted. Characteristic, it seems, is the tableau composed of statuesque figures set at different levels, the higher being regarded as the more remote, in a landscape indicated by sparse hillocks and shrubs; there was no diminishing perspective, and line drawing supplemented by flat colour still remained the medium, though an uneven wash was allowed for rocks and some other accessories. Fairly soon architectural perspective appeared and there are hints of a more sympathetic treatment of landscape; both architecture and landscape were used as background scenery in the theatre. Because so many surviving examples are incorrect it is usually thought that the Greeks never understood perspective; but, after all, Anaxagoras and Democritus, two acute scientists of this period, wrote treatises on its theory. Even so, it seems true enough that the great Classical painters used perspective only for settings and did not apply it to figures, which they kept properly in the foreground. It was man that interested the Greeks.

The next big advance was made shortly before 400 BC, when Apollodorus developed the use of shading to model male forms and drapery, though by a curious convention the flesh of women was not shaded for another fifty years. About the same time, in the middle of the fourth century, the technique of high-lighting was discovered. The art had now passed from coloured drawing to an illusionist painting, which with its figures grouped in the foreground and modelled by a clear and evenly diffused light pleased later connoisseurs more than the strong chiaroscuro and atmospheric effects of its Hellenistic successors. Apelles, active in the second half of the fourth century, was usually reckoned the greatest of Greek painters. Some idea of a masterpiece of this time, though copied in a clumsy and unpictorial medium, may perhaps be found in the Alexander mosaic, now in Naples.

Plate 87

POTTERY

The Athenians evacuated their city in 480 BC and when they returned the next year found it ruined. The interruption did not affect their dominance in the production of fine pottery, and the same masters continued in the same style. But in a few years a new Classical style arose, less decorative and more decorous. A little experiment showed that the advances in pictorial art were not altogether suited to the scale, fields and technique of red-figure vase-painting; though line-drawing was modified, composition kept to late Archaic principles. Cautiously progressive, vase-painting could no longer be rated a major art. At the end of the fifth and round the middle of the fourth centuries some workshops attempted a bolder and grander style. But in general the average quality declined and at Athens red-figure came to an end in the 320's. The 'white-ground' style, which became important around 460 BC and lasted till about 400, had more promise. This style was more or less confined to narrow flasks intended only as offerings in graves and so could use colours that were not durable. Many

Plates 81–83

Plate 84

Plates 79–80

Fig. 31

of the earlier pieces have a quiet and restrained harmony; later work is usually more ambitious and less competent.

Attic red-figure maintained its primacy till the end and was exported widely, though probably in decreasing quantity. Imitation in Boeotia began slowly in the second quarter, in Corinth at the end of the fifth century. But the only big competitors of Attic were in Italy. In Etruria a sort of red-figure style appeared early in the fifth century, prospered in the fourth, and lasted into the third. In South Italy around 440 BC vase-painters trained at Athens started local manufacture and early in the fourth century we can distinguish four main schools – Apulian, Campanian (with Sicilian), Paestan and Lucanian. Their prolific and artistically inferior products are to be seen in almost every museum. South Italian too survived into the third century. A popular side-line was the so-called Gnathian ware, with mainly vegetable decorations in white, yellow and purple on a black ground; it began rather before the middle of the fourth century and continued for about a hundred years. These South Italian wares captured their local market, and had some sale further west.

The subjects of Classical vase-painting ranged from mythology to daily life. Quiet scenes and conversation pieces were much commoner than in Archaic, partly because of greater knowledge of the human form, and in the fourth century a sensual taste became obtrusive. It is interesting that in this and the display of emotion vase-painting was ahead of sculpture; presumably mural and panel painting was still further ahead.

The dating of Classical pottery is fairly safe. Useful historical events are the sack of Athens in 480–79 BC, the refounding of Camarina in 461, the 'purification' of Delos in 426 or 425 (when the Athenians shifted the contents of graves in that island to an enclosure on Rheneia), the grave of the Lacedaemonians in Athens of 403, the destruction of Olynthus in 348, the refounding of Gela about 340, and the founding of

Alexandria in 331. There are also parallels with datable sculptures, a few contexts with datable coins, and some untypical Attic pots of the middle part of the fourth century which have painted on them the year of manufacture.

SCULPTURE

The surviving examples of Archaic sculpture are almost all originals. That is because the Archaic style was never admired much between its own time and the present century. But Classical sculpture remained classical throughout antiquity, and in the late Hellenistic and Roman periods copies and adaptations of its major and minor works were produced in very great numbers. This popularity, as it turned out, lessened the chances of survival of original statues; more of them were still above ground when the Middle Ages set in and ancient masterpieces came to be valued in terms of scrap metal and lime. Even in Rome, where some municipal organisation continued, the looters could not be stopped; during the fourth century AD an official census noted 3,785 bronze statues in public ownership, a thousand years later only three or four were still to be seen. With losses on this scale, the student of Classical sculpture is obliged to take notice of the copies, which make up the bulk of most collections of ancient statuary and turn so many casual visitors against mature Greek art. Copies are helpful for pose and major features, but generally their detail is harsh and summary and the surface of the marble (which is their usual material) has a frigid glossiness. In originals the execution is careful, the modelling is subtle (especially in the fourth century), and where the material is marble the surface has a diffuse and opaque sheen.

The Archaic sculptors, concentrating in the typical way of Greek artists on one problem at a time, had mastered the general anatomy of the human body and begun to loosen its posture. Their Classical successors improved the detailed structure, relaxed the poses, and experimented cautiously with mood.

Fig. 30, Plate 61

But they kept to the old principles of composition: statues were designed for a principal view from in front, and in reliefs movement was still along the plane of the surface even though the human figures were not often in full profile. Further, there was no attempt at individual peculiarities in face or body, which had an equal importance. Classical sculpture was 'ideal', that is it aimed at perfect types of humanity, so much so that only attributes or context show what god or man is represented or even whether god or man, and in spite of the convincing appearance of its figures it would be foolish to trust them far as evidence for the physical characteristics of the Greeks of that time.

Plates 57, 58

Classical sculptors were not afraid of spoiling their marble by painting it, and as their anatomy became more natural so did their colouring of drapery, hair, eyes, lips and even cheeks. In bronze the eyes at least were filled in. Our present distaste for such embellishments is accidental: in the Renaissance, when ancient statuary was collected and studied, its paint had perished. But it is still easy to appreciate on reliefs how a blue cloak or red background would set off the white of struggling bodies, and by a great but useful exertion one may imagine the effect of a temple where colour was applied systematically to emphasise both architecture and sculpture.

Plate 52

Plate 57

Plate 29

The development in style was logical. In the standing male statue the stage of transition from Archaic to Classical is shown by the Critian boy, where the old rigidity is broken by a slight shift in balance and turn of the head. A generation later, in the 440's, Polyclitus made his bronze Doryphorus (or man carrying a spear) and wrote a book about it. In this statue, known to us only through copies, the change to the Classical type is complete. The weight is wholly on the right leg while the left hangs free, the left arm is raised and the right slack, the head tilts round towards its right. The effects of these actions on the body are observed faithfully; the median

Plate 44

Fig. 30

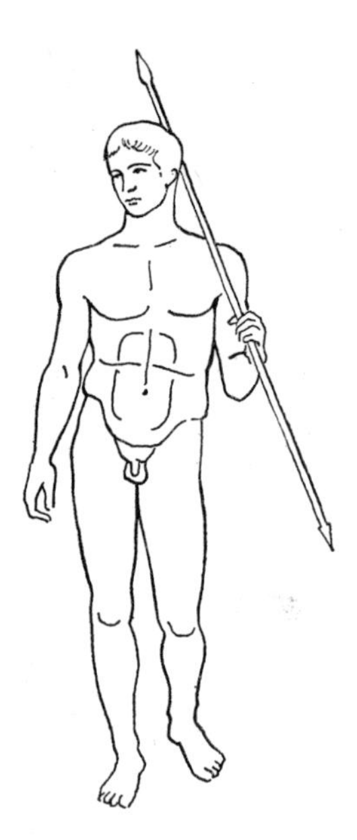

Fig. 30. The Doryphorus of Polyclitus, 450–440 BC. *Height (without spear) 2·12 m.*

line has a light curve and the axes through knees, hips, chest, shoulders and eyes are carefully divergent. A century later relaxation could be carried as far as languor. The Hermes from Olympia, with its sinuous median line, perhaps needs a support. In free-standing figures more extended poses are uncommon. One of the most extreme is the Artemisium statue, of about 460 BC and not the only bronze original salved from ancient shipwrecks. But even here the extension of the figure is in one vertical plane, as if it had been cut out of a relief, and the moment represented is not action, but the pause before action. In the details of the body progress was steady. The Artemisium figure displays a broadly accurate anatomy, on the Hermes the ripple of flesh has been mastered. A curious and universal convention is the bulge of muscle along the lower edges of the male abdomen.

Plate 61

Plate 49

Study of the female figure was slower. The central personage on the so-called Ludovisi throne, a provincial work of about 460 BC, does not bear anatomical inspection. The handle of a

Plate 50

bronze mirror in Copenhagen, some ten to twenty years later, is too decently draped to be revealing, though the thrust of the slack thigh proves that here too the weight is on the right leg. The Victories of the Nike balustrade, a little before 400 BC, show a sensitive appreciation of female form. But it was not till the middle of the fourth century that Praxiteles introduced into European statuary the now indispensable female nude. The copies of his famous Cnidian Aphrodite are too unpleasant to illustrate, but other works of the time share its sensual inspiration.

Plate 51

Plate 59

Plates 55, 84, 87

Most female statues were clothed and some males too, especially old men and charioteers, who raced in full, ankle-length dresses. Early Classical drapery tended to fall in heavy folds, V-shaped on the chest and vertical down the skirts. About 460 BC, for variety, one thigh was thrust forward to flatten or disperse the folds above it. Further development went various ways: folds were diversified or bunched – the Demeter of Cnidos shows how strong such effects could be in the mid fourth century – or the material became clinging or transparent.

Plate 51

Plate 33

Plate 60

Plate 59

The Classical Greeks gave no over-riding emphasis to the head, and (excepting the special cult requirement of herms) had no more use for busts than they had for torsos. Early Classical faces tend to look vacuous: examples are the Delphi charioteer and the emerging goddess of the Ludovisi throne. The Alba head, a second-rate work not much after 450 BC, is more expressive, though the skin still seems leathery, and it possesses already the slightly melancholy and reserved air of breeding that characterises the Classical style. The trend was to softer and rounder forms, and with Praxiteles the flesh seems palpable. Emotion and passion, alien to the Classical ideal, were rarely represented by more than a slight frown or a conventional gesture: on a frieze from the Mausoleum of Halicarnassus, where Greeks fight Amazons, the action is violent

Plate 52

Plate 50

Plate 53

Plate 54

Plates 55, 61

Plates, 56, 58

Plate 57

but the faces, though intent, are controlled. This intensity of expression, obtained by sinking the eyes and parting the lips, becomes common in the fourth century, when severe standards were loosening. The development in hair is similar.

Plate 54

The sculptures put in the pediments of Doric temples show the same style, but inevitably poses were freer and figures were grouped, sometimes even in successful repose. But free-standing statuary regularly avoided groups. Several figures might stand on the same base, but they remained independent; and where two figures are combined, as in the Hermes of Olympia with its Classically unchildish child, the second figure is a minor accessory.

Plate 61

In relief sculpture the possibilities and principles of composition were very different and, since it was coloured, a connection with painting might be expected. In fact, though there are a few painter's tricks (like the outlining of the further legs of the attendants on the Ludovisi throne), Classical sculptors generally ignored the pictorial advances in representing depth and setting. The Ludovisi throne, in spite of some ineptness, has more delicacy than the statues of the 460's. The gods of the frieze of the Parthenon (to be understood as seated side by side) have a full share of the Classical ideal of innate and easy courtesy. Thirty years later, at the end of the fifth century, the figures of the Nike balustrade aim more frankly at grace. In scenes of action, relief sculptors took full advantage of their liberty: the vigour of the fighters of the Mausoleum is paralleled even in the fifth century.

Plate 50

Plate 56

Plate 59

Plate 57

A special class of reliefs are those on gravestones, which grouped on family plots lined the roads outside cities. Here the normal scene is one of idealised home life. In the fifth century expression is calm and restrained; during the fourth, hands clasp and eyes lock in pathos, though often no particular occasion is intended nor is it always clear who is mourner and who mourned. Such expressions of sentiment had appeared

Fig. 32

Plate 58

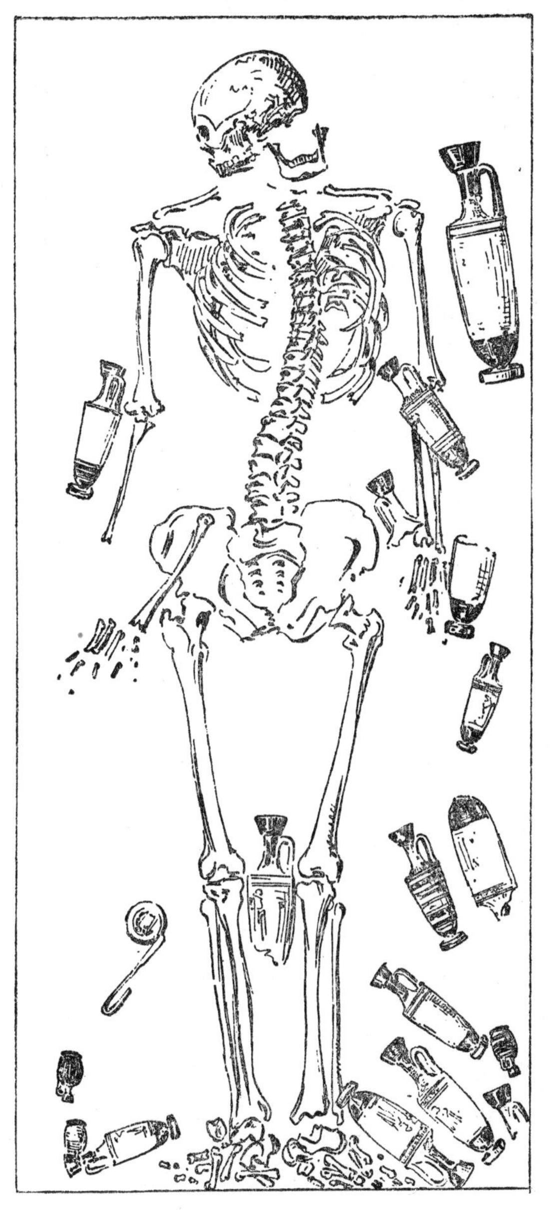

Fig. 31. Plan of inhumation grave at Athens, mid fifth century BC.

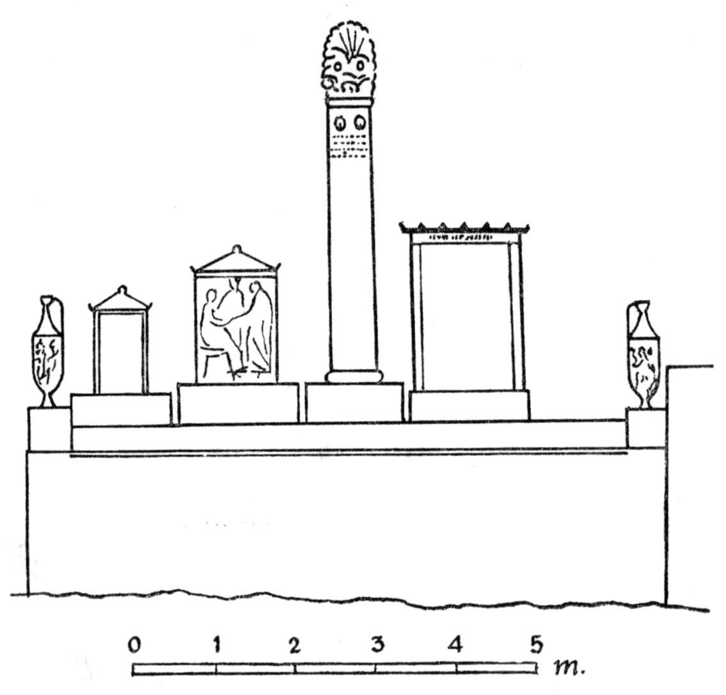

Fig. 32. Family burial plot at Athens, fourth century BC.

more than a generation earlier in white-ground vase-painting and perhaps for the same reason: both were funerary art of an especially private nature. Even so, there was no more attempt at portraiture than in public monuments.

The purpose of Classical sculpture was on one side civic display, and civic feeling or taste largely governed even private patrons. On the other side it was aesthetic: subjects needed to be only vaguely appropriate – the choice of Greeks and Amazons on the Mausoleum, as elsewhere, is for the spirited contrast of male and female bodies – and even the great temple statues had no special religious sanctity: the veneration of the devout and the robe brought by the Panathenaic procession

Plate 57

were given not to Phidias's gold and ivory Athena in the Parthenon, but to the primitive and probably artless wooden idol in the Erechtheum.

The personalities of Classical sculpture – among them Myron, Phidias, Polyclitus, Scopas, Praxiteles, and Lysippus – can be discerned now only vaguely. Of these Lysippus, it seems, makes the transition to Hellenistic, at least in regard to pose: his Apoxyomenus (or man scraping himself) is shown in the process of shifting his weight, reaches forward in space, and is no longer designed for a principal single view. But most attempts to group anonymous originals and copies round a particular master are not convincing. Still less convincing are the alleged local schools of Athens, Argos, Sicyon and elsewhere; the major sculptors travelled and took pupils from other cities, so that their differences may well have been personal and not geographical. Inferior, provincial workshops of course existed, and in western Asia there is throughout the period the curious phenomenon of Greek sculptors working for foreign

Fig. 33

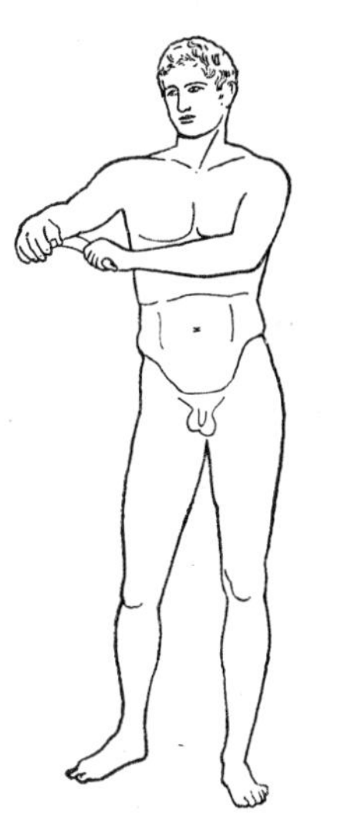

Fig. 33. The Apoxyomenus of Lysippus, about 330 BC. *Height 2·05 m.*

kings or magnates and sometimes devising new subjects or attempting depth and perspective as they would never have dared to do in Greece itself.

The technical methods of Greek sculptors must be inferred from their surviving works, finished and unfinished. The hollow casting of bronze had been mastered by the middle of the sixth century, and in the fifth that metal became the preferred medium for free-standing statues. The usual process was to make a careful model in wood and envelop it in clay; then the wood was removed, the clay jacket (or mould) was coated inside with wax, and the wax in turn was lined with a clay core. Figures were regularly made in many pieces to be joined when cast. Afterwards molten bronze was poured in through a hole in the top to replace the wax. Next the casing was broken off and the clay core too could be picked out, and finally the bronze cast was worked over. Bronze was kept polished, so preventing the patination now admired. For marble the principal tools were punches, held at right angles to the final surface; when that was nearly reached, chisels were used; and finishing was done by rasps and emery, without any high polish. Drilling was used with restraint in the Archaic and Classical periods, and not so much more freely in the Hellenistic until the first century BC; then, to meet the demand for copies, pointing was introduced and the punch was replaced by the drill and chisel, and sometimes the marble was polished to the high gloss now thought natural to it. At the same time it became common practice to complete one part of a statue at a time: earlier sculptors worked evenly all round a figure, removing a single layer as if they were peeling an onion.

The types of Archaic statues were square and so straightforward that outlines drawn on the four sides of a block could have been a sufficient guide for the sculptor. But many students argue for models in the Classical period, since its poses were more complex, especially in pedimental statuary, and there too the relation of figures to each other required careful planning and measuring. The same may be said of bronze statues (or rather their preliminary wooden forms). Yet the method of carving round the figure implies that the sculptor viewed his work as a whole at all stages and so was not simply copying a model; and red-figure vase-painters made preliminary sketches only as rough aids. It is wisest not to be dogmatic on whether and when Classical carvers used models or how detailed and of what scale they were: even practising sculptors give different verdicts.

OTHER ARTS

The major arts of the fifth and fourth centuries were sculpture and painting (and, of course, architecture). But the other arts accepted the same principles and forms, with some additions of floral and abstract ornaments, and since craftsmanship was highly skilled they too can illustrate the Classical ideal.

The most important of these lesser arts was metalwork, of bronze, silver and gold. The finest productions were in relief and decorated a variety of articles from armour to jewellery. Engraving, inlay and filigree were practised too, and cast pieces were often incorporated in utensils. With gems, as might be expected, the standard of cutting was excellent and some surviving examples show an almost un-Classical imagination. Coins vary in quality. The widely accepted currencies of important states tended deliberately to repeat the familiar old-fashioned types, but some minor or commemorative issues show die-cutters of the first rank. Since coinage was regarded as a sign of independence, every Greek state (except Sparta) had its own separate issues, however small. On both coins and gems heads are frequent; this breach of the Classical rule can be excused by the smallness of the field.

Plate 85

Plate 87

Plate 51

Plate 86

Figurines of bronze, cast solid, are usually of fair to good quality. But most of the countless terracottas, so frequent in

Plate 51

sanctuaries, are poor and nasty: they can also be very provoking archaeologically, since moulds might continue in occasional use for fifty years or more and be replaced at any time by remoulds from their casts.

Arts that are almost completely lost are the inlay of ivory and wood, much used on boxes and furniture, and the woven and embroidered decoration of textiles: both indulged in figures. Vase-painting has been described separately, less for its artistic than its archaeological value. Mosaics, mainly in black and white pebbles, were attempting figures before the end of the fifth century, but the mosaic technique was by its nature too coarsely reticular for the advanced linear or pictorial styles that it copied; even the most satisfactory Greek examples, those of the late fourth century from Pella, need strips of lead to give clarity to important contours.

A claim for aesthetic status can be made even by inscriptions, which especially in the public decrees of Classical Athens exhibit not only simplicity and clarity in their lettering, but also a neat sense of spacing. This regularity has its usefulness too, since the student attempting restoration can often calculate how many letters are missing from a broken or damaged line.

Plate 88

Most of these arts existed before Classical times. Metal reliefs and metal and terracotta figurines go back as far as the eighth century. Gem-cutting worthy of the name reappears not much later and coins begin a little before 600 BC. Vase-painting and textiles have a much greater antiquity, though mosaics and calligraphic inscriptions are new. But in general it was in the Classical period that the minor arts reached maturity; and, as in the Renaissance, the great masters of sculpture and painting sometimes turned their hands to lesser tasks.

ARCHITECTURE AND PLANNING

The principles of the Doric style had been established in the sixth century and the Classical period improved the subtlety of the details. The most remarkable development was in the 'refinements', so happily studied by the Athenian architects of the third quarter of the fifth century. In their larger temples, such as the misnamed 'Theseum', there is no major line that is strictly horizontal or vertical. The platform curves up from the corners towards the centre, the axes of the columns slope in-wards, the entablature too slopes inwards and curves up to its middle. These deviations, which have been verified, are too small to be discernible in any ordinary view – in the 'Theseum' again the rise of the platform is rather less than 1 in 700 at the ends and 1 in 1,000 at the sides – and since no practical function is served, the purpose must be visual. How the vision is affected and how Greek architects calculated such refine-ments are questions still to be answered completely. The change in proportions is more easily comprehended: the column becomes slimmer, its echinus smaller and steeper, the entabla-ture lower. Another trend is to shorter temples: the 'Theseum' soon after 450 BC was given the normal six columns on the ends and thirteen on the sides, but seventy years later the temple of Asclepios at Epidaurus had six by only eleven. Generally speaking the Doric style aimed at sturdiness in the sixth century, in the fifth it attained harmony, and in the fourth turned towards elegance.

Plates 28, 30
Fig. 25

The Ionic style was slower at settling down and it was prob-ably at Athens, the wealthiest Greek city in the fifth century, that a Classical standard was set. What that was can be seen in the illustrations. There is a general trend towards higher columns and the ornateness inherent in the style continued to find new expressions, among them the Corinthian capital. This form, which apparently began in metalwork, was trans-ferred to stone architecture in the late fifth century and used from time to time for an interior colonnade. Its first known occurrence outside is on the Choregic Monument of Lysi-crates, put up about 334 BC and more a decorative composi-tion than a building. Early Corinthian capitals show a lively

Plates 31–33

Plate 34

variety in detail and even in structure; the standard was not fixed till the late first century BC.

During the later fifth century it was becoming common for buildings externally Doric to have an Ionic order inside, if extra height was wanted. This practice was not limited to temples, where one style was outside and the other within the cella, but became regular for stoas, although both rows of columns could be seen at once and the inner series was spaced twice as widely as the outer. Further, in a few Doric temples Ionic features were allowed outside the cella, as for instance the friezes of the 'Theseum' and the Parthenon.

Fig. 25

A few new types of structures received architectural treat-ment in the Classical period and occasionally particular build-ings posed unusual problems. Of these the Propylaea of the Acropolis at Athens, built by Mnesicles in the 430's, is worth detailed study, especially for the balancing of the two projecting wings on the west and their relation to the main block. The Erechtheum near by, some twenty years later in date, was only partly successful. It is a pity that Classical architects did not have more opportunities for exercising ingenuity on buildings of difficult shape or site. Of the new or newly fashionable types the most attractive was the small round hall or 'tholos'. In its elaborate form the circular wall is surrounded by a circular colonnade; inside there is another ring of columns, free or attached, and the roof is conical (whether in one or two stages) and crowned by a suitable finial. The shaping of the pavement blocks and also of the tiles allowed neat experiments in design. The gymnasium or palaestra was a place for athletic exercise and, incidentally, philosophical study. The new standard was a rectangular yard, surrounded by low colonnades behind which were dressing rooms, washrooms and halls. The outer walls were blank. Large closed halls such as the council-house ('bouleuterion') were less suited to the character of Greek architecture with its emphasis on exterior effects. The task here

Plates 20, 21

Plate 35

Plate 18

Plates 35, 36

was to construct a room where some hundreds of people could sit and take part in discussion. Inevitably this meant a squarish building with tiered benches, and these were arranged either on three or all four sides or, through unhappy imitation of the theatre, in a semicircle. The roof was supported inside by columns or piers; sometimes these were arranged radially, so that the view of the platform was not obscured too much.

Theatres, often used for assemblies of the citizens as well as for dramatic and choral performances, are the most regularly impressive remains of ancient Greece; they have survived the best and their siting makes them intelligible at first look. The familiar stone or rock-cut type was established in the late fifth century and soon became universal. Most of the theatres built in the Classical period have suffered later alteration, especially in the orchestra and the stage, but fortunately the best preserved, that at Epidaurus, is also the least modernised. Since usually they had to accommodate thousands of spectators, theatres were open to the sky and good acoustics were essential. In the centre was a circular orchestra, where choruses and choirs performed. Round this rose tiers of seats, divided radially and extending for rather more than a semicircle (if that term may include a curve with varying centres). On the opposite side of the orchestra was a low shallow stage, separated from the auditorium by wide passages. In the Hellenistic period stage buildings became more important, and the orchestra was reduced; later remodellings were still more extensive. Economy, supported by tradition and perhaps aesthetics, determined that the Greek theatre (unlike the Roman) was regularly set into a hillside, so that it had little substructure or back wall, but the architect could show his quality in the vertical inclinations and horizontal curvature of the auditorium, the access to the seats, and the precision of the masonry. A similar precision was expected even in fortifications where the appropriately rough-faced stonework of towers had accurately drafted edges.

Plate 17

Plate 25

Fig. 38, Plate 36

For Classical houses ancient literature and the paintings on pottery do not help much and the only considerable remains are at two outlying cities – Olynthus in Chalcidice, founded in 432 and destroyed in 348 BC, and Priene, which was laid out on a new site around 350 BC. Both these cities were planned with rectangular plots, so that their houses were more regular and uniform than those of the old Greek towns. Further, the type of house at Olynthus is different from that at Priene, and there may well have been other types elsewhere. But even so we have some notion of middle-class housing of the fifth and fourth centuries, still unostentatious but more comfortable than before. Country homesteads are likely to have been more

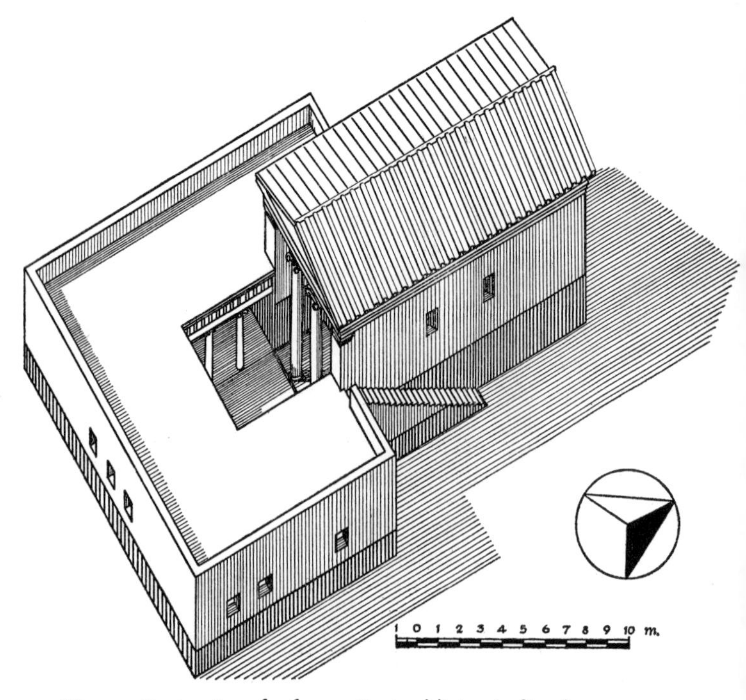

Fig. 34. Restoration of palace at Larisa (?) in Aeolis, about 500–450 BC.

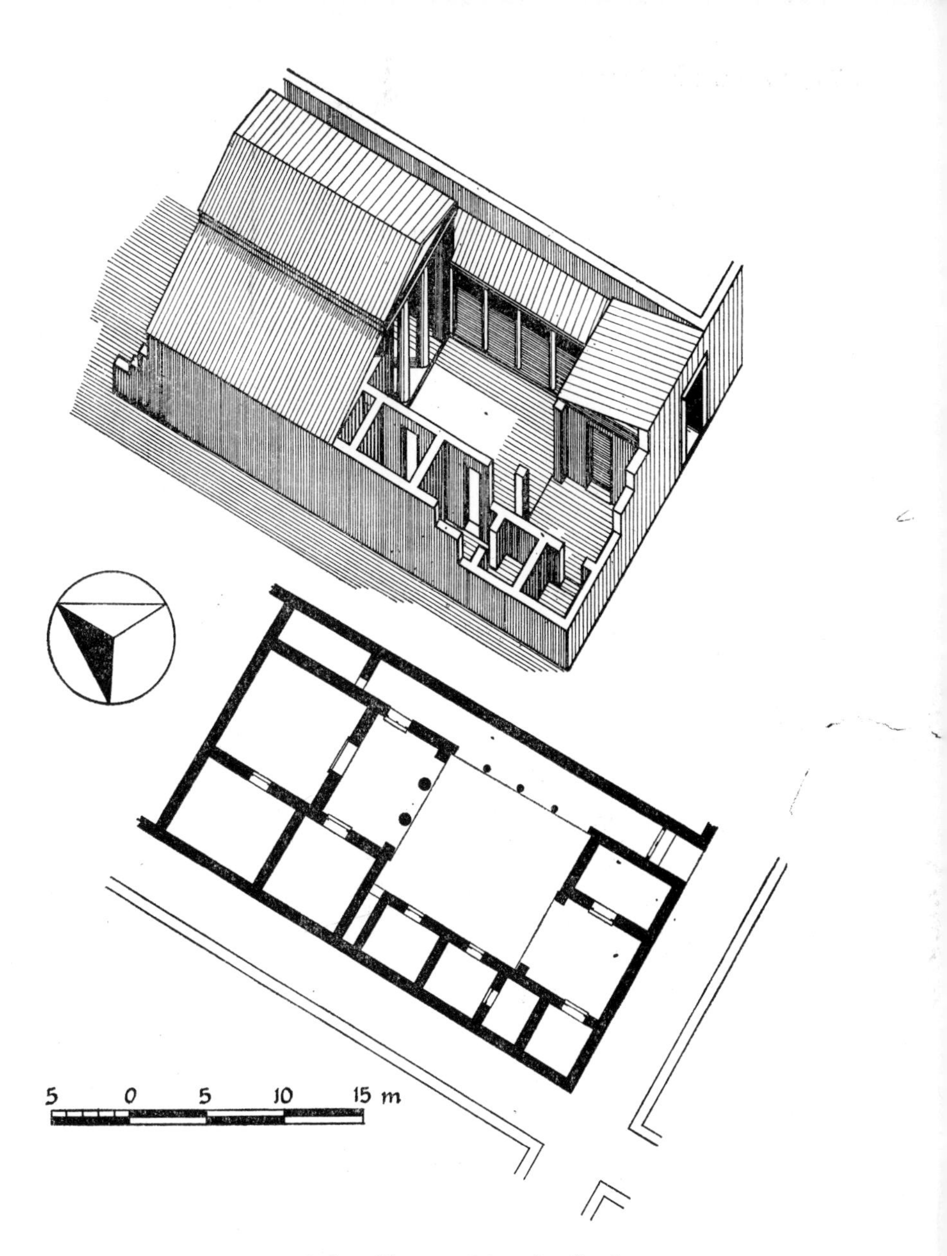

Fig. 35. Restoration and plan of house at Priene, late fourth century B.C.

sprawling, and it is not hard to imagine the dwellings of the poor. The illustrations show a standard fourth-century house at Priene: it measures 58 by 77½ feet in plan. The comparable houses at Olynthus are squarer with a normal area of 56 by 56 feet: this is less than at Priene, though there subdivision of plots was or became common. Both types of house have an internal courtyard with the main suite to the north; its deep portico gave shade in summer, but let in the low winter sun. At Olynthus this portico is continued beyond the edges of the court, more or less across the plot; and in a few larger houses the court has a colonnade (or 'peristyle') on all four sides. Something similar had occurred already in the palace at Larisa in Aeolis: there, about 450 BC, a sort of peristyle court was added to an older building that seems to have relatives in Priene. In these houses living rooms and dining rooms were, of course, large. The other compartments served as kitchen, bedrooms, storerooms, and a primitive latrine which might have a channel connecting with the street. Some Classical houses had an upper floor, but not necessarily over all the ground-floor rooms. The street entrance was usually quite simple, and windows were very few and small except in upper storeys, which might also have balconies. The normal building materials were sun-dried bricks, timber and terracotta roof-tiles; at Priene, rather exceptionally, the walls were to some height of stone. Interior decoration was generally simple; walls might be painted in plain colour (especially red) or in deep contrasting bands, of which the lowest sometimes imitated squared masonry, and floors were sometimes surfaced with hard stucco or a mosaic of pebbles set in simple or complex patterns. Water was fetched in jars from a public supply or drawn from a private well or cistern. For heating, charcoal braziers usually had to do.

Fig. 35

Fig. 34

Plate 76

In the design of their buildings the Classical (and Hellenistic) architects of Greece took care not to concentrate the spectator's interest on a single part of a structure or on a grand axial vista. With the temple the position of the cella door was not advertised by the colonnade and the main approach from the sanctuary gate was oblique. The ascent to the Propylaea of the Athenian Acropolis was along a narrow zigzag path – the present imposing flight of steps is a characteristically Roman addition – and on the Acropolis itself the main buildings, put up in the short period of forty years, are not all in alignment with each other although there was no difficulty from the terrain or tradition – the Erechtheum, in particular, is not even on the same site as its predecessor. A similar principle governs

Fig. 36

Plate 20

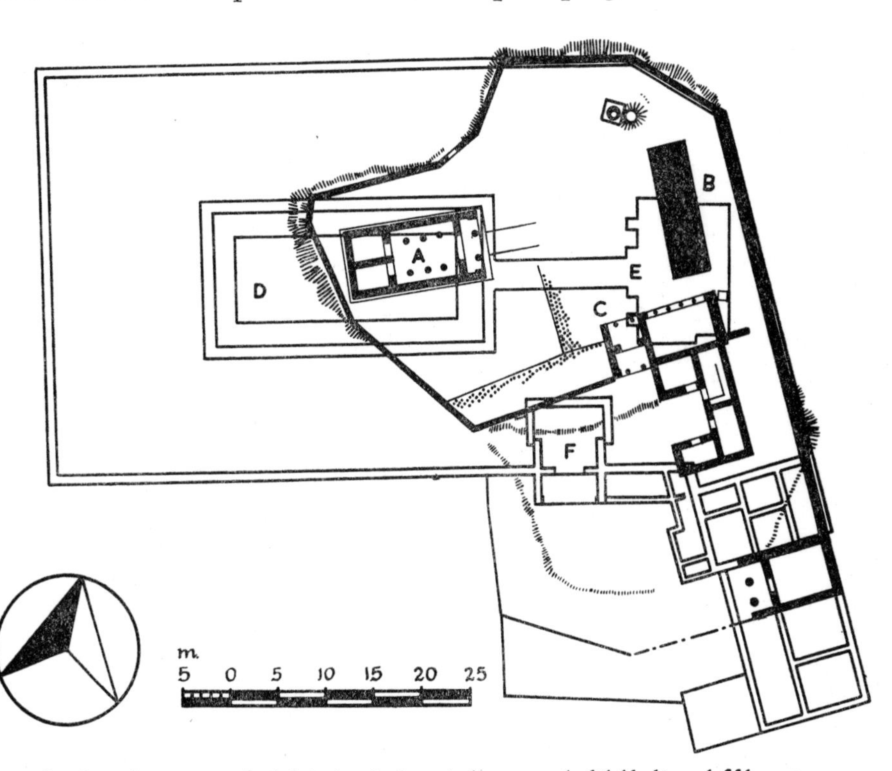

Fig. 36. Plan of sanctuary of Aphaia in Aegina, sixth century (solid black) and fifth century BC. *(in outline): A and D, temples; B and E, altars; C and F, gateways*

the planning of public squares when these became monumental and (through the use of stoas) rectilinear. The west end of the Agora at Athens, though free for development in 479 BC, was a piecemeal grouping of buildings of different shapes and sizes; but even the Agora of Priene, designed as a whole and on a rectangular plan, is not composed symmetrically nor are its entrances in the centres of the sides.

Plate 35

Fig. 38, Plate 36

Early Greek towns grew up haphazard with narrow, winding streets and irregular building plots. But when new cities were founded on virgin sites, as with many of the colonies, it must often have been convenient to lay out the streets and divide the plots on a rectangular plan. Aristotle credited the

Fig. 37

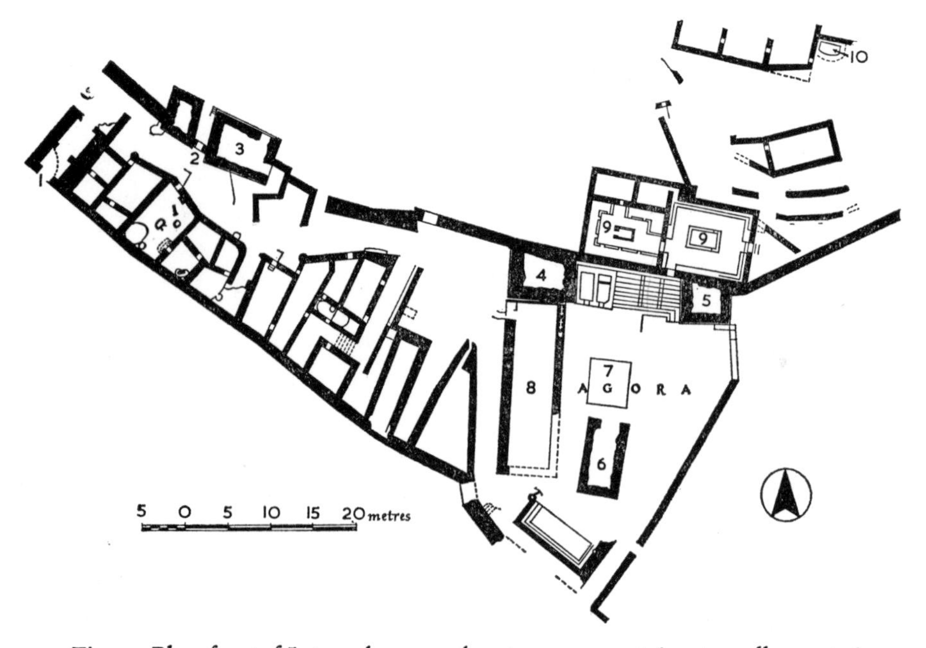

Fig. 37. Plan of part of Lato, perhaps seventh century BC*: 1, gate in outer wall; 2, gate in inner wall; 3–5, towers of inner wall; 6, sanctuary; 7, cistern; 8, stoa; 9, town hall; 10, cistern*

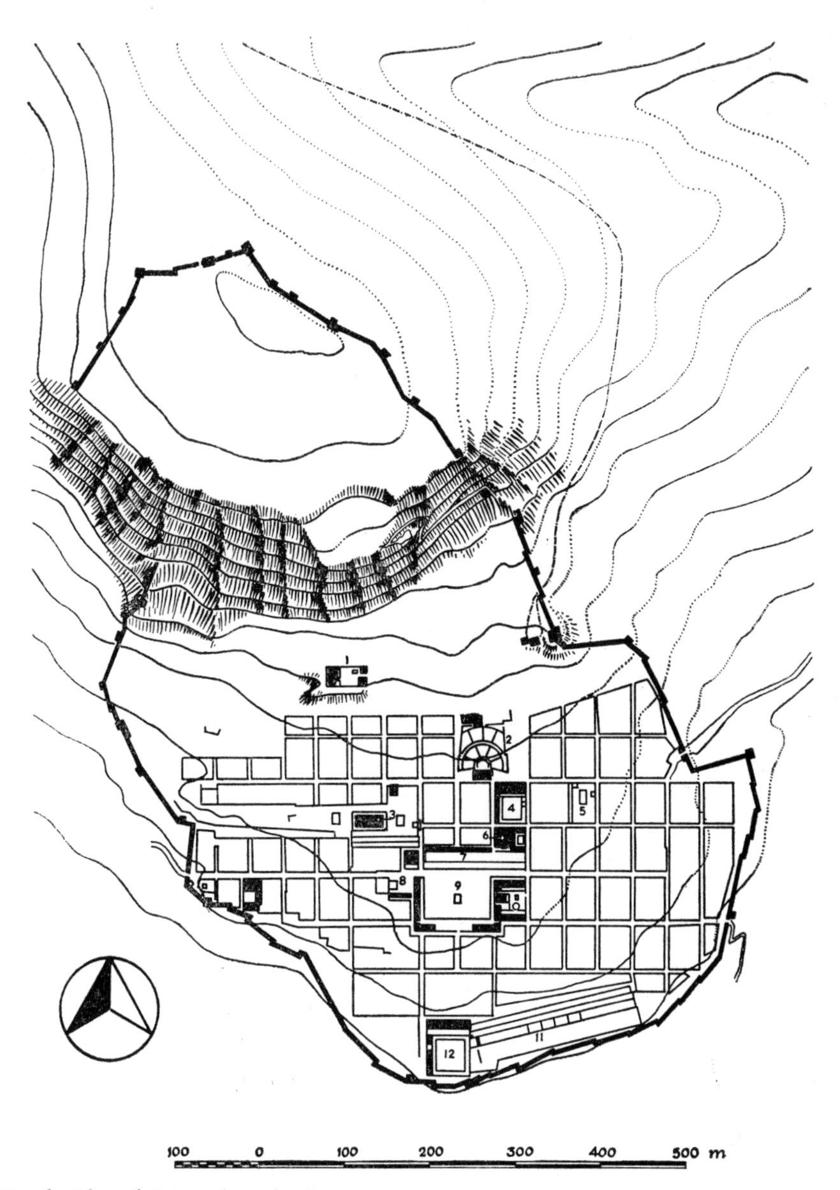

Fig. 38. Plan of Priene, later fourth century BC. *Contours at 25 metre intervals. 1, temple; 2, theatre; 3, temple; 4, gymnasium; 5, temple; 6, council house; 7, stoa; 8, fish and meat market; 9, Agora; 10, temple; 11, stadium; 12, gymnasium*

invention of the grid system to Hippodamus, who planned the Piraeus in the mid fifth century: perhaps he introduced the grid to Greece itself or made it more rational. Priene, a century after Hippodamus, is a planned city, divided by streets into blocks of standard size, though two or more of these units may be combined for a public place. The Agora is near the middle, as a market place should be, and temples (like parish churches) are put in different parts of the town. The city wall alone disregards the grid – rightly, since it must follow the best line for defence. A peculiarity of Priene is the steepness and length of the slope on which it was built: so by Classical standards the acropolis is abnormal. In old cities complete replanning was impracticable, but often public spaces and sanctuaries were tidied, as (though this was outside the city) in Aegina. The Agora at Elis is a rather countrified lay-out of the fifth century for an uncongested little town.

Fig. 38, Plate 36
Fig. 36
Fig. 39

Greek architects, to judge by building inscriptions, were paid the same day-rate as a skilled mason, and their position and status were presumably those of a clerk of the works. But the best of them did not rest only on experience and skill, but thought closely about the theory of their craft. That theory is lost and even the facts were not known accurately by Vitruvius, whose erudite treatise on architecture, written at the end of the first century BC, was admired but not too literally accepted in the Renaissance. But we can discover something by precise observation of existing remains and their setting.

Plate 29

The best preserved Classical buildings are the 'Theseum' at Athens (which still has its cella and perhaps for that reason disappoints most modern visitors), the temple of 'Concord' – also with its cella – at Acragas (Agrigento) in Sicily, the temple of 'Posidon' at Paestum, the Parthenon at Athens, the Propylaea of the Athenian Acropolis, the temple of Apollo at Bassae, the temple of 'Juno Lacinia' at Acragas, and the unfinished temple at Segesta also in Sicily. All these are Doric

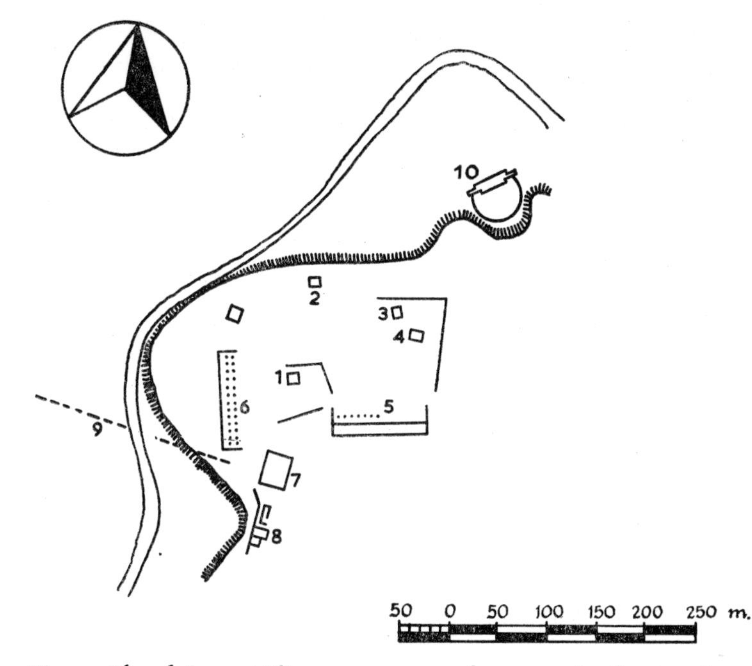

Fig. 39. Plan of Agora at Elis, 470–420 BC*: 1, altar; 2–4 and 7–8, sanctuaries; 5–6, stoas; 9, road; 10, theatre*

and of the fifth century: the Sicilian examples are of much coarser stone. For the Ionic style the finest survivors are the Erechtheum and the little temple of Nike (Victory) on the Acropolis of Athens, and for the Corinthian variant the Choregic Monument of Lysicrates in the town below. Theatres, thanks to their structure, are still numerous, but that of Epidaurus is the most perfect and Classical. Priene offers the best examples of houses and town-planning. Good examples of fortifications are accessible at Aegosthena, Eleutherae (if that was the name of the site which commands the ancient and modern road from Athens to Thebes) and Messene. There are other structures too which can be reconstructed more or less

Plate 32
Plate 34
Plate 17
Plate 25

completely, especially if the style and workmanship are fine; because of the rules of proportion one fragment of an order can give the scale of a building, and the methods of jointing not only show which face of a block is which, but also – since it was not till it was in position that the holes for clamps and dowels were cut – careful comparison of cuttings may allow a student to detect blocks which originally were joined to each other. Though finicky, such investigations often pay.

Fig. 26

CONCLUSION

The greatest service of the Greeks of the Classical period was that they created the first modern civilisation. Their habits of thought, political and moral attitudes, personal ideals, art and literature are as intelligible to us as those of most foreign countries of Europe to-day. This cannot be said of the ancient Assyrians or Egyptians, or even of our own medieval ancestors. The reasons for the Greek achievement, as of most historical revolutions, cannot be demonstrated tidily. But it is hard to doubt that they lie in the city state, where the community was not unmanageably large and the individual could think and act for himself without being too much shackled by any religious or political hierarchy. Certainly the largest contribution to Classical civilisation – a contribution out of all proportion to the number and prosperity of its inhabitants – was that made by Athens, where radical democracy gave the widest measure of effective freedom and opportunity.

Greek civilisation did not end with the Macedonian conquest. In some ways it developed further, especially in scholarship, mathematics, astronomy and mechanical science, while sculpture, painting and even architecture continued to flourish and experimented vigorously. But generally the Hellenistic Greeks were more concerned to hold the positions reached by their Classical predecessors. Alexander had conquered the East as far as Pakistan, and when he died his generals set up several large empires, staffed by Greeks but populated by foreigners. A principal task of these Hellenistic rulers was to 'hellenise' or impose Greek culture on their subjects; and though often that culture was accepted willingly, diffusion usually meant dilution. The new Greek cities of the East had the regular institutions of the city state, but their powers were no more than municipal and their function educational. Even in the old Greek lands the surviving states did not often risk their precarious independence by any bold or revolutionary innovation. The spirit of the new age can be judged by the welcome it gave to Stoicism and Epicureanism, both preaching decent, if not aggressively logical, submission of man to the world around him; though reckoned as philosophies, they were rather creeds.

It was from Hellenistic civilisation that the Romans took most of their cultural and some of their political stock, and part of this survived into and through the Middle Ages, wretchedly distorted in the West but with more direct comprehension in the Greek-speaking East. The Eastern or Byzantine tradition was almost completely destroyed in the mid fifteenth century, when the Turks took Constantinople. But by then the West, already stimulated by Arabic translations, was beginning to study the ancient writings of the Greeks. The direct benefits of this study do not matter much; what was important to the Renaissance was the opportune acquaintance with freer and more rational modes of thought.

A question worth considering is why the civilisation of Classical Greece advanced no farther than it did. The answer is partly technological, but behind this was a social attitude. The Classical ideal was leisure, with as a corollary a contempt of manual labour. Unfortunately there was no belief that material progress was inevitable or even possible; and since the total stock of wealth seemed limited, the only way in which a state and its citizens could become richer was predatory. Much of the prosperity of Athens in the fifth century resulted from its empire, and it was for or against imperialism that the main wars of the fourth century were fought. Though as time went on feeling grew stronger against the wasteful combats between Greek states, the alternative proposed (and attempted before both by Athens and by Sparta) was a united expedition to plunder the Persian territories. When the Macedonians had mastered Greece, such an expedition was indeed prepared by their king Philip and after his assassination carried out by his son and heir Alexander. But whatever Alexander's motives, his organisation of his conquests showed a bold and even liberal vision – to unite the world in a homogeneous empire where Greeks were not superior to barbarians – and though his successors had less exalted ideals, they too were obliged to widen the concept of Hellenism. Even this autocratic self-interest was beyond the resources, material and imaginative, of those close corporations, the Greek city states.

Plate 89

At the side of the main road from Athens to the north, at the place called once again Chaeronea, a gigantic marble lion faces the battlefield where in 338 BC Philip and Alexander crushed the defenders of the liberty of the Greek city states. Appropriately the monument has no inscription, so that the passer-by may well wonder whom he should commemorate, the victors or the defeated.

Notes on the Figures

1 Physical map of Greece. The annual rainfall, mostly in the period November–March, averages up to 20 inches on the east side of Greece and 40–50 inches on the west.

2 Political map of Greece. The places marked have been chosen partly for their importance, partly because they are mentioned in the text. The district round Athens is Attica, not named on the map through lack of space.

3 Section of grave, Ceramicus cemetery, Athens. About 740 BC. The bronze vessel below contained the cremated remains of the dead person. The large clay pot (krater), which protrudes from the ground, presumably served as a marker and conceivably, though not certainly, as a funnel for offerings: it is decorated in the Attic Geometric style (*cf.* Figures 4 and 5, Plate 66–67). After *Athenische Mitteilungen* 1893, 92 Figure 4.

4 Drawing of soldier. About 750 BC. The equipment is plumed helmet, shield, two throwing spears, sword and dagger. From the same pot as Figure 5.

5 Restored drawing of a warship. About 750 BC. The ship has a ram, collapsible mast with square sail, and steering oar (or more likely a pair of such oars—*cf.* Figure 16). The line above the gunwale probably represents a narrow deck along the side of the ship, used as a platform to fight from; the oarsmen, here twenty to a side, sat under this deck and rowed through the spaces between the stanchions. Above the stern project three long boarding spears. Attic Geometric style. After Louvre A.527 and A.538 and fragments in Athens, National Museum, all probably from one clay pot (krater) like that of Figure 3.

6 Restored terracotta model of apsidal building. Late eighth century BC. Since it was dedicated in a sanctuary, it is more probably a temple than a house. The twisted spine and steep pitch of the roof suggest thatch.

The decoration is taken from contemporary pottery and need not have been used on buildings (*cf.* Plate 39). From Perachora near Corinth, and probably Corinthian work. Athens, National Museum. After H. Payne, *Perachora* I, Plate 9*b*.

7 Gold diadem. About 725 BC. Thin gold leaf with decoration in relief; the exact repetition of units shows the use of dies. Geometric style. From a grave at Athens. Copenhagen, National Museum 741. After *Archäologische Zeitung* 1884, Plate 9.1.

8 Bronze brooch. Eighth century BC. This type —the 'spectacle fibula'— occurs widely, but not frequently, in Greece in the eighth and seventh centuries and is found, presumably about the same time, in Italy, Hungary and Yugoslavia as well. It is one of the very few apparent connections between Greece and Central Europe in the early Iron Age, and its significance (if any) is not clear. Olympia 8835. After E. Curtius and F. Adler, *Olympia* IV, Plate 21 no. 359.

9 Bronze brooch. About 700 BC. This type of fibula, with oversized catch-plate (here decorated on both sides), occurs in the late eighth and early seventh centuries, especially in Boeotia. Geometric style. Probably from Boeotia. Berlin 7979. After *Jahrbuch des deutschen archäologischen Instituts* 1888, 362 Figure.

10 Restoration of bronze tripod and cauldron. Mid eighth century BC. Geometric style. From Olympia. After *Olympia* IV, Plate 34*c*.

11 Map to illustrate extent of Greek colonisation. The total number of independent colonies was not less than 200.

12 Phoenician, Greek and Latin alphabets. All Phoenician and some early Greek writing was from right to left, but for convenience in comparison the forms given here are all set out from left to right. The early alphabets vary much more than is shown in this table.

13 Greek inscription in Ionian alphabet cut by a mercenary on the leg of colossal statue of Rameses II at Abu Simbel in Egypt. 591–589 BC.

The translation is 'When King Psammetichos came to Elephantine, this was written by those who sailed with Psammetichos son of Theocles and came above Kerkis, as far as the river allowed. Potasimto led the foreign-speakers and Amasis the Egyptians. Archon son of Amoibichos and Axe son of Nobody wrote me.' From H. Roehl, *Imagines Inscriptionum Graecarum Antiquissimarum*[3], 18 no. 1.

14 Bronze helmet. Late seventh or early sixth century BC. The helmet is of the type known as Corinthian. The holes round the edge are for securing a leather lining. From Olympia. Olympia Museum. After *Olympia* IV, Plate 62 no. 1015.

15 Back-piece of bronze corselet with engraved decoration. About 650 BC. The style is close to that of the drawings on Corinthian pottery of that time. In the main scene, perhaps Zeus and Apollo (with lyre) and other deities. Probably from Olympia. Stolen in World War II from Crowe collection, Patras. After *Olympia* IV, Plate 59.

16 Restored drawing of a warship. About 570 BC. The ship is of 'penteconter' type, though the true penteconter had twenty-five oars on each side. The mast is shipped. From paintings on Attic pots. After A. Furtwängler and K. Reichhold, *Griechische Vasenmalerei,* Plate 13, with supplements from vase-paintings of the next generation.

17 Drawing of Athenian gentleman. About 690 BC. His outfit is long dress (reaching to the ankles), cloak, sword and spear (rather than staff). Attic style. From the neck of an amphora, New York 21.88.18.

18 Moulded terracotta relief (dotted lines for restorations). Height 34 cm. About 530 BC. Scene from drinking party: two men reclining on a couch, piper, wine-bearer, pet monkey, dog gnawing bone, cock. Details in black and red. The relief is part of an architectural revetment. From Buruncuk in Aeolis, identified (perhaps wrongly) as the ancient Larisa of Aeolis. Stockholm. From J. Boehlau and K. Schefold, *Larisa am Hermos* I, Figure 28.

19 Restored drawing of bronze cauldron and stand. About 700 BC. The griffin heads are ornamental, the 'sirens' (hybrids between man and bird)

are elaborated handles. This set was probably not Greek, but imported from the East. From Olympia. After *Olympia* IV, Plate. 49*b*.

20 Bronze head of griffin from a cauldron (*cf.* Figure 19). Middle of seventh century. Greek work, developed from such clumsy Oriental prototypes as on Figure 19. From Olympia. Athens, National Museum (Olympia 3884). After *Olympia* IV, Plate 47 no. 805.

21 Corinthian clay cup (kotyle). First half of seventh century B C. The style is Subgeometric – that is, in a weak Geometric tradition at a time when a more advanced style was already established. From *Notizie degli Scavi* 1893, 474 Figure.

22 Shapes of Corinthian clay oil flasks (*a–d*, aryballos; *e*, alabastron). These small pots are very frequent and their evolution is most useful for the dating of deposits in which they occur. Shape *a* is typical for 725–700, *b* for 700–650, *c* for 650–625; *d* and *e* are new types which appear about 625 B C.

23 Shapes of Archaic clay cups. *a*, seventh century; *b*, 585–570; *c*, 565–535; *d*, 560–525; *e*, 535–500; *f*, 520–450 B C. Though *a* is Corinthian and the others Attic, the series represents the main development of the low cup from the Geometric shape of Plate 65.

24 Plans of temples of various types. *a*, temple of Themis at Rhamnus: porch consisting of two columns ('distyle') between the ends of the walls ('in antis'); this is a common plan for treasuries. *b*, temple of Asclepios at Epidaurus: cella and porch of same type, surrounded by a colonnade ('peripteral'); it is also 'hexastyle', that is it has the standard number of six columns on the ends. *c*, temple of Zeus at Olympia: the same type as *b*, but (as is usual) with a false porch added at the back of the cella. *d*, the Parthenon at Athens: the porches of the cella block composed of a free row of columns ('prostyle') instead of columns 'in antis'; the surrounding colonnade has, exceptionally, eight columns at the ends.

25 The 'Theseum' at Athens, restored axonometric drawing from north-east. Width at top of steps, 44 ft. 11¾ in. (13·71 m.). Marble. About 445 B C.

The drawing explains itself. The style is Doric, but abnormally there is an Ionic frieze above the front porch of the cella and this is continued to join the entablature of the surrounding colonnade. The temple was fairly certainly dedicated to Hephaestus and not to Theseus, but the name 'Theseum' is hallowed by custom and it is pedantic to change it. For a view *cf.* Plate 29. Drawing by Dr W. H. Plommer.

26 System of masonry for important buildings. *a*, lifting boss to hold ropes or tongs. *b*, smooth projecting band ('anathyrosis') to ensure precise join. *c*, pry hole for levering upper block (that with boss *a*) into position. *d*, iron dowel set in lead to tie upper and lower courses; it is sunk into the lower block. *e*, iron clamp set in lead to tie adjacent blocks (*cf.* Figure 25); the varying shapes of clamps give some help in dating. *f*, projecting protective surface to avoid damage in erection. *g*, band dressed back to final surface and polished to ensure precise join. After all the blocks had been set and fixed in position, the lifting bosses (*a*) and protecting surfaces (*f*) were normally picked and polished away to give a level smooth face; but occasionally this process was omitted (*e.g.* on the string course of Plate 23) and sometimes, especially in later years, the protective surface might be left deliberately for the aesthetic effect of drafted edges.

27 System of tiling for roof of temples and other important buildings. This example is taken from the temple of Aphaia in Aegina (*cf.* Plate 29). After J. Durm, *Handbuch der Architektur*[3] II.1, Figure 178.

28 Aeolic volute capital. Trachyte. Second half of sixth century B C. This type of capital is sometimes called Proto-ionic, but it is not at all certain that the true Ionic capital is derived from it. From a temple at Klopedhi (perhaps the ancient Nape) in Lesbos. Istanbul, Museum of Classical Antiquities. After R. Koldewey, *Die antiken Baureste der Insel Lesbos,* Plate 16. 2–3.

29 Plan of fortifications of Athens and Piraeus. Constructed 479–450 B C. The long walls connecting Athens with Piraeus and the coast have now disappeared, but their approximate line is known.

30 The Doryphorus (man with spear) by Polyclitus the sculptor. 450–440 B C. The original, now lost, was in bronze. This drawing is based on a marble copy of the Roman period.

31 Plan of grave, Ceramicus cemetery, Athens. Middle of fifth century B C. The dead man lay, surrounded by oil flasks (of the 'lekythos' type—*cf.* Plates 79–80), in a sarcophagus made up of slabs of marble. From *Athenische Mitteilungen* 1893, 180, Figure 33.

32. Restored drawing of family plot in Ceramicus cemetery, Athens. Fourth century B C. Each gravestone and urn commemorates a separate grave. Based on E. Curtius and J. A. Kaupert, *Atlas von Athen,* Blatt 4.

33 The Apoxyomenus (man scraping himself) attributed to Lysippus; the attribution is not entirely certain. About 330 B C. The original, now lost, was of bronze. The man is using the scraper ('strigil') to clean oil and dirt off his right forearm. He holds a dice in his right hand. The drawing is based on a marble copy of the Roman period.

34 Tentative reconstruction of palace at Larisa (?) in Aeolis. The main block was built about 500, the rest added about 450 B C. The lower courses were of stone with, probably, mud-brick above. From *Larisa* I, Figure 39.

35 Plan and tentative reconstruction of house XXXIII at Priene. Late fourth century B C. Stone, perhaps continued in mud-brick. The smaller houses here have the same narrow plan. After T. Wiegand and H. Schrader, *Priene*, Figures 298–299.

36 Plan of sanctuary of Aphaia in Aegina. Stages of sixth and fifth centuries B C. The inevitable cistern is in the north-east corner. This sanctuary stood on a hill six miles east of the town. For the temple of the fifth century see Plate 28. After A. Furtwängler, *Aegina,* Figure 402.

37 Plan of part of city of Lato in Crete. The lay-out seems to go back to the seventh century B C. Lato was a small and unimportant state. After *Bulletin de la Correspondance Hellénique* 1903, Plates 4–5.

38 Plan of Priene. The lay-out is of the third quarter of the fourth century BC. For a reconstruction of the city see Plate 36 and for a typical house Figure 35. The city wall follows a scarp on the south, makes good use of the contours as far as the cliff, where it becomes unnecessary, and then takes in the summit above. A winding path goes up the cliff from just inside the east wall. After *Priene*, Plan.

39 Plan of Agora of the city of Elis. 470–420 BC. The theatre is characteristically fitted into a bay in the scarp. After *Jahreshefte des oesterreichischen archäologischen Institutes* XXVII, 68, Figure 77.

Bibliography

GENERAL REFERENCE WORKS

A. PAULY, G. WISSOWA and W. KROLL, *Real-Encyclopädie der Classischen Wissenschaft* (Stuttgart, 1893–). The standard encyclopaedia.

The Oxford Classical Dictionary (Oxford, 1949). A good one-volume encyclopaedia.

L. WHIBLEY (ed.), *A companion to Greek Studies*[3] (Cambridge, 1916). Longer entries on various topics, still valuable for reference.

J. A. Nairn's Classical Handlist[2] (Oxford, 1939). Useful classified bibliography, though in need of revision.

GEOGRAPHY

Graecia (Murray's Handy Classical Maps) (London). The best map of ancient Greece.

Murray's Classical Atlas for Schools[2] (London, 1917). The best atlas in English.

H. BENGTSON and V. MILOJČIĆ, *Grosser Historischer Weltatlas* I (Munich, 1954). The best atlas for the money.

H. KIEPERT, *Formae Orbis Antiqui* (Berlin, 1894–1910). The most comprehensive set of detailed maps.

A. PHILIPPSON and E. KIRSTEN, *Die griechischen Landschaften* (Frankfurt-am-Main, 1950–). A full and detailed study.

M. CARY, *The Geographic Background of Greek and Roman History* (Oxford, 1949). The best short survey.

J. O. THOMSON, *History of Ancient Geography* (Cambridge, 1948). For ancient knowledge of geography.

Bibliography

HISTORY, POLITICS AND SOCIETY

GENERAL

J. B. BURY and R. MEIGGS, *A History of Greece to the death of Alexander the Great*[3] (London, 1952). A sound if pontifical survey, which concentrates on political and military events.

N. G. L. HAMMOND, *A History of Greece to 322 BC.* (Oxford, 1959). A sensible but occasionally partisan survey, also emphasizing political and military history.

The Cambridge Ancient History V – VI (Cambridge 1927). An uneven account of the classical period.

P. JOUGUET and others, *Les premières civilisations* I (Paris, 1950). A good brief summary.

G. GLOTZ and R. COHEN, *Histoire grecque* (1925–38). Broadly and soundly conceived, though unreliable in details.

H. BENGTSON, *Griechische Geschichte* (Munich, 1950). A compact and intelligent survey with full bibliography and references.

K. J. BELOCH, *Griechische Geschichte*[2] I – III (Berlin & Leipzig, 1912–27). The most intelligent account of Greek history, though often obsolete or perverse.

SPECIAL

M. I. FINLEY, *The World of Odysseus* (London, 1956). An illuminating reconstruction of Early Iron Age society from Homer alone.

A. ANDREWES, *The Greek Tyrants* (London, 1956). A judicious study of Archaic political development.

A. H. M. JONES, *Athenian Democracy* (Oxford, 1957). A shrewd appraisal of political conditions in Classical Athens.

H. MICHELL, *Sparta* (Cambridge, 1952). The sanest book on Sparta.

G. GLOTZ, *The Greek City and its Institutions* (London, 1929). Valuable for sources and interpretations.

V. EHRENBERG, *The Greek State* (Oxford, 1960). The best short account of Greek political evolution.

A. E. ZIMMERN, *The Greek Commonwealth*[5] (Oxford, 1931). A good discussion of politics and economics in Athens in the fifth century.

H. F. CLINTON, *Fasti Hellenici* (Oxford, 1834). Useful for literary evidence for the traditional dates.

ECONOMICS AND TECHNOLOGY

J. HASEBROEK, *Griechische Wirtschafts – und Gesellschaftsgeschichte bis zur Perserzeit* (Tübingen, 1931). Sane and well-informed.

J. HASEBROEK, *Trade and Politics in Ancient Greece* (London, 1933). The best work in English on Greek trade.

G. GLOTZ, *Ancient Greece at Work* (London 1926). A short general study of economics.

H. MICHELL, *The Economics of Ancient Greece*[2] (Cambridge, 1958). A useful, but uncritical compilation.

R. J. FORBES, *Studies in Ancient Technology* (Leyden, 1955–). Comprehensive and intelligent, but not always accurate.

H. BLÜMNER, *Technologie und Terminologie der Gewerbe und Künste bei Griechen und Römern* (Leipzig 1875–87). A useful collection of evidence, in part obsolete.

WAR

F. E. ADCOCK, *The Greek and Macedonian Art of War* (Cambridge, 1958). Short and sensible.

J. KROMAYER and G. VEITH, *Heerwesen und Kriegführung der Griechen und Römer* (Munich, 1928). The standard work.

AENEAS TACTICUS. A professional treatise of the mid fourth century BC on the defence of a besieged city.

ATHLETICS

E. N. GARDINER, *Athletics of the Ancient World*[2] (Oxford, 1955). A sound and well-informed survey.

RELIGION AND PHILOSOPHY

W. K. C. GUTHRIE, *The Greeks and their Gods* (London, 1954). Sound and clear.

H. J. ROSE, *A Handbook of Greek Mythology*[6] (London, 1958). A useful survey.

E. R. DODDS, *The Greeks and the Irrational* (Beverley and Los Angeles, 1951). A penetrating study of Greek modes of thought.

A. H. ARMSTRONG, *An Introduction to Ancient Philosophy*[3] (London, 1957). The most convenient short survey in English.

E. ZELLER, *Outlines of the History of Greek Philosophy*[13] (London 1931). Deeper, but less up to date.

G. S. KIRK and J. E. RAVEN, *The Presocratic Philosophers* (Cambridge, 1957). A thorough and critical examination with all the relevant passages in text and translation.

A. E. TAYLOR, *Plato*[6] (London, 1952). A sound summary and discussion of Plato's work.

G. M. A. GRUBE, *Plato's Thought* (London, 1935). A sound analysis by topics.

D. J. ALLAN, *The Philosophy of Aristotle* (London, 1952). A short general interpretation.

W. D. ROSS, *Aristotle*[2] (London 1930). A sound summary and discussion of Aristotle's works.

S. SAMBURSKY, *The Physical World of the Greeks* (London, 1956). A good account of Greek physics.

E. BARKER, *Greek Political Theory*[5] (London, 1960). Discursive, but informative.

LITERATURE

LOEB CLASSICAL LIBRARY (London and Cambridge, Mass.). The most complete series of English translations; the Greek test is printed opposite.

PENGUIN BOOKS (Harmondsworth). Generally livelier but less accurate translations.

A. LESKY, *Geschichte der griechischen Literatur* (Berne, 1957–9). A good survey of Greek literature and its development.

(Since it is better to read than to read about literature, the many special studies are not listed here. An exception may, though, be made for D. W. LUCAS, *The Greek Tragic Poets*[2] (London, 1959), a sensible and useful discussion of a branch of Greek literature which more than any other interests non-specialists.)

ARCHAEOLOGY

(Special works are not listed; they can be found from the bibliographies of the more reputable works.)

ART, GENERAL SURVEYS

G. M. A. RICHTER, *A Handbook of Greek Art* (London, 1959). A workmanlike introduction.

F. MATZ, *Geschichte der griechischen Kunst* (Frankfurt-am-Main, 1950–). A fuller and more complex account.

VASE-PAINTING

A. LANE, *Greek Pottery* (London 1948). A good, short and well illustrated survey.

R. M. COOK, *Greek Painted Pottery* (London, 1960). A systematic introduction.

A. RUMPF, *Malerei und Zeichnung* (Munich, 1953). A concise and intelligent survey.

F. VILLARD, *Les Vases grecs* (Paris, 1956). Short and useful.

J. D. BEAZLEY, *Attic Black-figure Vase-painters* (Oxford, 1956). Lists of painters and works attributed to them.

J. D. BEAZLEY, *Attic Red-figure Vase-painters* (Oxford, 1942). Lists of painters and works attributed to them.

R. LULLIES, *Griechische Vasen der Reifarchaischen Zeit* (Munich, 1953). The finest collection of photographs of Archaic Attic red-figure pots.

M. ROBERTSON, *Greek Painting* (Geneva, 1959). Large coloured details of Attic vase-paintings and a sympathetic commentary.

P. E. ARIAS and M. HIRMER, *A History of Greek Vase Painting* (London, 1961). A large selection of excellent plates, with descriptive notes.

PAINTING

A. RUMPF, *Malerei and Zeichnung* (Munich, 1953). Includes the best account of Greek painting, though brief.

A. RUMPF, *Journal of Hellenic Studies* 1947, 10–21. Lucid and intelligent.

M. PALLOTTINO, *Etruscan Painting* (Geneva, 1952). Useful for illustrations of the wall-paintings in Etruscan tombs.

SCULPTURE

R. LULLIES and M. HIRMER, *Greek Sculpture*[2] (London, 1960). A good introduction with short text and worthy illustrations.

G. M. A. RICHTER, *The Sculpture and Sculptors of the Greeks*[3] (Oxford, 1950). A sound general account.

A. W. LAWRENCE, *Classical Sculpture* (London, 1928). Less systematic, but on the Classical period more penetrating.

G. LIPPOLD, *Die Griechische Plastik* (Munich, 1950). Invaluable for references to museums and publications.

R. CARPENTER, *Greek Sculpture* (Chicago, 1960). A deep and subtle appreciation.

BRONZEWORK

J. CHARBONNEAUX, *Greek Bronzes* (London, 1961). A brief but useful account with a good bibliography.

W. LAMB, *Greek and Roman Bronzes* (London, 1929). A convenient introduction, but needing revision.

A. FURTWÄNGLER in E. CURTIUS and F. ADLER, *Olympia* IV (Berlin, 1890). A large and still important publication of bronze objects from Olympia; the dates etc., of course, need to be checked.

F. WILLEMSEN, *Olympische Forschungen* III (Berlin, 1957). A modern study of early tripods.

E. KUNZE in *II Bericht über die Ausgrabungen in Olympia* and subsequent volumes (Berlin, 1938–). Excellent studies, especially of armour.

E. KUNZE, *Olympische Forschungen* II (Berlin, 1950). A fully illustrated study of Archaic reliefs on shield bands.

TERRACOTTA FIGURINES

R. A. HIGGINS, *Catalogue of the Terracottas in the Department of Greek and Roman Antiquities, British Museum* (London, 1954–). A sensible catalogue of a representative collection which can serve also as a general survey.

GEMS

J. D. BEAZLEY, *The Lewes House Collection of Ancient Gems* (Oxford, 1920). A good catalogue that can serve as a general account.

A. FURTWÄNGLER, *Die Antiken Gemmen* (Leipzig and Berlin, 1900). The only comprehensive study and still the standard work.

JEWELLERY

P. COCHE DE LA FERTÉ, *Les Bijoux antiques* (Paris, 1956). A convenient introduction.

COINS

C. SELTMAN, *Greek Coins*² (London, 1955). A useful introduction.

ARCHITECTURE AND PLANNING

W. B. DINSMOOR, *The Architecture of Ancient Greece*³ (London, 1950). The fullest and most expert survey.

A. W. LAWRENCE, *Greek Architecture* (London, 1957). The best illustrated of the handbooks; the text is unequal, but intelligent.

W. H. PLOMMER, *Classical Architecture* (London, 1956). A brief introduction, also intelligent and unequal.

D. S. ROBERTSON, *Greek and Roman Architecture*² (Cambridge, 1945). Has the merits and faults of orthodoxy.

F. C. PENROSE, *An investigation of the Principles of Athenian Architecture*² (London, 1888). A meticulous and fundamental study for specialists.

L. T. SHOE, *Profiles of Greek Mouldings* (Cambridge, Mass., 1936). A corpus of measured drawings with an informed commentary.

R. E. WYCHERLEY, *How the Greeks built Cities* (London, 1949). A sensible account of the planning of towns and the main types of buildings.

AESTHETICS

R. CARPENTER, *The Esthetic Basis of Greek Art* (London, 1959). This short book, which first appeared in 1921, is a singularly honest and shrewd essay on aesthetics.

K. CLARK, *The Nude* (London, 1957). A vigorous and salutary expression of aesthetic beliefs.

R. D. MARTIENSSEN, *The Idea of Space in Greek Architecture* (Johannesburg, 1956). A thoughtful and novel investigation.

EPIGRAPHY

A. G. WOODHEAD, *The Study of Greek Inscriptions* (Cambridge, 1959). A sound and useful guide for beginners.

SITES

(For references to particular sites the student may try the first five items below and W. B. DINSMOOR, *The Architecture of Ancient Greece*[3], 357–384).

PAULY, WISSOWA and KROLL, *Real-Encyclopädie*. The entries are not all recent.

Bulletin de Correspondance Hellénique, 'Chronique des Fouilles'. An accurate and useful annual survey of current excavations in Greece.

Fasti Archaeologici. A comprehensive and well-arranged annual catalogue of published studies and excavations, but the entries are much shorter and not always well-informed.

Archaeological Reports for (year) (replacing *Archaeology in Greece*). The counterpart in English of 'Chronique des Fouilles', shorter and less informative.

E. KIRSTEN and W. KRAIKER, *Griechenlandkunde*[2] (Heidelberg, 1956). A selective, but reliable guide-book.

Grèce (Les Guides Bleus: Paris, 1956). More comprehensive, but less scholarly than the last item. The English edition is remarkable for its grotesque translation of technical terms and mis-spelling of names.

I. T. HILL, *The Ancient City of Athens* (London, 1953). A generally sound work of reference.

W. JUDEICH, *Topographie von Athen*[2] (Munich, 1931). Full and scholarly, though obsolete in parts (especially for the Agora).

M. HÜRLIMANN, *Athens* (London, 1956). Perhaps the best of the many photographic albums of Greek sites and scenery.

MISCELLANEOUS

N. MITCHISON, *Cloud Cuckoo Land* (London, 1925). A remarkably credible novel of Greek life in the later fifth century BC.

Abbreviations in General Use

(mainly for Classical Archaeology)

AA	*Archäologischer Anzeiger* (bound in with *JdI*)
ADelt	*Archaiologikon Deltion* (Greek)
AE	*Archaiologiki Ephemeris* or *Ephemeris Archaiologiki* (Greek)
AJA	*American Journal of Archaeology*
AM	*Athenische Mitteilungen* (=Mitteilungen des deutschen archäologischen Instituts, Athenische Ableitung).
Anz	=*AA*
ASA	*Annuario della Scuola Archeologica di Atene*
BCH	*Bulletin de Correspondance Hellénique*
bf	black-figure
BSA	*Annual of the British School at Athens*
CIG	*Corpus Inscriptionum Graecarum*
CRAI	*Comptes Rendus de l'Académie des Inscriptions et Belles Lettres.*
CVA	*Corpus Vasorum Antiquorum*
Delt	=*ADelt*
DS	C. Daremberg and E. Saglio, *Dictionnaire des Antiquités grecques et romaines*
EA	=*AE*
FA	*Fasti Archaeologici* (polyglot)
FD	*Fouilles de Delphes*
FGH	F. Jacoby, *Fragmente der griechischen Historiker*
FHG	C. Müller, *Fragmenta Historicorum Graecorum*

Hesp	*Hesperia*
IG	*Inscriptiones Graecae*
Jahreshefte = *ÖJh.*	
JdI	*Jahrbuch des deutschen archäologischen Instituts*
JHS	*Journal of Hellenic Studies*
MA	*Monumenti Antichi*
NSc	*Notizie degli Scavi*
ÖJh	*Jahreshefte des oesterreichischen archäologischen Institutes*
PW	= Pauly-Wissowa = *RE*
RA	*Revue Archéologique*
RE	A. Pauly, G. Wissowa and W. Kroll, *Real-Encyclopädie der classischen Altertumswissenschaft*
REG	*Revue des Études grecques*
rf	red-figure
SEG	*Supplementum Epigraphicum Graecum*
SIG	= *Syll*
Syll	W. Dittenberger, *Sylloge Inscriptionum Graecarum*
wg	white-ground

2
3

6
7

10

11

12

3

15

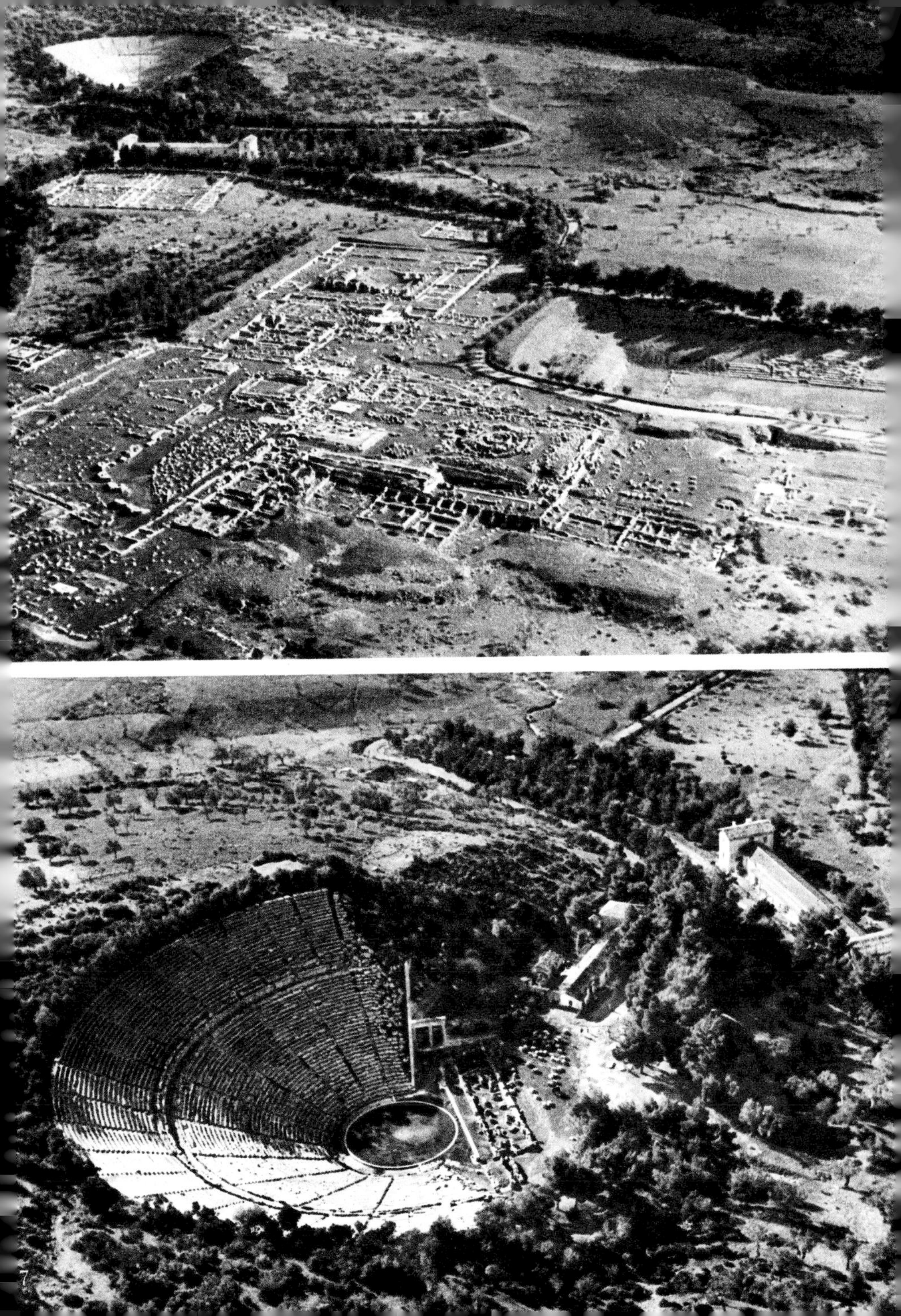

18
19

20

21

22
23
24

27

28

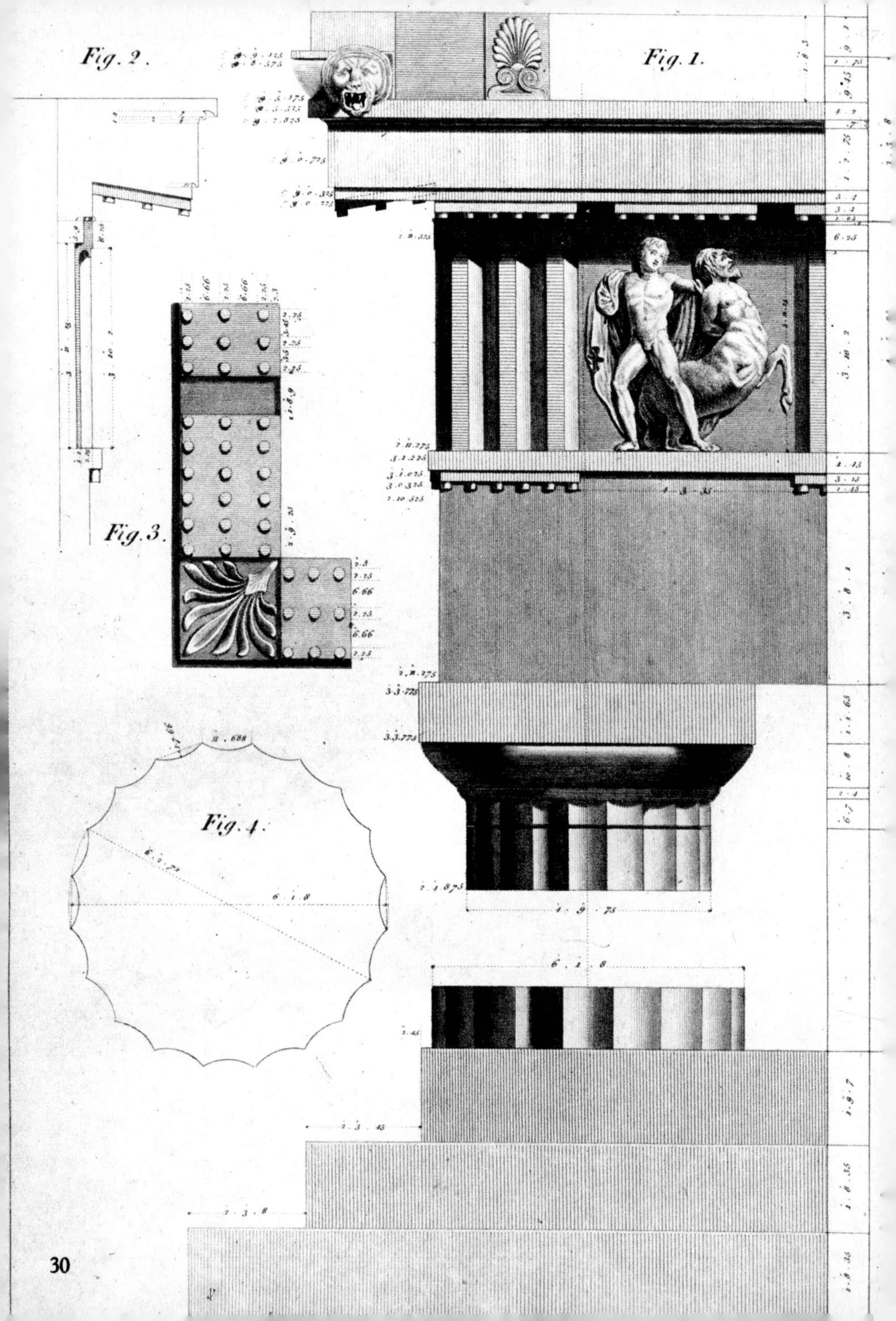
Fig. 1.
Fig. 2.
Fig. 3.
Fig. 4.

Fig. 3.
Fig. 4.
Fig. 2.
Fig. 1.

35

6

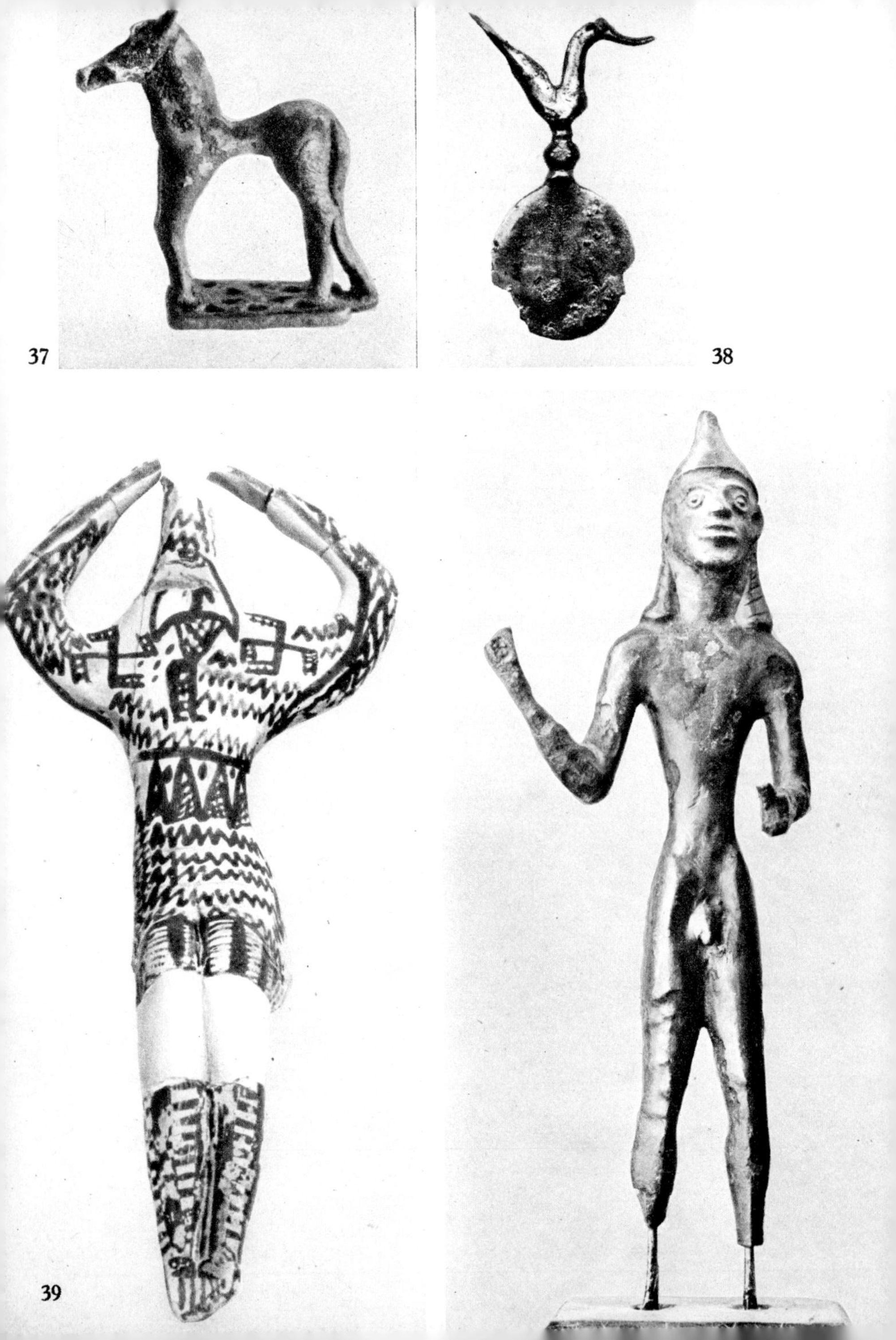
37
38
39

42

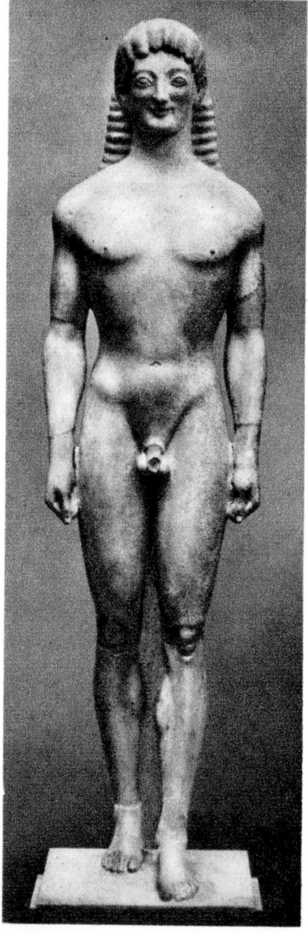

43

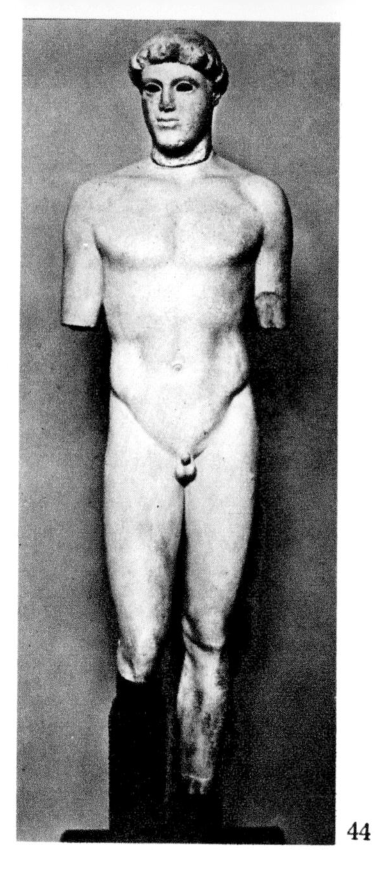

44

45

46

47

48

49
50

51

52
53
54
55

58

60

61

62

65

63

66

64

8

9

71

72

73

75

77

78

9

80

1

82

83

85
86
87

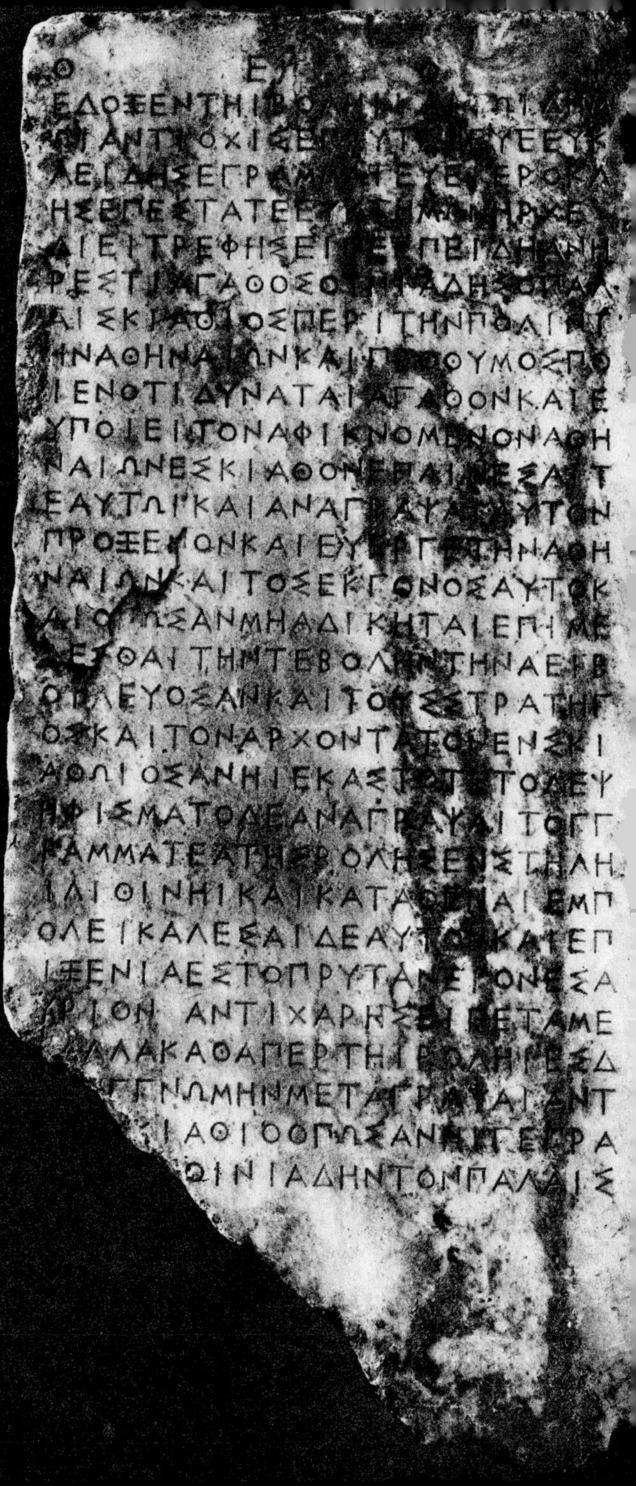

Θ Ε Ο Ι

ΕΔΟΞΕΝΤΗΙΒΟΛΗΙΚΑΙΤΩΙΔΗΜ
ΩΙΑΝΤΙΟΧΙΣΕΠΡΥΤΑΝΕΥΕΕΥΚ
ΛΕΙΔΗΣΕΓΡΑΜΜΑΤΕΥΕΙΕΡΟΚΛ
ΗΣΕΠΕΣΤΑΤΕΕΥΚΤΗΜΩΝΗΡΧΕ
ΔΙΕΙΤΡΕΦΗΣΕΙΠΕΕΠΕΙΔΗΑΝΗ
ΡΕΣΤΙΑΓΑΘΟΣΟΙΝΙΑΔΗΣΟΠΑΛ
ΑΙΣΚΙΑΘΙΟΣΠΕΡΙΤΗΝΠΟΛΙΝΤ
ΗΝΑΘΗΝΑΙΩΝΚΑΙΠΡΟΘΥΜΟΣΠΟ
ΙΕΝΟΤΙΔΥΝΑΤΑΙΑΓΑΘΟΝΚΑΙΕ
ΥΠΟΙΕΙΤΟΝΑΦΙΚΝΟΜΕΝΟΝΑΘΗ
ΝΑΙΩΝΕΣΚΙΑΘΟΝΕΠΑΙΝΕΣΑΙΤ
ΕΑΥΤΩΙΚΑΙΑΝΑΓΡΑΨΑΙΑΥΤΟΝ
ΠΡΟΞΕΝΟΝΚΑΙΕΥΕΡΓΕΤΗΝΑΘΗ
ΝΑΙΩΝΚΑΙΤΟΣΕΚΓΟΝΟΣΑΥΤΟΚ
ΑΙΟΠΩΣΑΝΜΗΑΔΙΚΗΤΑΙΕΠΙΜΕ
ΛΕΣΘΑΙΤΗΜΤΕΒΟΛΗΝΤΗΝΑΕΙΒ
ΟΛΕΥΟΣΑΝΚΑΙΤΟΣΣΤΡΑΤΗΓ
ΟΣΚΑΙΤΟΝΑΡΧΟΝΤΑΤΟΝΕΝΣΚΙ
ΑΘΩΙΟΣΑΝΗΙΕΚΑΣΤΟΤΕΤΟΔΕΨ
ΗΦΙΣΜΑΤΟΔΕΑΝΑΓΡΑΨΑΙΤΟΓΓ
ΡΑΜΜΑΤΕΑΤΗΣΒΟΛΗΣΕΝΣΤΗΛΗ
ΙΛΙΘΙΝΗΙΚΑΙΚΑΤΑΘΕΝΑΙΕΜΠ
ΟΛΕΙΚΑΛΕΣΑΙΔΕΑΥΤΟΝΚΑΙΕΠ
ΙΞΕΝΙΑΕΣΤΟΠΡΥΤΑΝΕΙΟΝΕΣΑ
ΡΙΟΝ ΑΝΤΙΧΑΡΗΣΕΙΠΕΤΑΜΕ
ΑΛΛΑΚΑΘΑΠΕΡΤΗΙΒΟΛΗΙΕΣΔ
ΓΓΝΩΜΗΝΜΕΤΑΓΡΑΨΑΙΑΝΤ
ΙΑΘΙΟΟΠΩΣΑΝΗΙΓΕΓΡΑ
ΟΙΝΙΑΔΗΝΤΟΝΠΑΛΑΙΣ

Notes on the Plates

1 Mount Olympus, on the coast at the north-east of Thessaly. This is the highest mountain in Greece (about 9,500 feet) and though remote was regarded by the Greeks as the home of their principal (Olympian) gods. Photograph Boissonas.

2 Patmos, view of the harbour from the monastery. The general effect of houses and cultivation should be much as in the more settled periods of antiquity. Photograph by Mr F. G. Mirfield.

3 Seriphos, air view from the east. For safety against pirates and raiders this island town clusters at the top of the hill, which is terraced for cultivation. Windmills, which appear to the right of the town, were unknown in antiquity. Part of the town is shown on Plate 24. Photograph the Air Club of Greece.

4 The bay of Itea from Delphi. Below are the olive groves of the valley of the Pleistos and the plain of Amphissa. In the far distance are the mountains of the Peloponnese. Photograph Foto Marburg.

5 The valley of the Peneus and the Pindus range, view from the north-east from Meteora in western Thessaly. Photograph Foto Marburg.

6 The promontory of Perachora opposite Corinth, view from the east. The small harbour (Plate 7) appears below and on the left of the lighthouse. Beyond is the coast of the Peloponnese.

7 The harbour of Perachora from the west. On the left are the foundations of the small temple of Hera Akraia (Hera of the Promontory) of the third quarter of the sixth century B C; beyond, those of a stoa of the late fifth or early fourth century B C. Photograph the British School of Archaeology at Athens.

8 Lycosura in Arcadia. In the foreground are the ruins of the temple of Despoina (the Mistress—in this instance almost equated with Persephone) built in the second century B C. The view shows good upland country at about the 2,000-foot contour. Photograph Foto Marburg.

9 Watercourse on Mount Olympus. Such watercourses, normal on the Greek mountains, are empty, except after rain. On this terrain there is pasturage only for goats.

10 Bay near Cape Sunium. The hillside, rough and infertile, is typical for much of the coast. Photograph by Roger Viollet.

11 View east over Sparta and the Eurotas valley from Mistra. The narrow plain is unusually fertile. Beyond are the waterless and barren foothills of Mount Parnon. Photograph by Mr E. A. Lane.

12 Delphi, air view from the south. The sanctuary of Apollo is at the middle right, with the theatre visible at the top. Further left and higher is the stadium. The circular marks in the centre are threshing floors. To the left is the modern village. Photograph the Air Club of Greece.

13 The stadium at Delphi. The stone seating (for 7,000 persons) was put in by the millionaire Herodes Atticus in the mid second century A D. Previously there had been only an embankment for the spectators. This stadium was used for the Pythian games. Photograph Foto Marburg.

14 Delphi, the theatre and the temple of Apollo. The theatre, which seats 5,000, was built in the fourth century B C, but modified later: in particular the stage building was built forward to encroach on the orchestra (*cf.* Plate 17, where the orchestra has kept its original form). The temple is that built in 369–329 B C after the destruction of its predecessor by earthquake. Photograph by Mr. R. Goold-Adams.

15 Sunium, air view from south. The temple, dedicated to Posidon, is in the Doric style and was built about 440 B C. A little to the right of it runs

a fortification wall, built in the late fifth century BC and restored in the third: though barren, the promontory was an important naval station. Photograph the Air Club of Greece.

16 Epidaurus, air view of the site from the north-west. In the foreground is the sanctuary: the round building is the Tholos, the light-coloured ruin to the left of it is the temple of Asclepios, and below both stretches a long portico (the Abaton) where sick pilgrims slept in hope of a cure. Above and to the right is the stadium. The square ruin below the theatre is the hotel with 160 rooms. Most of these buildings are of the fourth century BC; the hotel is Hellenistic. Photograph the Air Club of Greece.

17 Epidaurus, air view of the theatre from the west. This theatre, seating about 14,000, was constructed by Polyclitus the architect around 350 BC. Though the stage building was remodelled, the theatre still has a Classical character; the orchestra is circular, the auditorium extends far more than a semicircle, and the stage was detached. Photograph the Air Club of Greece.

18 Model of the sanctuary (Altis) at Olympia, viewed from the north. The big building in the centre is the temple of Zeus, built about 460 BC. To the right and nearer, the temple of Hera (Plate 26) of about 590 BC is partly visible. To the right and beyond the round building is the Hellenistic *palaestra,* a training place for athletes. On the left of the temple of Hera and seen in back view is a row of Archaic 'treasuries'. Still further left is the beginning of the stadium. Photograph Ehemals Staatliche Museen, Berlin.

19 Olympia, air view of sanctuary from the south-west. In the centre is the temple of Zeus and on the left among the trees the temple of Hera. Photograph the Air Club of Greece.

20 Model of the Acropolis of Athens, viewed from the north-west. The approach (from bottom right) is up a zigzag ramp to the entrance gate (the Propylaea). On the extreme right is the little temple of Athena Nike or Nike Apteros (see Plate 32). At the top is the Parthenon. On the left is the Erechtheum. Immediately behind it is the altar of Athena. The

lay-out and the principal buildings are of the second half of the fifth century B C. The enclosing wall, defensive as well as decorative, is a little earlier. This view, of course, was impossible from the ground and presumably was not taken into account by the architects. This model is in the Royal Ontario Museum, Toronto. Photograph by Professor J. W. Graham.

21 Acropolis of Athens, air view from the south-west. On the Acropolis itself, from left to right, the Propylaea, Erechtheum and Parthenon stand up clearly, and between the last two there are visible the foundations of a temple of the sixth century, partly destroyed in 480 B C. Below the Acropolis to the right appears the theatre of Dionysus, the home of Attic tragedy; the auditorium received its present form at the end of the Classical period, but the rest was remodelled later. At the bottom left is the Odeum of Herodes Atticus of the mid second century A D. Photograph the Air Club of Greece.

22 Apsidal building at Antissa in Lesbos: width inside, about 17¼ ft. (5·25 m.). Rough polygonal masonry. Perhaps eighth century B C. In the foreground is the apse, with a blocked door. In front on the right are two buttresses, and on the left the remains of a pavement. The two cross-walls of a much rougher masonry belong to an earlier building. Photograph by Mr J. K. Brock.

23 Tower and curtain wall of citadel of Larisa (?) in Aeolis: height to string-course about 8 ft. (2·50 m.). Good polygonal masonry. About 500 B C. On several blocks of the string-course the lifting bosses remain (*cf.* Figure 26). This string-course is of a reddish andesite, the rest of the wall of grey andesite.

24 Modern houses on Seriphos (*cf.* Plate 3). Such flat-topped boxes must have been as common in ancient times. Note the piles of clay for maintaining the mud roofs.

25 Aegosthena, view of citadel wall from the south-east. Limestone and conglomerate. Aegosthena, at the north-east corner of the Corinthian gulf, was a small settlement, but important strategically since it lay at the

end of the only practicable route from Attica to the western sea. The towers are set at intervals of about 50 yards and that on the left still stands to its full height of about 46 ft. Since at this corner the approach is relatively easy, this tower is built solid for the lowest 20 ft. The date of these fortifications is thought generally to be of the early fourth century, though they seem unnecessarily strong for the siege methods of that period. In the background is Mount Cithaeron. Photograph by Miss Alison Frantz.

26 Temple of Hera, Olympia, viewed from the north-east. Width at top of step 61½ ft. (18·75 m.). Shelly conglomerate. About 590 B C. Originally many or all of the columns were of wood, which were replaced in stone at various dates to show an extraordinary variety of proportions and contours. The walls of the cells were of stone to their present height and above were of mud-brick. The entablature was of wood, sheathed in painted terracotta. The platform has, exceptionally, only one step. This is the most primitive Doric temple of which much is preserved, but may have been backward for its time. Photograph by Miss Marjorie Webb.

27 Stoa of Zeus in the Agora of Athens, restored elevation (*cf.* Plate 35). Width 152 ft. 8¾ in. (46·55 m.). Marble. Built in the Doric style in the late fifth century B C. The wings projecting forward are very unusual. Drawing by Mr J. Travlos for the American School of Classical Studies at Athens.

28 The temple of Aphaia in Aegina, restored elevation of west end. Width at top of steps 45 ft. 2 in. (13·77 m.). Limestone. About 490 B C. The style is Doric. The restoration of the pedimental sculpture is incorrect, but not misleading. For the siting of the temple see Figure 36. From C. R. Cockerell, *the Temples of Jupiter Panhellenius at Aegina and of Apollo Epicurius at Bassae,* Plate 4.

29 The 'Theseum' viewed from the south-west. The bottom step is concealed. This is the best preserved of Greek temples; only the roof is not original. For a reconstruction see Figure 25 and for its ancient setting Plate 35. Old photograph, taken before 1875.

30 Doric order of the Parthenon, Athens. Marble. Built 447–432 BC. Figure 1, steps, column and entablature. Figure 2, section of cornice and frieze, showing undercutting of mouldings. Figure 3, underside of cornice (at a corner). Figure 4, plan of column at its bottom. These and other measured drawings of Athenian buildings were made in 1751–1753 and published from 1762 onwards; they represent the first accurate study of Greek antiquities and had a strong influence on classicising British architects. From J. Stuart and N. Revett, *the Antiquities of Athens* II, Chapter I, Plate 6.

31 Ionic order of north porch of the Erechtheum, Athens. Marble. Built 421–405 BC. Figure 1, column and entablature. Figure 2, anta. Figures 3 and 4, elevation and plan of bed of cornice. This is an elaborate example of Attic Ionic; the floral band at the top of the shaft of the column and the cables just below the volute member and on the base are unusual additions. From Stuart and Revett II, Chapter II, Plate 8.

32 The temple of Athena Nike (Athena-Victory) or less correctly Nike Apteros (Wingless Victory) at Athens, viewed from the east. Width at top of steps 17 ft. 8½ in. (5·4 m.). Built originally about 420 BC, dismantled by the Turks in 1687, and reassembled in 1838 and again in 1940. This little building is a singularly pure example of Attic Ionic: the pediment can be completed on the analogy of Plate 33 (without, of course, its cap). For the site see Plates 20–21. The Nike balustrade, from which comes Plate 59, fenced the bastion on which this temple stood. Photograph by Mr F. G. Mirfield.

33 Sarcophagus of the Mourning Women. Marble. Height (with lid) 5 ft. 11 in. (1·80 m.). About 360 BC. The effect of this end is more or less that of a temple 'in antis' (that is, with columns between the projecting walls of the cella); but the flat-topped cap above the pediment is foreign to architecture and instead of the base there should be steps. This is a fair illustration of the developed Asiatic variety of Ionic, with dentils instead of a deep frieze, and should be compared with the European treatment (Plate 32). Greek work for a Phoenician client. From Sidon. Istanbul, Museum of Classical Antiquities, 10. Photograph by Max Hirmer.

34 The Choregic Monument of Lysicrates at Athens, elevation. Marble. Height 34 ft. (10·36 m.). 334 BC or soon after. Originally the finial was surmounted by a bronze tripod (a more elegant version of the type of Figure 10). The order is Corinthian (which differs from Ionic in its capital) but the roof is fanciful. The monument commemorates the victory of Lysicrates in a public musical contest, where he 'led the chorus' or, in other words, had been elected as a wealthy man to pay the cost of training and production. Its only function is to support the tripod given as the prize. From Stuart and Revett I, Chapter IV, Plate 3.

35 Model of the west end of the Agora at Athens, viewed from the south-east. From left to right are the Tholos (a dining hall for the presiding officials), the Metroon (including a temple of the Mother of the Gods and the state archives) with the Bouleuterion (Council chamber) behind it, the temple of Apollo Patroos, and the Stoa of Zeus (see Plate 27). On the knoll at the back is the 'Theseum'. The buildings are of various dates from the fifth to the second centuries BC. Photograph the American School of Classical Studies at Athens.

36 Model of the central part of Priene, viewed from the south-east. For the plan and identification of buildings see Figure 38 and p. 181. Photograph Ehemals Staatliche Museen, Berlin.

37 Bronze figurine of a horse. Height 6·8 cm. Probably late eighth century BC. Such animals were regular dedications at Olympia at this time. Probably from Olympia. Cambridge, Fitzwilliam Museum GR.3.1957. Photograph the Fitzwilliam Museum.

38 Bronze bird and disc. Height 6 cm. Probably late eighth century BC. Purpose unknown: there is a hole for suspension through the base of the neck of the bird. Cambridge, Museum of Classical Archaeology. Photograph by Mr R. Johnson.

39 Terracotta figurine (made up from parts of a pair). Width at arms 6·9 cm. Late eighth century BC. From the handle of a pot. Woman mourning (*cf.* Plate 68). The decoration, in Attic Geometric style, is not relevant to the subject; it does not indicate a close-fitting garment, though the patterns

may well have appeared in textiles, and still less is it evidence for tattooing. From Athens. Athens, Agora Museum T.807. Photograph the American School of Classical Studies at Athens.

40 Bronze figurine of a soldier. Height 20·5 cm. Early seventh century BC. From Athens. Athens, National Museum 6613. Photograph Foto Marburg.

41 Restored and coloured cast of the 'Auxerre goddess'. Limestone. Height 65 cm. About 640 BC. So-called Daedalic style. Incised lines on the drapery show the boundaries between the original colours, and there are traces of red paint on the chest: the restoration gives a credible effect. Paris, Louvre 3098: the cast is in Cambridge, Museum of Classical Archaeology. Photograph by Mr R. Johnson.

42 Bronze male statuette. Height 19·7 cm. About 635 BC. So-called Daedalic style. These two figures represent the stock male and female types of Archaic sculpture, and belong to its very early stage: the coiffure is taken from Oriental models. From Delphi. Delphi Museum. From *Fouilles de Delphes* V.1, Plate 3.

43 Marble statue (the 'Apollo of Tenea'). Height 153 cm. About 560 BC. Presumably Corinthian work. The pose is that of the last figure, but the anatomy has progressed. From a tomb at Tenea near Corinth: the figure then should represent, in a general way, the man buried there. The name 'Apollo' was given to all statues of this type in the later nineteenth century and in some instances has stuck: the modern term, not much better, is 'kouros'. Munich, Glyptothek 168. Photograph Staatliche Antikensammlungen, Munich.

44 Marble statue of youth (the 'Critian boy'). Height 86 cm. About 480 BC. Attic work. The anatomy has advanced further and the Archaic stiffness of pose is now slightly relaxed. The current name of the statue comes from its close resemblance to the copies of the Tyrannicides, made by Critios and Nesiotes in 477 BC. From the Acropolis at Athens. Athens, Acropolis Museum 698. Photograph Foto Marburg.

45 Marble relief from the base of the statue. Height 32 cm. About 510–500 BC. Traces of red paint for the background. The figures show the new views and foreshortenings of this time (contrast the figures of Plate 48). The subject is some kind of ball game. From Athens. Athens, National Museum 3476.

46 Marble figure of Athena from the centre of the west pediment of the temple of Aphaia on Aegina (*cf.* Plate 28). Height 168 cm. About 490 BC. The holes drilled in the marble are to attach ornaments of metal. The style is late Archaic, where the interest in eleborate hair and drapery is weakening. Munich, Glyptothek A.19. Photograph Staatliche Antikensammlungen, Munich.

47 Marble statue of woman. Height 180 cm. About 530 BC. Considerable traces of colour; the hair, it may be noted, was red, the eyebrows black. This Archaic type of standing woman is now usually called 'kore', the female counterpart of 'kouros' (see note on Plate 43). At this stage sculptors were besotted with finicky coiffures and drapery. Here, as often, the left hand bunches the skirt to give radial folds stretching tightly across the legs and buttocks. From the Acropolis at Athens. Athens, Acropolis Museum 682. Photograph Foto Marburg.

48 Part of the north frieze of the Siphnian Treasury at Delphi. Marble. Height 64 cm. About 525 BC. The background was painted blue, and there are other traces of red and blue paint. In the foreground Apollo and Artemis shoot at three giants; in the background another giant runs away. This giant shows clearly the unresolved contrast between frontal thorax and profile hips (contrast the figures of Plate 45). Delphi Museum. Photograph Foto Marburg.

49 Bronze statue from Cape Artemisium. Height 209 cm. About 465 BC. Early Classical style. The identity of the figure is disputed: some think it Zeus with a thunderbolt, some Posidon with his trident, and some an athlete throwing a javelin. The position of the first finger of the right hand, crooked to rotate a shaft, favours an athlete. Recovered from an ancient shipwreck off north Euboea. Athens, National Museum 15161. Photograph by Max Hirmer.

50 The front of the Ludovisi throne. Marble. Width 143 cm. About 460 B C. Provincial, probably south Italian, work in the Early Classical style. The subject is uncertain—perhaps a goddess bathing or Aphrodite rising from the sea. The 'throne' is three-sided, with reliefs on the other sides also, and may have been a sort of fender at one end of a big altar. A corresponding 'throne', probably from the same structure, is now in Boston. Both were found in Rome, but presumably had been brought there from some Greek site. Rome, Museo delle Terme 8670. Photograph by Max Hirmer.

51 Bronze mirror. Height 47·8 cm. 450–440 B C. The disc was originally kept polished. This type of mirror with a figure for the handle is common in the late Archaic and early Classical period (for another type of mirror see Plate 87). The pose, though necessarily frontal, is not stiff and the forward thrust of the left thigh gives variety to the fall of the now severe drapery. Copenhagen, National Museum Chr. VIII 936. Photograph the National Museum, Copenhagen.

52 Head of the Charioteer of Delphi. Bronze, eyes inlaid (with brown iris). Height of whole figure 180 cm. About 470 B C. From a group of a chariot drawn by four horses: the lower part of the charioteer, often admired for the uncompromisingly vertical folds of the long racing costume, was partly concealed by the car of the chariot. The sternness of the face shows the reaction from Archaic cheerfulness. The group was dedicated by the tyrant Polyzalos of Gela in Sicily to celebrate a victory in the Pythian games. From Delphi. Delphi Museum 3484. Photograph Foto Marburg.

53 Female head (the 'Alba head'). Marble. Height about 27·5 cm. 450–440 B C. The marked asymmetry of the face and the neglect of the hair above the band suggest that the figure came from a pediment. Madrid, Alba collection 571. Photograph (from a cast) by Mr R. Johnson.

54 Head of a charioteer from a frieze of the Mausoleum at Halicarnassus. Marble. Height of head 10·5 cm. About 350 B C. The rounded forms, deep-set eyes and parted lips, which give a feeling of intensity, are an innovation of the fourth century attributed to Scopas. The Mausoleum

was the vast architectural tomb of Mausolus, a Carian king who was influenced strongly by Greek culture. London, British Museum 1037. Photograph the British Museum.

55 Female head (the 'Bartlett head'). Marble. Height 28·8 cm. Late fourth century B C. The style is in the tradition of Praxiteles. Boston, Museum of Fine Arts 03.743. Photograph the Museum of Fine Arts, Boston.

56 Part of the east frieze of the Parthenon at Athens. Marble. Height 106 cm. About 440 B C. Posidon, Apollo, Artemis. The photograph is of a cast made for Lord Elgin in 1799 and now in the British Museum, London. The original, which he left on the Parthenon to suffer further damage and weathering, is in the Acropolis Museum, Athens. Photograph the British Museum.

57 Part of a frieze of the Mausoleum at Halicarnassus. Marble. Height 89 cm. About 350 B C. Greeks fighting Amazons. London, British Museum 1015. Photograph the British Museum.

58 Gravestone. Marble. Height 121 cm. About 380 B C. A chip has broken away from the bridge of the nose of the seated woman, which should have the same profile as the standing woman's. Mistress and maid. From the Piraeus. *Cf.* Figure 32. Athens, National Museum 726. Photograph by Mrs S. A. Adam.

59 Part of the Nike Balustrade, Athens. Marble. Height 105 cm. About 409 B C. Nike (Victory) unfastening her sandal. The balustrade ran as a parapet round the bastion on the Acropolis on which stood the temple of Athena Nike (see Plate 32), and the reliefs were on the outside. Athens, Acropolis Museum 12. Photograph by Max Hirmer.

60 The 'Demeter of Cnidos'. Marble. Height 153 cm. 340–330 B C. The drapery shows the dramatic effects that became more popular in the fourth century. London, British Museum 1300. Photograph the British Museum.

61 The 'Hermes of Praxiteles'. Marble. Height 213 cm. Style of about 350 B C. Both legs of Hermes below the knees, his left foot and the lower

part of the tree trunk are restored. The subject is Hermes with the infant Dionysus. This statue was seen by Pausanias in the mid second century AD. and described by him as the work of Praxiteles. But because of the glossy finish of the surface, the tree trunk, and tool marks on the back, some good judges regard it as a later work, whether a copy of an original by Praxiteles, a new creation perhaps by another Praxiteles, or an original that was later worked over and modified: the first of these theories seems to me most likely. Olympia Museum. Photograph by Max Hirmer.

62 Cup of Attic Protogeometric style. Height 14·5 cm. Brownish clay, dark paint (in some places diluted to a medium brown). Tenth century BC. The concentric circles are drawn with compasses and a multiple brush. The clean regularity of the decoration contrasts with the carelessness of late Mycenaean. The shape with conical foot is peculiar to Protogeometric. Athens, Ceramicus Museum 3475. Photograph the German Archaeological Institute, Athens.

63 Oinochoe (jug) of Corinthian Protogeometric style. Height 20·3 cm. Brownish clay, dark paint. About 900 BC. Corinth Museum C.33. 1439.

64 Amphora (two-handled jar) of Attic Protogeometric style. Height 46 cm. Yellowish slip over brownish clay, dark paint. Tenth century BC. The shape, system of decoration, and the semicircles are characteristic of Protogeometric. Athens, Ceramicus Museum 586. Photograph the German Archaeological Institute, Athens.

65 Cup of Corinthian Geometric style. Height 6·7 cm. Brownish clay, dark paint. Later ninth century BC. The shape is normal for Geometric (contrast Plate 62 and Figure 23*a*). Corinth Museum CP. 865.

66 Oinochoe (jug) of Attic Geometric style. Height 27·3 cm. Brownish clay, dark paint. Middle or late ninth century BC. Contrast for shape and system of decoration the Protogeometric oinochoe (Plate 63). The hatched meander is the typical ornament of the Geometric style. Athens, Agora Museum P.18622. Photograph by the American School of Classical Studies at Athens.

67 Amphora of Attic Geometric style. Height about 42 cm. Brownish clay, dark paint. About 725 B C. For the style of the horse compare Plate 37. The loosening system of decoration shows the decline of the Geometric style. Athens, National Museum 18138. Photograph by Miss S. Benton.

68 Detail of large krater (mixing-bowl) of Attic Geometric style. Height of field about 18 cm. Brownish clay, dark paint. About 740 B C. Mourning: the dead man lies on a bier with a pall lifted for artistic clarity, below and probably not part of the same scene is a two-wheeled chariot, on the left women (as their breasts show) stand wailing, at the bottom on the right there are men wearing swords. Athens, National Museum 990.

69 Detail of an aryballos (oil-flask) of Corinthian style. Height of field 3 cm. Pale yellowish clay, dark paint (here outlined) and some added purple (here shaded); details incised (here shown by darker lines)—these conventions for copying vase-paintings are regular in Classical Archaeology. By the Ajax painter. About 680 B C. Zeus (with thunderbolt) attacking a giant. Boston, Museum of Fine Arts 95.12. From H. G. G. Payne, *Protokorinthische Vasenmalerei,* Plate 11.1.

70 Detail of an olpe (sagging jug) of Corinthian style. Height of field about 5 cm. Pale yellowish clay, blackish paint with accessory white, purple and flesh colours. By the Ekphantos painter. About 640 B C. Battle between hoplites. The elaborate subject and the use of a flesh colour are abnormal in vase-painting and may perhaps imitate mural and panel pictures. The evasion of depth (since the two lines should be parallel to each other) is regular throughout Greek vase-painting and sculpture (*cf.* Plate 56). The shape of this pot is like that of Plate 71. The period of Corinthian vase-painting to which this and the preceding piece belong is known as Protocorinthian. Rome, Villa Giulia 22697 (the 'Chigi vase'). From *Antike Denkmäler* II, Plate 44.

71 Olpe (sagging jug) of Corinthian style. Height 27·5 cm. Pale yellowish clay, blackish paint with some added purple and yellow. Perhaps by the Sphinx painter. About 630 B C. Oxford, Ashmolean Museum 1879.100. Photograph the Ashmolean Museum.

72 Oinochoe (jug) of Wild Goat style. Height 33 cm. Pale yellowish surface, darkish paint with some added purple. 625–600 BC. The animals of this East Greek (probably Rhodian) piece should be contrasted with the Corinthian animals of Plate 71. Oxford, Ashmolean Museum (lent by Sir John Beazley). Photograph the Ashmolean Museum.

73 Detail of bowl of Attic Black-figure style. Height of field about 20 cm. Brownish clay, blackish paint with some added purple. By the Gorgon painter. About 590 BC. Heroic duel; the equipment is contemporary, the way of fighting Homeric. The style is greatly indebted to Corinthian. Paris, Louvre E.874. Photograph Giraudon.

74 Olpe of Corinthian style. Height 27·8 cm. Pale yellowish clay covered with a reddish wash in the panel, blackish paint with accessory purple and white. About 570 BC. Thetis visiting Achilles; but if this is a reminiscence of the *Iliad*, it is muddled. The reddish wash imitates the colour of the surface of Attic pots of this time. Brussels, Musée du Cinquantenaire A.4. Photograph Musée du Cinquantenaire.

75 Amphora of Attic Black-figure style. Height 34·7 cm. Reddish brown clay with (originally) added purple and white. By the Amasis painter. 540–530 BC. In the main field, Dionysus and satyrs. Above, nymphs and satyrs. The one-piece shape, where the neck passes into the body in an unbroken sweep, came into favour about the middle of the sixth century: a similar development occurs later in the cup (see Figure 23) and the hydria (see the hydrias in the main panel of Plate 76). Würzburg, Martin von Wagner Museum K. 265. Photograph the Martin von Wagner Museum.

76 Hydria (water pot) of Attic Black-figure style. Height 57·5 cm. Reddish brown clay, blackish paint with added white and purple. By the A.D. painter. About 510 BC. The shape has two side handles and one vertical handle at the back. In the main panel, women at a fountain house of irregular Doric style—the irregularity may be evidence only for the vase-painter's carelessness. The animals below the main panel are the descendants of those of Plate 71: the Orientalising fauna is now rare and ex-

hausted. London, British Museum 43.11–3.49 (B.329). Photograph the British Museum.

77 Detail of inside of Attic Red-figure cup. Diameter of field 15 cm. Reddish brown clay, black paint (which is diluted to brown for some lines), and a little added purple. By Onesimos. About 490 B C. Woman (by her short hair a slave) preparing a bath. The shape of the cup is as Figure 23*f*. Brussels, Musée du Cinquantenaire A.889. Photograph Musée du Cinquantenaire.

78 Detail of inside of similar cup. Diameter of field 10·7 cm. Clay and paint as last. By the Elpinikos painter. 500–490 B C. Young man at drinking-party; he is lying on a couch, holding a lyre, and flicking the dregs from his cup in the game of 'kottabos'. Manchester, City Art Gallery (lent by the Manchester School of Art; Aa 24). Photograph Dr A. Cambitoglou.

79, 80 Details of lekythos of Attic White-ground style. Height of field 18·3 cm. White ground, blackish paint which is diluted to brown for some lines, purple for the fillets round the gravestone and in the woman's hand; the colour on the woman's dress has vanished. By the Achilles painter. 450–440 B C. Man and woman at grave. The interpretation of the subjects of these lekythoi and on gravestones is often difficult: here the figure on the left may be the dead man looking on in spirit. For the shape of this lekythos see Figure 31. Oxford, Ashmolean Museum 1947.24. Photograph the Ashmolean Museum.

81, 82 Loutrophoros-amphora of Attic Red-figure style. Height of field 22 cm. Clay and paint as for Plate 77. By Polygnotus (not the painter of murals). About 440 B C. Wedding; the attendants are holding torches. The loutrophoros-amphora was a ritual vase used at weddings. Toronto, Royal Ontario Museum C.935. Photograph by C. T. Seltman.

83 Stamnos (wine jar) of Attic Red-figure style. Height 44 cm. Clay and paint as Plate 77. By the Cleophon painter. About 430 B C. Soldier pouring a libation before leaving home. Munich, Museum Antiker Kleinkust 2415. Photograph Staatliche Antikensammlungen, Munich.

84 Detail of calyx-krater (mixing bowl) of Attic Red-figure style. Height of panel 22 cm. Clay and paint as Plate 77. About 360–350 B C. Ariadne and Dionysus and attendants. This more pictorial drawing is characteristic of the progressive Athenian vase-painters of the mid fourth century. Athens, National Museum 12592. Photograph by Miss Alison Frantz.

85 Silver-gilt plaque. Height 6·5 cm. Third quarter of fifth century B C. Nike (Victory) in a chariot. From a Thracian grave at Duvanli in Bulgaria. Plovdiv Museum 1654.

86 Chalcedony gem. Greatest length 2·2 cm. By Dexamenos (signed). About 440 B C. Woman and slave, who holds a mirror and a garland. Cambridge, Fitzwilliam Museum. Photograph (from a cast) the Fitzwilliam Museum.

87 Engraved bronze mirror cover. Diameter 18·5 cm. Second quarter of fourth century B C. Aphrodite and Pan playing knucklebones, with Eros looking on. Tentative shading on body of Pan and on drapery, but not body, of Aphrodite. London, British Museum 88. 12–13.1. Photograph the British Museum.

88 Inscribed marble slab. Height 62 cm. 407 B C. Stoichedon style (that is the letters are in strict vertical alignment): as was normal in Greek writing, there is no division of words nor punctuation. Decree of the Council and People of the Athenians, with an amendment. The formulation is regular. I give a full translation: 'Gods. It was decided by the Council and the People in the month when the tribe Antiochis was presiding and Euclid was secretary, on the day when Hierocles was chairman, and in the year when Euctemon was archon, on the proposal of Diitrephes, that since Oeniades of Old Skiathos is good in his dealings with the Athenian state and eager to do whatever good he can and helps any Athenian who arrives at Skiathos he be commended and he—and his descendants—be registered as honorary consul and benefactor of the Athenians, and that the Council at the time in office and the generals and the commissioner in Skiathos whoever he may be at any time shall take care that no wrong is done to him. The secretary of the Council is to write up this decree on a stone slab and put it on the Acropolis. Further,

Oeniades is to be invited to dinner in the Town Hall tomorrow. It was also decided on the proposal of Antichares that the rest should be as in the Council's resolution, but to alter the word 'Skiathos' so that the decree reads 'Oeniades of Old Skiathos'.' Found on the Acropolis of Athens. Athens, Epigraphical Museum 6796. Photograph the German Archaeological Institute, Athens.

89 The Lion of Chaeronea. Marble on a limestone base. Height (with base) about 28 ft. (8·50 m.). Between 338 and 335 BC. This monument, according to Pausanias in the second century AD, was set up by the Thebans in memory of their soldiers killed in the battle of Chaeronea. It was broken up in 1818 by the intermittently patriotic brigand Odysseus in hope of finding treasure inside it. Finally it was restored in 1904. Photograph by Dr F. Willemsen.

Index

Achaeans, 23, 25, 58, 74, 118
Acropolis (definition), 27
Administration, 25–6, 66, 126, 256–7
Aegina, 23, 59
  sanctuary of Aphaia, 110, 115, 167, 245
Aegosthena, 171, 244–5
Aeolians, 24, 25, 46
Aeolic capital, 112, 179
Aeschylus, 145
Aetolians, 23, 135
After-life, 33, 85–6
Agora, 82, 168, 170
Agrarian troubles, 29, 64
Agriculture, 17, 28–9, 47–8, 57, 59, 63–4, 131, 133–4, 241, 242
Alabastron, 43, 178
Alexander the Great, 48, 120, 142, 174
Aliens (resident), 25, 71, 122, 124, 125, 131
Al Mina, 59
Alphabet, 55, 97, 176
Altars, 35, 106, 167
Amphora, 43
Anaxagoras, 140, 147
Anaximander, 86
Anaximenes, 86
Animism, 32
Apelles, 148
Aphrodite, 31, 139
Apollo, 30, 31, 32, 33, 72, 248
Apollodorus, 148
Arcadians, 20, 23, 119
Archers, 37, 38, 77, 135
Archilochus, 88
Architects, 170
Architectural refinements, 108, 110, 161
  terms, 103–4, 108–9, 123, 178–9, 246
Architecture, 39–40, 102–16, 160–72, 175–6, 179, 244, 245
Ares, 31
Argos, 17, 23, 26, 31, 65, 73–4, 118
  pottery, 46, 95
Aristocracy, 25–6, 29, 42, 47, 62, 65–7, 85
Aristophanes, 145
Aristotle, 142–3
Arms and armour, 37, 74–8, 175, 177
Art, 40–6, 89–102, 146–60
Artemis, 30, 31
Artillery, 78, 136–7
Artistic conventions, 45, 78, 98, 100
Aryballos, 43, 178
Asclepios, 139
Assembly of commoners, 25, 65, 70, 71, 126
Assyria, 50, 51, 57, 90
Atê (doom), 86, 144

Athena, 30, 31, 32
Athens, 22, 23, 31, 51–4, 57, 59, 67, 71, 73, 80, 117–20, 121, 124, 125–7, 129, 135, 140, 172, 173, 174
  Acropolis, 167, 243–4
  Agora, 168, 247
  empire, 118–9, 122, 124
  pottery, 44–6, 63, 93–6, 148–50
Athletics, 30, 81, 82, 83–5, 87, 127, 162, 242
Attica, *see* Athens

Babylonia, 50, 51, 61
Bacchus, *see* Dionysus
Barbarians, 72
Baths, 127, 255
Bireme, 79
Black-figure technique, 90
Black Sea, 54, 57, 61, 69, 97, 120, 129, 132
Boeotia, 17, 20, 23, 47, 118, 119
  pottery, 46, 96, 149
Books, 88, 146
Bouleuterion, 162–3, 247
Building, *see* Architecture
  methods, 39, 102–3, 106–8, 133, 172, 175–6, 179, 244, 245
Burials, *see* Funerary practices

Carians, 24, 60, 77
Carthage, 54, 57, 69
Castor, 31
Cavalry, 38, 75, 77, 125, 135
Centaurs, 32
Chaeronea (battle), 120, 174, 257
Chalcis, 23, 55, 58, 59, 73
  pottery, 96, 97
Chariots, 29, 37, 45, 84, 85, 134
Chronology, 45, 63, 88–90, 115, 116, 149–50
Cimmerians, 51, 54
City state, 27–8, 65–72, 120, 121–3, 125–7, 143, 172, 174
Clans, 26
Cleisthenes, 71
Climate, 17, 175
Coinage, 64–5, 159
Colonies, 24, 54, 57–9
Colour in architecture, 109, 113
  sculpture, 99, 151, 248, 249
Comedy, 145
Commerce, *see* Trade
Commoners, 25, 26, 47–8, 62, 65–8
Communications, 17–9, 126, 134
Constitutions, 25–7, 65–6, 68, 69, 71–2
Copies of sculpture, 150, 158
Corinth, 23, 57, 58, 59, 61, 67–8, 73, 78, 80, 100, 102, 112, 118, 124, 129, 135
  pottery, 45, 46, 63, 90–3, 149
Corinthian capital, 161–2, 171
Corn supply, 57, 60, 61, 69, 120, 129, 131
Council, 25, 65, 70, 71, 126
  chamber, 162–3, 247
Crafts, 27, 28, 133
Crete, 23, 24, 100, 102
  pottery, 46, 96
Croesus, 51, 72, 115
Cups, 178
Cynics, 141
Cyprus, 29, 46, 50, 55
Cyrenaics, 141

Daedalic style, 100
Dead, cult of, 33, 255
Dedications, 35, 43, 78

Delos, 24, 30, 33, 35, 100, 149
Delphi, 32, 35, 57–8, 72, 73, 86, 119, 139, 242
Demeter, 31, 32, 35, 85
Democracy, 70–2, 74, 121–3, 129, 172
Democritus, 140, 147
Demosthenes, 130, 146
Diet, 127
Dinner parties, 82–3, 177
Diolkos, 61
Dionysus, 30, 31, 32, 35, 85, 86, 139
Dioscuri, 31
Divination, 32
Dodona, 32
Dorian invasion, 20, 21
Dorians, 20, 23, 24, 25, 36
Doric order, 108–12, 115–6, 160–1, 162, 170–1
Drainage, 126, 166
Dress, 80, 127, 177
Drink, 127
Drinking parties, 83

East Greek Architecture, 112
  definition, 96
  pottery, 46, 96–7
  sculpture, 101
Economics, 17, 28–9, 59–65, 129–32
Education, 48, 81–2, 83, 127, 128
Egypt, 50, 51, 58, 59, 60, 61, 90, 100
Eleans, 23, 26
Elis (Agora), 170
Emigration, 24, 57–9, 123
Empedocles, 140
Ephors, 71
Epic, 46–8, 87
Epidaurus, 139, 163, 243
Epigraphy, 120, 256–7
Epirus, 23, 26, 32, 65
Eretria, 23, 51–2, 58, 59, 73
  pottery, 96
Eros, 31, 139
Etruscan art, 97, 147, 149
Etruscans, 54, 55, 57
Euclid, 143
Euripedes, 145
Eusebius, 116

Fate, 32, 47
Fertility cults, 30, 31, 35
Festivals, 30, 35, 36, 42, 48, 69, 83–5, 126
Figurines, 40, 102, 159–60
Fikellura pottery, 97
Finance (public), 25, 38, 61, 66, 68, 125–7
Food, 127
Foreshortening, 96, 147
Fortifications, 27, 78–9, 135–7, 163, 171, 244–5
Fountain houses, 106, 126
Funerary practices, 30, 33, 37, 45, 83, 99, 175, 180, 255

Games (indoor), 82–3
  (outdoor), *see* Sport
Gems, 159, 160
Geometric art, 38–46
  period, 21, 39
  pottery, 44–6, 252–3
Geometry, 55, 86, 87, 143
Gift conventions, 42
Gnathian pottery, 149
Gods, 30–3, 47–8, 85–6, 138–9
Gorgias, 146

Grave goods, 33, 37, 43, 77–8
Greek (definition), 21, 50
Gymnasium, 127, 162

Hades, 31
Helladic, 21
Hellenic, 21, 24–5
Hellenistic, 21, 172–3
Hephaestus, 31
Hera, 30, 31
Heraclitus, 86–7
Hermes, 30
Herodotus, 116, 144, 145–6
Heroes, 33
Hesiod, 25, 27, 28, 29, 30, 32, 47–8, 54–5, 64, 87
Hestia, 31
Hetaera, 81
Hippocrates, 144
History, 65, 144
Homer, 25, 28, 29, 30, 32, 35, 41, 42, 46–7, 48, 59, 62, 72, 87
Homosexuality, 81
Hoplite, 59–60, 64, 74–8, 134–5
Houses, 39–40, 80, 106, 127, 164–6, 171, 180
Hybris (excess), 86, 144
Hydria, 43

Iliad, 46–7
Illyrians, 23
Industry, 28, 57, 62–3, 130–1, 132, 133
Infantry, 37, 59–60, 64, 74–8, 134–5, 175
Inscriptions, 120, 160, 256–7
Ionian migration, 23, 24
Ionians, 24, 25, 26, 36, 47, 51, 96
Ionic order, 112–5, 116, 161, 162, 171, 179, 246
Iris, 30

Justice, 27, 58, 67, 68, 69, 126, 141

Kings, 25–6, 36, 65, 71
Kore, 99–100, 249: *see also* Persephone
Kotyle, 93
Kouros, 99–100, 248
Krater, 43

Laconia, 23, 24, 26, 100, 102; *see also* Sparta
pottery, 96
Landscape in art, 147
Language, 20, 23, 24, 25
Lato, 168, 180
Laws, *see* Justice
Leagues, 36, 74, 118, 134
Leisure, 82–3, 128–9, 173
Lekythos, 43, 180
Lesbos, 24, 80
Leucippus, 140
Leuctra (battle), 119
Light-armed troops, 37, 75, 77, 135
Literacy, 28, 46, 65, 81, 127
Literature, 46–8, 87–9, 144–6
Loans, 130, 131
Luxury, 55, 80
Lydians, 50–1, 59, 64, 69
Lyric poetry, 72, 87–9, 144
Lysippus, 157

Macedonians, 17, 23, 26, 46, 65, 72, 120, 129, 174
Magic, 32, 48

Magistrates, 25–6, 65, 70, 71, 126, 131–2, 256
Marathon (battle), 52, 117
Marriage, 29, 80, 123, 128, 255
Mathematics, 87, 143
Medicine, 58, 127, 139, 143–4
Megara, 23, 57, 58, 59, 73, 74, 118, 135, 137
'Megaron', 40
Mercenaries, 60–1, 65, 77, 119, 123, 135, 138
Messenia, 23, 65, 74, 119
Metalwork, 39–41, 159, 160, 176
Metics, 71, 124
Miletus, 24, 51, 58, 86
Mining, 17, 68, 125, 129, 131, 132, 134
Mortality, 123
Mosaics, 160
Muses, 31
Music, 42, 81, 84, 89
Mycenae, 27, 73, 78
Mycenaean pottery, 44
Mycenaeans, 20, 21, 23, 24, 25, 28, 29, 41, 59, 111
Mysteries, 35, 85, 139
Mythology, 25, 26–7, 33

Nationalism, 72–3, 121–2
Natural resources, 17
Naucratis, 58, 60, 62
Naxos, 24, 59, 73, 100, 102

Odyssey, 46–7
Oenochoe, 43
Offerings, 33–5, 43
Officials, 25–6, 65, 70, 71, 126, 131–2, 256
Oligarchy, 66–71, 74, 121–2
Olympia, sanctuary, 35, 72, 83–5, 243
  temple of Hera, 109, 111, 115, 245
Olympian Gods, 30–1, 241
Olympic games, 49, 83–4
Oracles, 32–3, 139
Orders of architecture, 108–15, 160–2
Oriental influences, 54–5, 59, 90, 100, 178
Orientalising (definition), 90
Orphism, 85–6

Painting (on walls and panels), 42–3, 98–9, 146–8, 149
Palaestra, 162
Pan, 31–2
Panhellenism, 48, 54, 72–3, 85, 120, 122, 174
Parmenides, 139–40
Peloponnesian league, 74, 118
  war, 118–9, 138
Penteconter, 79, 80
Persecution, 36, 87
Persephone, 31
Persian invasion, 52–4, 89–90, 117–8
Persians, 51–4, 61, 69, 117–9, 174
Perspective, 147, 158, 253
Phalanx, 75–8, 135
Phidias, 157
Phidon, 73–4
Philip II of Macedon, 120, 122, 135, 174
Philosophy, 86–7, 138, 139–43
Phocians, 23, 119
Phoenicians, 29, 50, 54, 55, 90
Phrygians, 24, 51, 59
Pindar, 144
Piracy, 25, 38, 61

Pisistratus, 68–9
Plataea (battle), 53–4, 117
Plato, 141–2, 143, 146
Pluto, 31
Poetry, 46–8, 87–9, 144–5
Police, 125, 126
Polis, *see* City state
Politics, 25–7, 65–72, 121–3
Pollux, 31
Polyclitus (architect), 243
  (sculptor), 151
Polycrates, 69, 80
Polygnotus, 147
Population, 123–4
Posidon, 30
Pottery, 43–6, 62–3, 89–98, 130–1, 148–50
  industry, 62–3
  names of shapes, 43
  technique, 43–4, 90, 94–6
Praxiteles, 152, 153, 154, 252
Priapus, 31
Priene, 124, 164, 166, 170, 171
Priests, 25, 35, 36
Propylon, 104, 162
Prose, 88, 145–6
Prostitution, 81
Protoattic pottery, 93
Protocorinthian pottery, 90–3
Protogeometric period, 21, 38–9
  pottery, 44, 45–6, 252
Public works, 61, 67, 69
Pythagoras, 83, 86, 87
Pyxis, 43

'Racial' composition, 20
Reading, 146
Red-figure technique, 94–6
Religion, 30–6, 47, 54–5, 85–7, 138–9
Rhodes, 24, 100, 122
  pottery, 46, 96–7

Sacrifice, 33–5
Salamis (battle), 53, 80, 117
Samos, 24, 69, 80, 100, 115
Sanctuaries, 35, 126, 167, 170
Sappho, 62, 80, 88
Satyrs, 31–2
Science, 86, 133, 143–4
Sculpture, 40, 99–102, 150–9, 248–52
Scythians (South Russia), 51, 54, 57, 58
Serfs, 24, 25, 28, 71, 74
Shading, 148, 256
Ships, 38, 45, 79–80, 134, 137, 175, 177
Sicilian colonies, 57, 69, 90, 121
  expedition, 118–9
  pottery, 97, 149
Sicyon, 59, 98
Sieges, 78–9, 126, 136–7
Slaves, 25, 60, 71, 122, 124, 129, 131
Smyrna, 27, 78
Social life, 29–30, 42, 55, 80–3, 127–9
  organisation, 26–7, 62, 68, 83, 127
Socrates, 139, 141
Solon, 62, 64, 68, 88
Sophists, 128, 138, 140
Sophocles, 145
Sources of knowledge, 21–2, 37, 49, 65, 77–8, 88–9, 116, 120–1, 138, 146–7
South Italian colonies, 57, 83
  pottery, 97, 149
Sparta, 17, 65, 69, 71, 74, 78, 80, 83, 117–9, 121, 124, 159, 174; *see also* Laconia
Sport, 29, 30, 81, 82, 83–5, 87, 162, 242

Stele, 99
Stoa, 104–6, 162
Subgeometric, 45, 178
Subjects of art, 33, 45, 98, 149, 156
Submycenaean pottery, 44
Survival of literature, 88–9
Syria, 50, 55, 58, 59, 60, 90, 100

Taxation, 61, 68, 125–6
Technique of building, 39, 102–3, 106–8, 133, 172, 175–6, 179, 244, 245
  pottery, 43–4, 90, 94–6, 133
  sculpture, 158
Technology, 132–4
Temples, 35, 39–40, 103–4, 178
Ten Thousand (march of), 119
Thales, 86
Theatres, 163, 171, 242, 243
Thebes, 23, 73, 119, 120, 124, 135
Theogony, 47
Theophrastus, 143
Thessalians, 17, 20, 23, 24, 46, 73, 118, 120, 121
Tholos, 162, 247
Thracians, 23–4, 51, 54, 120, 129
Thucydides, 116, 118, 144, 146
Town planning, 166–70, 171, 180–1
Trade, 28–9, 57, 59–63, 98, 129–30, 132
Tragedy, 69, 126, 143, 144–5
Transport, 134
Treasuries, 104
'Tribes', 26–7
Tripods, 41–2
Trireme, 79, 80
Tyranny, 61, 67–70, 74, 121
Tyrtaeus, 88

Urbanisation, 27–8, 123

Vase-painting, *see* Pottery

Walls, *see* Fortifications
Warfare, land, 36–8, 74–9, 125–6, 134–8
  sea, 38, 79–80, 137, 175, 177
Water supply, 69, 106, 126–7, 166
Weaving, 30, 42, 133, 160
Weapons, *see* Arms
Welfare, 125, 127
Wild Goat style pottery, 96–7
Wine, 34, 43, 60, 127, 129
Women (position of), 30, 55, 71, 80–1, 81–2, 83, 127–8
Works and Days, 29, 47–8
Worship, 33–5
Writing, 55, 81, 127, 133

Xenophanes, 48, 64, 87
Xenophon, 119, 128, 146

Zeus, 30, 31, 32